Aberdeenshire Library and Information Service
www.aberdeenshire.gov.uk/libraries
Renewals Hotline 01224 661511

GILL, Charan

Tikka look at me now

TIKKA LOOK AT ME NOW

CHARAN GILL MBE

THE AUTOBIOGRAPHY

BLACK & WHITE PUBLISHING

First published 2006
by Black & White Publishing Ltd
99 Giles Street, Edinburgh, EH6 6BZ

Hardback Edition
ISBN 13: 978 1 84502 099 6
ISBN 10: 1 84502 009 5

Paperback Edition
ISBN 13: 978 1 84502 100 9
ISBN 10: 1 84502 100 2

Typeset by RefineCatch Ltd, Bungay, Suffolk
Printed and bound by Creative Print and Design Group Ltd

ACKNOWLEDGEMENTS

Many thanks to all the people who have worked with me at Harlequin over the past twenty years – without them I never would have been able to achieve the success of which I write.

I also want to thank my many friends who helped to jog my memory as I tried to recollect my journey – a difficult task as I had never bothered to keep notes.

My wife Parminder and my children should be thanked for allowing me the peace and quiet to make my wish of writing a book become a reality.

A special thanks to my numerous mentors from whom I drew my inspiration including the early immigrants whose personal stories became my motivation.

Not least, I want to thank the people who helped me in my hours of need and believed in my ability to repay them.

DEDICATION

My grandfather, Sajjan Singh Gill, has been my guiding light. He instilled in me a great belief that I would achieve whatever I set out to do and his words are what give me the confidence in my ability. The stories he told me as a little boy are still a driving force.

In life, he was my greatest inspiration – in death, he is my guardian angel.

WHY?

Have you ever wondered why
Most birds don't reach where eagles fly?
Why sheep just bleat and lions roar,
Why planes just fly and rockets soar,
Why some birds chirp while others sing?
What makes a slave?
What makes a KING?
People say it's destiny –
They say it's how it's meant to be.
God is wise – his team was picked
Long before a ball was kicked.
Are you like them or more like me
And question how it's meant to be?
For I can top the eagle's flight –
Though just a man, a lion fight.
Like nightingales, I too can sing
And, in my world, I am a king.

So walk with me and share my dream –
I know there are places in God's team.

Charan Gill

CONTENTS

INTRODUCTION

All tales must have a beginning, a middle and an end. My beginnings were simple, my middle more complex and my end, hopefully, still some way away.

I left my home in the Punjab at a very young age and with my mother and my three brothers flew to Scotland to join my father. This did not make me unique; in fact I was just one of the millions of kids who tagged along with their parents who emigrated to new shores each year. Whether they travelled from Ireland to America, Scotland to Canada or from China to Europe, all immigrants were driven by the same desire to make lives more prosperous for themselves and their families. The very fact that they left familiar shores and their loved ones, in search of new horizons, made them entrepreneurial in spirit. They were risk-takers by nature who had no fear of any dangers that might lurk around the corner. The ones who were afraid stayed at home.

These people put up with shocking prejudices, which would never be accepted in today's civilised society. They made massive sacrifices to chase and realise their financial dreams. Were they 'economic migrants' who had only come to this country to improve their financial standing? Of course they were: what other reason would anyone have to leave their home and their loved ones? Some made it big in life, while others struggled at the bottom of the food chain. I was one of the people who happened to make it, but as I look around me at my fellow immigrants, I see many who are living a life that was not what they had envisaged when they came to Scotland, working long hours in menial jobs. I take my hat off to each and every one of these courageous people, because life is about trying to achieve that ultimate goal. It's what makes life as exhilarating as being on the biggest roller coaster in the world, the thrill of which can only be appreciated by those who have the balls to go on the ride in the first place. It takes great courage to embark on such journeys into the unknown and at least they can all take pride from the fact that they tried.

This is my story, and apart from its finale, it is no different from that of any of my fellow immigrants who toil long and hard. We have all had similar experiences, felt the same pains and joys. We have cried at our misfortunes and tried to hold up our heads when things have been tough and laughed every time we have achieved a new goal or milestone in life's journey.

This is my story.

Chapter One

THE SALE

As I sat in my office with Sanjay Majhu that Monday afternoon, and we waited patiently for the call that would have us dashing down to our solicitor's offices, my thoughts wandered back on the road I had travelled and the hurdles I had overcome to reach this point in my life. It had been a remarkable journey in which I had experienced every emotion that is possible in one's lifetime. Now, I was about to sell my business but it was not just a business – this was my baby and I still wasn't quite sure if I was doing the right thing. I could tell that Sanjay was tense; he was probably thinking that I might still change my mind and call the whole thing off. The deal was supposed to have been signed that morning and it was now two o'clock in the afternoon and three sets of lawyers were still drafting and redrafting documents. He had been waiting for this moment for many years and was still not sure if it would happen. He wanted it so bad, and it showed.

'Surely nothing can go wrong now,' he kept saying. 'It's going to be all right, isn't it?'

'Yes, it's going to be all right,' I answered.

Even if I had wanted to, I would never have gone back on my word and changed my mind at this late stage. We tried to make light of the situation by having a rubber band fight. It's the sort of thing guys do when they are under pressure. We had known each other for a very long time – I had shown him how to pour his first pint of lager and pull his very first bird – and a rubber band fight was very appropriate. It must have been a strange sight to someone on the outside looking in: I was just about to sell my company, my life's work, everything I had lived and breathed over the past twenty years and Sanjay was just about to acquire a company that only a few years ago, he could not even have dreamed of owning. And here we were passing the time by having a rubber band fight.

The deal didn't get signed that day. In fact, it didn't get signed until eight o'clock the following evening, and it had been a long and tense day with frayed tempers. The bank's lawyers wanted some redrafting done to documents because a couple of things were not in alphabetical order – which I thought was a strange request from a company calling themselves DLA Solicitors.

'Is that short for "delay"?' I asked, trying to ease the tension but realising that they didn't think I was as funny as a few of the room's occupants did. Solicitors get a lot of flak but I guess they have a job to do and DLA were just making sure they got it right for the bank. The bank came back at the last minute and told Sanjay that, if he wanted the funds for the deal to go ahead, he would have to increase his personal guarantee to £1 million. This was typical of the bank. Bring a man to the point of where he could not go back by saying yes to everything he asked for and deliver the sucker punch at the last moment. Sanjay had no option but to say yes.

Once the button had been pressed to transfer the money from the bank into my account and we had gotten rid of the bank's lawyers, Nick Naddell and George Frier, who were acting for me on the deal along with two other colleagues, cracked open some bottles of champagne and poured out numerous glasses. The deal was finally done. The money was transferred into my account the following morning and I had more money in the bank than most people can only dream about.

I still felt that I was the boss because I was around the office to ease the takeover. The transition would not be easy for me; after all, Sanjay and all his team had been working for me for many years prior to this and looked to me for advice in the months after the takeover. At the same time they wanted to make changes to the way things had been done, and rightly so. Even then, it was frustrating for me to sit in on meetings when decisions were being taken to change certain strategies and, with mutual agreement, I stopped attending the meetings. I don't know who felt more relieved by this: me, or the rest of the team.

Closure for me finally came about five weeks later when the official press release was sent to the media and the story appeared in all the press and the news on television. On the evening of the press release Sanjay had a party in one of the restaurants and the restaurant was wall-to-wall with people that we both knew. Old habits die hard and I always like my staff to look smart, so when I saw a guy with a white shirt and black trousers in behind the bar without a bow tie, I took him aside and told him that I was not very pleased with his scruffy appearance.

'The least you can do,' I told him, 'is to wear a bow tie.'

He went off and spoke with the restaurant manager who looked over at me curiously as he handed the chap a bow tie. Later in the evening I saw the guy with a large camera taking photographs of all the guests. I asked the manager who this chap was and I was left feeling a wee bit embarrassed when told that he was the official press photographer.

Some of the people in the restaurant that evening were suppliers I had dealt with since I first went into business and it was great having them in the one room to say my thanks. I was asked to say a few words, which I did, making sure that I kept it short and simple because this was not my night. I said that I felt like a proud father who had just married off a beautiful daughter; I had brought her up well, I had groomed her, and she was beautiful. I had a heavy heart but was pleased that I felt that the groom was more than capable of keeping her in the manner to which she was accustomed. The dowry he had paid had helped to ease my pain.

I thanked the people in the room for coming and thanked them for the roles they had played in my success and then introduced the new Chief Executive of Harlequin Leisure Group to our guests and handed over to the new man. I finished my glass of champagne and went home with my wife – my business was sold and I was now a wealthy man.

Chapter Two

MY FIRST RESTAURANT CURRY

My first visit to an Indian restaurant is one I will remember for the rest of my life. The restaurant was located in Sauchiehall Street, on the first floor of a building which also housed a cinema. This was no ordinary cinema because this one showed continuous blue movies and I discovered, when I went the loo, that the two establishments also shared common toilets, making it possible to take in a part of a movie between your bhoona lamb and the gulab jamin. It was quite common to take long breaks in between courses.

A busy wee place it was too. Reputable-looking guys with pinstripe suits considered it was better to pretend they were going for a businessman's lunch, as opposed to something saucier, and enter the cinema through the restaurant entrance. The place had been recommended to me by Ashy Aziz, a friend of mine who regarded himself as a man about town, and he decided to take me under his wing. The only thing I remember about the decor was that it was mostly maroon and green and the ventilation system was obviously turned off during quieter periods to save a bit of money. The smell was quite overpowering and it hit you as soon as you started to climb the steps.

At the top of the stairs a waiter wearing a maroon jacket that matched the flock wallpaper greeted us. It was obvious the jacket was not his own as it was about three sizes too big, but he still wore it with great pride. We were shown to a table well away from the front door, which I thought was really nice, as it was freezing cold outside.

'Is that your daddy's jacket?' asked Ashy, at the same time giving me a wink to make sure the joke didn't go over my head.

'He thinks we are going to do a runner,' Ashy told me as he flipped through the massive menu, the size of which would have put the *Encyclopædia Britannica* to shame. Ashy regarded himself a bit of an expert in these matters because he had worked there previously as a part-time dishwasher.

The waiter kept his smile during Ashy's comments and I wondered if it was wise to slag off a guy who, for the next hour, would be handling everything that went into our mouths so I decided to go out of my way to be extra nice to him. The red cloth covering the rickety table had not seen the dry cleaners for some time and when Ashy asked the waiter if they ever changed the table covers, he replied that he wasn't sure as he had only worked there for a few months.

'We don't need these menus,' said Ashy with an air of confidence. 'Just get us two bhoona lamb and four chapattis.' Turning to me he said, 'We are OK because the lamb in here is halal.'

That was great for Ashy as he was Muslim but he gave no consideration to the fact that I was a Sikh and therefore should not really be eating halal. I didn't think about it at the time but this is something which has always irritated me about all my Muslim friends. When we have Muslim guests, we go out of our way to make sure that the food we serve them is halal. But to this day, no Muslim has ever asked me if I have a special dietary need and just assume that I will eat what I am given. For those interested, the Sikh form of ritual slaughter is known as *chartka*. The Sikhs do not believe that an animal should suffer as it slowly bleeds to death but that it should die with one single blow from a sharp sword which would decapitate the animal.

The waiter could sense I was a novice. 'Would you like your curry hot?' he asked, reaching for his pink order pad.

'The pink pads are the ones which never go through the till,' winked my mate. 'The taxman only gets to see the white ones.'

He was delighted that he could share with me this insider knowledge that not everyone had the privilege of knowing and I wonder to this day if I should have employed him as a consultant when I opened my first restaurant. I would have saved a fortune in VAT but would probably have spent a significant part of my life behind bars.

Do I want my curry hot? What a stupid question, I remember thinking: who in their right mind would eat a cold curry? My mother's food always came piping hot. Still, I thought perhaps in restaurants, one had to specify.

'Very hot, please,' I said with the confident tone of a regular visitor.

My companion nodded his proud approval with that 'he's my mate' look in his eyes.

'How hot exactly?' asked the waiter just to make sure I understood the implications.

'Well, as hot as possible,' I confirmed.

The waiter looked concerned as he walked away with the order, confirming with me as he went that I liked my curries served as hot as possible. I think he liked me.

I should have noticed the warning signals, especially when the kitchen door opened and I saw the waiter pointing me out to the chef. I gave a friendly wave. I was sure I had seen him before, possibly at the Sikh temple. The chef was curling his moustache with both hands and twirling it in an upward direction. Within seconds the tash resembled a bull's horns and he was ready for the battle. He didn't return the greeting and I realised later that he had been busy sizing up the opposition. He had been challenged; the gauntlet was down. In those days, 'customer care' were words Indian chefs were totally unfamiliar with. The gloves were off and he was going to 'take care' of this particular customer, no problem. Who the hell did

I think I was? He had been a chef for many years. The advert outside claimed that he had once cooked a Chicken Moghlai for Mahatma Gandhi. I had my doubts; I was sure I had read somewhere that Gandhi Ji was a strict vegetarian. This chef had taken on more formidable opposition than me and seen them off, time and time again. How dare I challenge him?

I became aware that the waiter was now wearing what looked like gloves made from asbestos as he brought the food to the table, similar to the ones I wore when I had to do a spot of welding in Yarrow's shipyards where I was serving my apprenticeship.

'It looks really good,' I said as he carefully placed it on the table, making sure none of it splashed his tablecloth. I also failed to notice the asbestos plate it had been served on and I realised later that, had it not been served in such a manner, there was a danger it could have burnt a hole through the table, melted my shoes and scalded my feet. It took only one mouthful before I started to feel a painful burning sensation in my mouth and my tongue swelled to about three times its normal size.

I was gasping for air and at the same time looking to my learned friend to do something magical and put me out of my misery. Water made little difference. I would not have put up any resistance if the staff, who by now had all gathered around to witness a scene most of them saw on a regular basis, had suggested I use the fire extinguisher to put out the flames in my mouth. My vision started to blur, and my last recollection of the evening was the chef standing by the kitchen door scratching his scrotum. The satisfied look on his face resembled that of an experienced gunslinger who had just seen off a new trigger-happy kid, and held on to his reputation as the fastest gun in town. The smell of that curry and the pain it gave me is what remains in my mind to this day. In fact, it is logged in my memory for all eternity.

Later in life I would discover that the only things that can quench a curry fire are dairy products like milk, yoghurt or ice cream; something to do with the fats in the dairy products binding to the hot-making molecules in the curry. But of course at that time I didn't have a BSc in Curryology or, for that matter, an MBE.

I had been eating my mother's home-made curries for many years but this was unique. That first experience didn't put me off that restaurant and the very next week I was back for more. There was also a new movie showing but that had nothing to do with my quick return. This time, the chef and I got talking and eventually we went on to become good friends. I had now moved a few steps closer to my destiny because even back then I loved the buzz of a busy restaurant and a hot smoky kitchen. Was that the inspiration I needed to go into the trade that would change my life or was it just my kismet that my grandfather had talked to me about when I was a little boy?

Chapter Three

ARRIVING IN GLASGOW

No two places could be more different than the plains of the Punjab and the western, industrialised city of Glasgow. The Punjab, the land of the five rivers, is lush agricultural land, known as the breadbasket of India. This is wheat country and that heritage is what gives Punjabi cuisine its chapattis, parathas and naan breads. Southern and eastern India is much more rice-based. We Jat Sikhs are sons of the soil, a farming caste, and generally own the land we farm. To come from this to the grime and smoke of Glasgow was more than a culture shock.

I didn't know how life would turn out when I first arrived in Glasgow with my mother and three brothers back in October 1963. My father had come over a few years before us, got himself a job driving the buses, bought a small room and kitchen in the Cowcaddens area near the city centre, then he sent for us. Well, I think he sent for us. It was not uncommon in those days for men to take on a second local wife, possibly setting up a new family here while keeping his ties back home. This was more common amongst the Muslim community as it seemed more acceptable in their religion and culture. When we arrived in Glasgow my dad brought home a *gori*, a white woman whom he introduced as his conductress. I was suspicious. Could this be the other wife? I thought. But I needn't have worried because that was the first and last time I saw her.

My first memory of Glasgow was stepping off the aeroplane and my father waiting for us on the tarmac. How different he looked, and at first I didn't recognise him. The beard and long hair that he kept beautifully groomed and were his pride and joy back in India were all gone. He was now clean-shaven and his hair were short, brushed back and held in place with Brylcreem.

'To get a job on the buses, we had to make these sacrifices,' he told us. 'They would not employ me if I wore a turban and had a beard so I got my friends to shave it all off.'

I thought it was very sad and wondered why we had come to such a damp horrible place. My thoughts then went back to the Punjab and how my grandfather had taken me to the barber a few weeks before we had boarded the plane to Glasgow. I had never had my hair cut in my life and I remember it being long, silky and flowing. My mother would always comment on how beautiful my hair was whenever she combed it. She would tie it up in a ball on the top of my head and put a white handkerchief over it, which was held in place with a rubber band. Getting my hair cut was a traumatic experience and I cried all the way home. Looking back now, I realise that it was just another requirement for me to fit in when I finally reached the land of flowing whisky.

Throughout history, Sikhs had given their lives rather than cut their hair. They had fought in many wars that were not of their making. During the two world wars, Sikhs had refused to remove their turbans and wear helmets and were praised for their bravery. Now, the people of this proud race were doing the unthinkable and visiting the barber, just to get a job on the buses.

'Don't worry, I'll grow it back at the first opportunity,' my father said. And years later he did – as soon as he retired from the buses.

Racism back then was something people seemed to accept as a part of everyday life. People like my father put up with shocking prejudices, which would never be accepted today. My father and his friends had to shave their beards and remove their turbans just to get a job. Banks wouldn't lend them money because they were Asians. Insurance companies said no because they were Pakistanis. There were no subtleties and the racism and bias was blatant. There were no laws to protect them so they suffered the humiliation and just got on with it. It was acceptable to be treated like second-class citizens and just get on with the business of bringing up their families.

Things have moved on and we now have a situation where the Glasgow humour has rubbed off on to the most diehard Asians, who quite often find themselves laughing at stories which in the past they would have found offensive. Like the story of the wee Asian boy who was so desperate to be white like all his pals at school that he walked into the kitchen one day as his mother was making chapattis, dipped his hands into the flour and rubbed the flour all over his face. 'Look, Mummy,' he said excitedly, 'I'm a white boy!'

The mother wasn't too pleased. 'I'll "white boy" you!' she shouted and slapped him around his head. 'Now go and show your father what you have just done.'

So the wee fellow walked into the lounge where his dad was watching television and said, 'Look, Dad, I'm a white boy.'

His father looked up and was furious. 'I'll "white boy" you!' he shouted and kicked the wee boy around the room. 'Go upstairs and show your grandfather what you have just done.'

So the wee guy went up to grandfather's bedroom and said, 'Baba Ji! Baba Ji! Look, I'm a white boy!'

The grandfather went berserk. ' "White boy"!' he shouted. 'I'll "white boy" you!' and he took the boy over his knee and spanked him until he was raw. 'Now go back to the kitchen and wash your face and don't ever do that again.'

When the wee boy walked into the kitchen his mother asked, 'What have you learnt today, my son?'

'What I've learnt, Mother, is that I've been a white boy for five minutes and I hate you Asians already.'

The liberal intelligentsia require me to have some angst about the clash of cultures that must resound in my brain. Somehow, having only one culture seems to be the preferred option. Why? It's like having only one TV channel to tune in to. And I remember the days when the BBC was all we had. Why not celebrate all the cultures that this marvellous world provides and invite them all to the party? If being a Sikh Scotsman is seen as a problem, then parochialism definitely rules.

Our first home was a tiny ground-floor tenement flat. It had a kitchen, with a sofa in it which could be converted into a bed at night. Unlike a lot of tenement properties, it had an inside toilet which we didn't have to share with the rest of the close and, because of this little luxury, my father was always reminding us of how lucky we were. My brothers and I never really liked the enclosed toilet as we found it very claustrophobic. When one is used to having thousands of acres of green lush farmland to use as a toilet then a wee five-foot-square box is not exactly a luxury. The kitchen was not large but it did have a recess, which held a double bed. There was only the one bedroom, with a couple of beds with very little space in between them, and one wooden wardrobe which, along with the rest of the furniture, had been purchased from the 'Barras', the famous Glasgow street market to which most immigrants went for all their household needs. This one wardrobe and a couple of suitcases held the whole family's worldly possessions.

I had three brothers when we first landed in Glasgow but within a couple of years two more siblings arrived. First another boy, Sukhdev, and then a girl, Sukhwinder, joined us in our one room and kitchen.

'You are living in a palace compared to what I had when I first arrived,' my father would tell us.

He had to share a room with several other guys and as far as they were concerned, a home was just a shelter and a place to sleep in between doing long shifts and working as much overtime as their gaffer could throw at them. He regarded himself lucky too because he had a good job compared to a lot of the other guys who worked as navvies. These guys would not only share a bedroom but also share a bed. One of them would be on the nightshift while the other worked during the day. This allowed them not only to share their beds but also their pyjamas, their work clothes and their shoes.

Their whole focus was to work hard, spend as little as possible and try to send home as much money as they could. That was the purpose of their existence and the reason they were born. They had responsibilities and they would not let down their families and bring shame upon their parents. Whenever my grandfather received money from my father he would sit in the meadow and boast about how well his son was doing in Scotland while waving around the latest money order and making his friends completely envious. If anyone had gone abroad and not sent money back to the family – and this happened now and then because the guy had gone off the rails and succumbed to the fruits of the Western world, which meant that he had started to drink or found himself a *gori*, a local Scottish girl – they would be the talk of the whole village. Their families would feel humiliated and would not be able to hold their heads up high amongst their peers.

Though we lived in such a small flat, the amazing thing was that I never felt that we needed any more space, especially after the stories our father had told us. In that tiny house we had all the space we needed; so much so that my brothers and I would play tag team wrestling on the kitchen floor while my mother went about her cooking.

The second day after we arrived we went outside to play on the pavement and a passing lady gathered us together and, pointing to her feet, indicated that we should go back inside and put on our shoes. For a while, we all believed that it was against the law to venture out in bare feet. It was normal for us to run around in bare feet and it took a while getting used to wearing shoes all day. In the village I only wore shoes when I went to school. We couldn't figure out why she felt it so important that we should wear shoes, while it was all right for her to walk around with nothing to cover her legs. None of us, including my mother, had ever seen stockings before. We used to talk about the pain that these poor women must go through to get the back of their legs stitched up.

Another strange sight was that of young couples walking along the street holding hands and kissing. Back in the village a boy would get castrated for even looking at a girl never mind going up to speak to her. In Glasgow, it was the swinging sixties and The Beatles were played everywhere. It was quite common to walk into your close and have to step around numerous young couples groping and snogging each other's faces off. My mother would sometimes guide us through the masses of bodies, telling us not to look, tutting while she did so and muttering in Punjabi that these people had no shame. '*Besharam!*' she would say, which means 'shameless'.

When I think back to my childhood, I remember a lot of happiness, especially growing up in Landheke, the village where I was born on 8 December 1954, according to my passport. I was two months premature which may not be a big deal nowadays but, in a remote village in the Punjab back in the fifties, it was a big deal. The death rate for newborns was shocking and for a child to be born two months premature and still survive was a miracle.

'You were a fighter from the day you were born,' my mother sometimes told me.

The one thing that she couldn't tell me, though, was my date of birth. All she knows is that it was the start of harvest but as to the year she said, 'Work it out for yourself.' And that is precisely what my grandfather did. Don't always believe what you read in a passport. I have always known that it was not my real date of birth. I have vivid memories of visiting the travel agent in Moga, the nearest town to my village. The travel agent asked my grandfather my date of birth to put on my passport, to which my grandfather replied that he wasn't sure.

'Just make one up,' he suggested.

I remember the agent measuring me with his eyes. 'He looks about eight – what do you think?' he said, trying to gain my grandfather's approval and even calling over some of his colleagues for a second opinion. 'Just call it nine – means he can start working sooner and bring in the money,' was my grandfather's response.

I have never forgotten those words and they often remind me of my reason for being in Scotland. Everyone in the office looked impressed by my grandfather's wisdom and foresight. I don't think they gave much thought to the fact that I had just aged a year, in just less than five minutes.

Although I always say that not knowing my birthday has never bothered me, it has left me with a small psychological scar. To this day, I find it difficult to understand why birthdays are so important to other people. 'It's just another day,' I argue. 'Why do you need a day off work just because it's your twenty-first birthday?' would be a question I often asked my staff in future years.

I realise now it's because I don't know how it feels to genuinely celebrate the day you were born, and so much so that I have gone to great lengths to find out my real date of birth, all to no avail. According to the records kept in the registry office in Faridkot, the city closest to my village where birth records are kept, I simply don't exist. Which would give me the other big chip on my shoulder in my teenage years and lead me to believe that I was adopted.

I couldn't blame my grandfather for increasing my age, because he perceived that to work and earn money was important in life. To my grandfather, wealth was all-important.

'No one is interested in a man without money,' he reminded me constantly. 'And people will judge you by your possessions. Money is power – it will earn you respect and some folk will even interpret it, and associate it, with wisdom.'

I guess this view is shared around the world because someone once told me that the only time a woman likes a man's company is when he owns it. I later realised how true my grandfather's words were, because as I became wealthier with my large house and fast cars, I was seen as a man of wisdom, and many people would travel long distances for my learned opinion. Most of the time, the wisdom comes with the experience of life and it is good when others can learn from your mistakes. I have come to know, though, that when people are looking for advice they are more often looking for you to endorse their own ideas and if you don't do this, quite often won't take your advice anyway. Therefore, sometimes you are telling people what they want to hear, which is not necessarily a bad thing as it gives them the confidence to go forward and achieve whatever they set out to do.

Of course, I realised as I started to rub shoulders with other affluent wise men and seek their advice that most of them were morons who, more often than not, had made their fortunes through fraud and embezzlement and didn't have a clue about making an honest living. But my grandfather was adamant and would support his theory by pointing out a poor man who lived in the village and had two wives. 'No wonder he is poor,' people in the village would say. 'The silly bugger has to feed and clothe two women.'

Then he would compare the villagers' opinions of the wealthy landowner with the big house in the middle of the village. 'He has done so well – a large house, a hundred acres of land, a foreign tractor ploughing his fields and he even has three wives.'

The rich man's wives became a part of his success story while they became the poor man's burden and downfall.

My grandfather, Sajjan Singh Gill, was my biggest inspiration. He had travelled to foreign lands with the British Army and fought in Burma, Japan and Singapore, and he always spoke highly of the British officers with whom he had served. He was impressed by their discipline and their honesty, by which he meant that they were not as corrupt as the people who took over when the British eventually left. My grandfather hated corruption. Through this association and what he had learnt on his travels, he always wanted his only son, my father, Mehar Singh, to emigrate to England because that, according to my grandfather, was the land of opportunity. The strange thing was, he did not want to come over himself. In his later years we encouraged him to visit but he would never come, saying that he had done all his travelling and seen all he had wanted to see.

'There is nothing here for you,' he would tell me. 'We are farmers, and as the land belonging to me will get passed down from generation to generation, from father to son, eventually, it will be divided up so often, there will be hardly enough left to go round and you can't grow or build new land.'

With this thought in mind, he worked hard to get my father the visa he required to get him to the UK.

'Why Scotland?' I asked my grandfather on one of my visits back home.

'Well, son, when I was in the army I had heard two rumours: the first, that the streets of London were paved with gold; the second, that the streams of Scotland flowed with whisky.' He confessed that he had foolishly shared this secret with my father and, when it came to the crunch, my father chose Glasgow. That explained why my father always took us hillwalking so often though I doubt if he ever found that stream.

I don't remember my father from my childhood in India. He had left us to come to Scotland when I was about four years old, or five, if you go by the age according to my travel agent, and the next time I set eyes on him was at Glasgow airport three or four years later. All my childhood memories are of the times spent with my grandfather. He loved being the centre of attraction. He was the village *Lambardar*, the leader of the council. He was an imposing figure, six feet three inches tall, and he always wore a white turban which added a couple of inches to his height. He had a long white silky beard and he always carried a double-barrelled shotgun. I only have memories of him with a white beard. Even all his photographs are with white hair, and this must be where I get my premature greyness.

Most afternoons, men would congregate on the meadow outside our house and I would quite often sit next to my grandfather while he held court. Those were genuinely happy times. I felt so safe, so secure. I think back and realise how fortunate I have been to have such a good life, even in my childhood. We were not rich but we had everything we needed. It is said that wealth can be measured by taking stock of the things one has in one's life that cannot be bought. I believe that now, but human nature also drives us towards material wealth and it's only when something goes wrong which money cannot fix that we realise how useless money can sometimes be.

My grandfather also encouraged me to sing. 'You will be a star one day and you will entertain thousands of people. It will give you a different perspective on life and people will love and admire you because everyone in the world, whether they be king or slave, wishes for this special talent that God gives only to his personal favourites.'

He would ask me to sing for him and his friends and, to this day, I can still see the pride in his face as I belted out the religious *shabads* which I recited from the holy book of the Sikhs, *Siri Guru Granth Sahib*. He was always keen for me to learn. Whenever I went back to visit on holiday, the highlight of the day for him, and for me, was when we sat together in the evenings and I would sing for him, as he sipped on his army-issued brandy, traditional songs of legendary lovers, their search for true love, each verse throwing up a fresh challenge to their quest, each line another tragedy, and finally their inevitable sacrifice or death, whichever was the more painful. He was right once again when he said that singing would give me a different perspective. Being able to sing made life so much easier. I used to lead the weekly school assembly, through which I became the teacher's pet, which had its rewards.

Believe me when I say this but you do not want to get on the wrong side of a teacher in a Punjabi village. I remember scenes from the school classroom which would have been regarded as brutal in a Japanese POW camp. Some of the kids were literally tortured and the practice still continues to this day. As a minor punishment, children were forced to stand in the scalding heat of a midday sun for hours on end and the cane was freely used to keep order in the classroom. The strange thing was that we all accepted it as the norm and I don't remember any debates about the long-term effects the beatings would have on the kids. It wasn't something I had to worry about, though, because I could sing and I was cute and that made me the teacher's pet. She liked me so much she used to give me apples.

Chapter Four

MY SCHOOL IN GLASGOW

The teacher at Garnetbank School in Primary Seven was the one that caused me the psychological damage. Mr Finlayson hated me with a vengeance, obviously not impressed by my singing voice, and he belted me most days for the slightest thing. We have all heard of teachers having pets but I know there is also a flip side, which is the pupil that the teacher just doesn't like. I remember he had a weird deformity and one of his hands was badly twisted so he couldn't use it. Bobby Watson sat next to me in the class and would sometimes translate things I couldn't understand.

'Imagine how bad it would be if the big bastard had two hands,' wee Bobby would say.

I suppose, without realising it, wee Bobby played his part in my character development. Things could always be worse, was Bobby's take on everything that happened. My first day at primary school in Scotland had been different from most nine-year-old kids; I had started in Primary One, which was where the five-year-olds normally started, whereas I was *nine* years old. I had short trousers and hairy legs and when I think back I realise that I must have frightened the life out of those wee lassies.

I couldn't speak a word of English, so I was put in with all the other kids who were just learning their alphabet. I couldn't understand a word of what was being said, but I did realise that I was the centre of attention for these five-year-olds who had never seen an Indian before and couldn't believe that someone, with a small moustache, could be so thick that they could not speak English or count past ten. Years after I had left school, I met Mrs Hutchison, a teacher from my primary school. She shouted my name from across the room, 'Charan Gill, I remember you!' and, in front of my business associates, she recounted how she had taught me to count when I was a lad in her class. In a way, I think she wanted to take a wee bit of credit for the way I eventually turned out.

'I was teaching him to count on his fingers in class one day,' she said loudly, making sure everyone could hear, 'and I asked him to repeat after me "Five fingers plus five fingers make ten fingers" which he did. I then said, "We have ten fingers and ten toes" and he shook his head and replied, "No, Miss, I have ten fingers but only nine toes." I failed to convince him that we all had ten fingers and ten toes but he just would not relent. Eventually, in front of the whole class, he took off his shoe and sock, put his left foot on the desk for everyone to see, pointed to his large webbed toe and said, "See, ten fingers but only nine toes." '

I often wonder why so much emphasis is put on the importance of the early education of children. I have heard it said that a child's most formative years are up to the age of six. By that age, according to experts, the basic character has already been established. I didn't even start school until I was nine. And as my children constantly reminded me when I shouted at them to do their homework, I hardly went to school and I didn't turn out too bad. I was a bad example to my kids when it came to making them do their homework. Bobby Watson would probably say, 'Aye, but just think of what you could have achieved if you had started school like us normal kids.'

Although I was a quick learner, the fact was I didn't catch up fast enough and after only three years of primary education I had to move on to secondary school. Back then, if you were smart you got to go to Woodside Senior Secondary with all the bright kids, but if you were not so smart you were sent to

St George's Road Junior Secondary. If Mr Finlayson had spent more time teaching me stuff to make me smart and less time beating me up, I might have made it to Woodside. But he hadn't, so junior secondary it was!

The difference between the two schools was the standard of education as well as the standard of the pupils. At Woodside you stayed on until you were eighteen and achieved your O levels and Highers, which made you university material. At St George's Road, your education would end after three years, and you would leave school and get a job as soon as you reached your fifteenth birthday, usually as a van boy or, if you were driven and ambitious, an apprenticeship.

'At least it will make your grandpa happy and you will start work sooner than anyone thought was possible,' quipped wee Bobby.

As it turned out, I did manage to catch up at St George's Road, this despite the fact that I didn't really like school too much due to my life being made difficult by school bullies. It was at this point that I realised how good a teacher Mr Finlayson actually was. I now knew what he meant when he said he was preparing me for secondary school as he beat the shit out of me in Primary Seven.

It was not so much the teachers who belted me at St George's Road; well, not any more than they belted the other kids. Big Alan Bryans, the school bully, took over where Mr Finlayson had left off. Even after all these years I am wondering whether it is a good idea for me to expose him like this in case he comes looking for me. I was his personal gofer and I spent three years at his beck and call. It did not affect my studies though, and each year my results improved until by the end of year three, I was top of my class.

The third year at school was the only year where we had a mixed class. We had girls sharing quite a lot of the periods during this final year and it made school a lot more interesting.

The girls did appreciate me and saw I was actually pretty smart for St George's Road and a lot of them would turn to me for help with their lessons. After a while, even big Alan Bryans started to take a liking to me when he needed help in the classroom. This change in attitude towards me would never last too long. Instead of beating me up for being a stupid darkie, Bryans was now inflicting punishment on me for being a swot. Bobby Watson was philosophical, although he felt sorry for me; his view was that if Bryans was busy beating me up, he was leaving Bobby alone.

The highlight of secondary school for me was the school dance. I had not been looking forward to it but it was my final year and I decided that I was going to make an appearance. I don't remember what I told my mother; I don't think I would have told her I was going to the dance. I would definitely have been grounded. It was not something good Punjabi boys did. We had been given weekly dance lessons in the gym for three weeks leading up to the dance and it was exciting dancing with all those pretty girls. I was so nervous walking into the gym that evening that I was almost physically sick.

I don't remember much about the evening except when it came to the ladies' choice. This one I had been dreading. There was no way any of the girls would want to dance with me. I expected to be the last one to be picked, though I don't know why that concerned me because I should have been used to being last picked as it happened every week at the football.

The boys sat at one end of the gymnasium in anticipation as the teacher announced that the next dance was a ladies' choice and asked the girls to take their partners. My heart was thumping so hard that I thought everyone in the hall would hear it and I feared it might explode. I couldn't believe it when Christine Gavin, the prettiest girl in the class, came straight towards me and asked if I would be so kind enough to dance with her. I felt my palms getting sweaty and quickly rubbed them on the seat of my pants as Christine reached out to take my hand. To this day, I still wonder if she did it because she felt sorry for me.

As if my night had not already been made, and at that point I would have died a happy wee boy, there was more joy to come my way. That particular dance was also one of the night's competitions, with all the couples having to dance a waltz while holding a Polo Mint between their noses without dropping it. It was an elimination process and the last couple left standing would win the prize. There was no way I was going to let that Polo slip from between our noses. We danced away while other couples dropped out one after another until only Christine and I were left standing. I had hoped the others would have put up a better challenge; it's not every day you get to dance so close to Christine Gavin. I wanted it to last for as long as possible. I was dancing on air and as she gave me a hug when we collected our trophy I wondered if that meant we were now an item. That night I could not sleep and I wanted the next morning to come so that I could go to school and see Christine again. As soon as I saw her the next day I gave her my best smile. She didn't even notice I was there. I obviously didn't have the effect on her that I thought and our feelings were obviously not mutual. No fears though; I could still worship her from afar.

The only really bad thing I remember doing at school was when Bobby Watson and I were given the classroom keys by our form teacher and asked to go and set up the room during a break. Bobby started going through the teacher's drawers, found some blank exam papers and decided that we should nick them and get ourselves 100 per cent in the forthcoming exams. I don't think that even if he had known the questions and memorised all the answers, Bobby had the capacity to score more than a pass mark. Quite instinctively, we took the papers and without even looking at them hid them behind a radiator. A couple of hours later, our form teacher came into the gym where we were doing

PE and spoke to our PE teacher. I knew from the way they were looking at us that we had been found out.

Bobby and I were separated and questioned about the missing papers. This was where Bobby's experience of being questioned by the police about one thing or another on a regular basis came in handy for him and he stuck to his guns and denied everything. Within minutes, though, I had broken down and confessed to the crime and told the teachers where the papers had been hidden. I got belted four times for that crime and Bobby, with his policy of 'deny, deny, deny', got off scot-free. It was even worse when I found out that the exam papers were not even for our class, so they would not have been of any use to us anyway.

The headmaster, Mr McDougall, called me to his office and my father was also asked to be present. My dad had spent the entire previous evening giving me the third degree after I had given him the letter from the 'heidie'. 'What the hell have you been up to now? If you embarrass me in front of your headmaster, you're dead!'

When my father said something like that, he meant it. I lost count of the number of times he had given my brothers and me a doing for one thing or another. I needn't have worried because it was good news.

'Your son has performed exceptionally well over the past year, Mr Gill, and he came first in the class. I would urge you to encourage him to continue with his education at Woodside so that he can achieve his Highers and go on to university.'

I could see my dad's chest swell with pride. The final decision was left to me: I could stay on or leave. I sometimes wish my father had played a bigger role at that time and told me to stay on at school, because if he had insisted then I would have done so and I often wonder how life would have turned out if I had got my university degree. But he didn't, and I was pleased to move on. I don't think I could have gone through three more years of bullying and weekly beatings.

Chapter Five

WORK, WORK, WORK

My father, like my grandfather, had his own agenda. Our sole purpose in leaving India and coming to Scotland in the first place was to get a job and start earning money as soon as possible. He probably thought that I was never going to be university material and was quite happy that I would at least have a trade to my name.

Work was nothing new to me; I got my first job as a milk boy when I was thirteen years old. I would get up at half past five and walk to the dairy to start work an hour later. I still don't know why I took that job. I don't remember any of my brothers doing it, or my father making me do it, so it must have been a decision I made by myself after being encouraged by Donald McGregor, who was also in my class and had been doing the milk round for a couple of months. It was all right for Donald as he stayed directly opposite the dairy but my house was a good twenty-minute walk that I had to do at six-thirty every morning in the freezing cold. Donald had spoken to the man who owned the dairy and had gotten me my first job so I wasn't going to let him down. The job only lasted a couple of months because I was quizzed by two plain-clothes police officers about my age. I didn't want to say that I didn't know as that may have sounded cheeky so I gave my official date of birth. I was then told to go home as I was too young to work, which really disappointed me because I had got used to the money. I have always been pretty independent when it comes to making choices regarding employment.

I was not unemployed for long. When I was still thirteen my father reckoned it was time for me, along with my elder brother Iqbal and my cousin Sadhu, to take on a job during our summer holidays. My mother complained about how difficult we were to handle during the long summer break and it was decided that a job would be good discipline. My father had friends who were door-to-door salesmen; most of them going around small farms and villages selling merchandise from suitcases. These guys were amazing. A lot of them couldn't read or write, not even in their own language, having never been to school. They travelled by bus and walked miles by foot, peddling their wares. They gave credit and never ever wrote anything down because they couldn't. Yet, they remembered everything. They always remembered who owed them money, when it was due to be paid and what the terms were. These guys carried their ledgers in their heads. My father had heard that farms required seasonal workers to gather potatoes during summer.

'What better work for the sons of a farmer than working the land?' I heard him say to my mother.

The first Sunday of our summer holidays, my mother gave us a week's supply of tinned food and Phuman Singh, a friend of my father's who could not only read and write but also had a driving licence, came to pick us up in his minivan. We travelled for what seemed like eternity and ended up at a farm in West Kilbride. I didn't realise that we were only about forty-five minutes from home because Phuman was doing his usual rounds, visiting numerous farms and conducting his business so he would get us to our destination in his own good time.

When we eventually arrived, the farmer's wife watched as three of us piled out of the back of the van and she tried to persuade Phuman to take us home. But he had his orders; my father had given him strict instructions to make sure we had jobs. It wasn't important which farm we were left at because, to my father, they were all the same. Phuman Singh took a bit of time to sell a few wares from his suitcase, bade us goodbye and drove off into the horizon. We were given bunk beds in a barn that we were to share with other workers who were all Irish. It was hard work and the first week my back hurt so much. The days were long; each minute felt like an hour and I cried myself to sleep every night.

'It takes a while getting used to it. You will be OK after the first week,' everyone kept telling us. Eventually I did get used to it, and the pain decreased but it was still the toughest job I've ever done. I wondered if I would have to go through my life working like this every day. We continued to work on the farm for six weeks of our holidays. Saturday afternoons, we would go home, where we would spend one night. The next morning we would get fresh supplies, which were to last us for the following week, and catch a bus back to the farm on Sunday afternoons.

I did that for three years. After the first year, my brother and cousin stopped going as they left school and went on to full-time employment. My younger brother Dippal and other friends took their places and joined me at the farm. I became the veteran and by the time I was fourteen I was leader of the gang. Although the work was tough I enjoyed those summers at the farm because after we finished work there was still plenty of time for play. The summer days were long and the weeks seemed to last a lifetime. Most evenings were spent lazing around the farm, playing football or kabaddi, an Indian game similar to rugby, the only difference being there is no ball in kabaddi, just rugby tackles.

I left school in December 1969 to start my working life. I had applied for three jobs as an apprentice. It wasn't important to me what I served my time as, as long as I had a trade and could earn good money. I was offered all three jobs and it was up to me to decide which one to take. There was such a demand for labour and tradesmen at the time that it was impossible not to get an apprenticeship. I don't know why I chose Yarrow's shipyard as the place to serve my time but I think the fact that it was easy to get to by bus in the mornings probably had something to do with it.

It was my father who told me the importance of having a trade. When I told him that quite a few boys from my class were going to work as van boys for companies who delivered goods to the shops because the pay was so much better, he said that long-term, the apprenticeship would definitely be the better option. I would have put money on him going for the better-paid job but I suppose I had underestimated his wisdom and foresight.

I started my proper working life as an apprentice turner in Yarrow shipbuilders in January 1970, and I worked there until the Easter of 1978. Yarrow's was an amazing place back in 1970; it employed thousands of people. Next door there was Barclay Curle, shipbuilder; on the other side was Harland and Woolf, another shipbuilder, and across the road in South Street was the Albion Motor Company. Between them, these companies employed tens of thousands. When all the workers poured into South Street at the same time, at four-thirty in the afternoon, the sight was awesome and as far as the eye could see, the whole street was a sea of bunnets.

Yarrow's was a seriously cushy number. After picking tatties, this was a doddle. For the duration of the four-year apprenticeship, we had to do three weeks at work in the shipyard, and every fourth week we would go to Anniesland College to learn the theory. The early seventies were a time when the trade unions ran the country. I couldn't be exact as to the actual number of times the whole yard downed tools and walked out, but there were numerous strikes during my apprenticeship. As apprentices we were not allowed to go on strike, but we were not allowed to work either as there were no tradesmen to provide supervision, so at those times our days would be spent playing cards or shove-ha'penny, a game played on a board with goals at each end using penny coins for players and a ha'penny as a ball. The object of the game was to score as many goals as possible.

The guys at Yarrow's took their shove-ha'penny seriously; scuffles quite often broke out if the referee gave a dodgy decision. Grown men had to be held apart by workmates to avoid some serious battles. There was even a league table and knockout cup tournaments with the finals being played in front of capacity crowds in the canteen at lunchtimes.

As well as the strike, there was also the three-day working week brought about by the infamous strikes of the early seventies. Lack of coal supplies affected every industry and every walk of life; there were power cuts every day and electricity was rationed. As places struggled to remain open an apprentice's life in Yarrow's became even easier.

I enjoyed my time at Yarrow's. It wasn't just an apprenticeship in shipbuilding; it was also an education in a way of life. It was odds-on that the majority of the men supported either Rangers or Celtic, usually depending on whether they were Catholic or Protestant. It was in Yarrow's that I discovered that, in Glasgow, the colour of your football scarf was more important than the colour of your skin and one of the first questions I got asked was whether I was a Tim or a Hun. To which I replied, 'Well, actually, I am a Sikh.'

Obviously not satisfied with my answer, my questioner asked, 'Aye, but are you a Tim Sikh or a Hun Sikh?'

I had realised at school that the easy way out was to say that you were a Partick Thistle fan. That way, even though you took a terrible slagging, everyone left you alone.

Then there was the economy within Yarrow's. The place had its own hairdressers, sweet sellers, cigarette wholesalers and bookies, to name a few. All of them were on Yarrow's payroll but they also did these wee jobs to earn some extra cash. There was very little that could not be sourced within Yarrow's.

The place was full of characters; the humour and the patter didn't allow time for stress or depression. I should confess at this time that I was also involved in a vocation that was over and above my normal working contract. I can't remember how I became the chosen one but I think that the fact that my lathe, which was the machine that I operated, was situated near the toilets may have something to do with it. One has to remember that the shipyards were full of macho male workers and the only females that were employed by Yarrow's were in the offices. The workshops were men-only and that meant there was a requirement for literature that featured naked girls posing in all sorts of erotic positions. When guys went to the toilet, they would take one of these magazines with them to flick through as they did their business, as only men do. When they came out of the toilet, they would hand me the magazine and ask that I keep it in my locker and give it to whoever needed it.

Within a few months I had a couple of dozen magazines. I was fast making a name for myself as the local librarian and I was fondly known as 'Big Singh, the Porno King'. I decided that, if I was to do the job properly, then I should start a proper club and have a list of rules and regulations. To join my club one had to bring along a brand-new girlie magazine, free of any stains, and one would then have access to the whole library. Within a short space of time the foreman allowed me to have an extra locker to stock my hoard of girlie magazines. I had them shelved in alphabetical order and then issue numbers. People came from all over the shipyard because word of the quality of my stash spread like wildfire and everyone was desperate to join my club. If the magazines came back with stains on them or were not in the same condition as they left my library, the guilty party would either have to bring in a brand new magazine or risk being thrown out of the club forever. I ran a tight ship and the library thrived.

By the time I left Yarrow's, I had a collection of hundreds of mags that I left for a friend to run but, sadly, when I visited Yarrow's at a later date, the library had all but disappeared due to the incompetence of my successor. I had subconsciously learnt my first business lesson – I should have chosen my heir more carefully. The other great thing about Yarrow's was the chance to work on the night shift, which we were asked to do from time to time. Some guys chose to do night shift permanently but I liked it just for a change. Instead of working five shifts we only had to do four ten-hour stints at night, which meant that the weekends lasted from Friday morning to Monday night.

The nightshift foreman was never very strict and the guys on the shift got away with murder. We were given some work to complete on every shift and once the work was done, which usually took about half the night, the rest of the time was used up playing cards. There were some conscientious guys who chose to work throughout the night but these were not large in numbers. Some of the guys would not play cards but instead chose to go to sleep instead. I had a wee hideaway which I would tuck myself into at around four o'clock in the morning and sleep for about three hours. I got very blasé and one night decided just to sleep next to my machine. I was lying down when I saw the foreman walking up the aisle. I tried to decide quickly what I should do because it was quite clear that I had been caught. I knew that if I got up then he would have to reprimand me so I decided to pretend to be asleep. I could sense him standing over me but kept my eyes firmly closed. He also knew that if he woke me up then he would have to suspend me. He obviously decided that he didn't want to do that so he just let me lie there and moved on up the aisle. He approached me the next night and said, 'The next time you decide to go for a kip, make sure you do it where I can't find you.'

I took his advice that night and, when it got to bedtime, I went back to my secret hideout.

I often think how much I have changed over the years and how much my outlook to life has changed. It really was a case of doing in Rome as the Romans do when I worked those nightshifts. Once I left Yarrow's, I would never have dreamt of going to sleep on the job and would have never allowed anyone else to do so either if I were their manager. Yet, when I was in Yarrow's, I took it as a perk of the job.

Outside of Yarrow's, I led a totally different life. I spent a lot of time at the Sikh temple in Nithsdale Road, quite often staying the whole weekend with my brothers and my friends. I don't think it had much to do with religion, more the social aspect. Sikh boys were not allowed to go anywhere interesting but my parents didn't mind us staying out all weekend as long as we were helping at the temple. It wasn't a bad place really and most evenings there was plenty of female talent to admire.

I learnt to play some musical instruments and on Sundays I played regularly in front of the congregation. I started to get more involved with my music. I was leading a double life: Friday nights I would be out getting drunk with my Yarrow's mates, getting thrown out of pubs, jumping on top of parked vehicles, and on Saturday I would be a totally different person, helping to serve food, assisting to clean and hoover the Sikh temple.

It was at the Sikh temple that I learnt to play the *dholaks*, a Punjabi drum in the shape of a small barrel with skin on both ends. I played it every Sunday with zest and I was a favourite of all the aunties in the temple. I was not liked by other Sikh boys of my age because after their mothers got home from the temple they would give their sons a good beating for not being more like me and playing the dholaks like I could.

Chapter Six

MAKING MUSIC

It was through my music that I got involved with a new set of friends. It was 1972 and, although I accompanied various people as a musician, I had not sung since I was a boy, back in the Punjab. My new friends were members of the Glasgow Indian Students Union studying at Glasgow University and each year they put together a show called *The Festival of India*. It was here that I met Balbir, the man who would one day become my mentor and my partner in business.

The show involved dozens of students and rehearsals started months beforehand. These were not actual rehearsals, just excuses for the boys to get together with the girls and sing romantic songs across the room. Everyone fancied someone but nobody ever got to know who fancied which person – sometimes not even the pair who fancied each other. It was worship from afar, a few stolen glances; everybody walked around like heroes from a Bollywood blockbuster. I was asked to go along and play dholak for the next show and I really enjoyed the company of my new friends. I loved the musical aspect and was really taken by how much they enjoyed their sing-songs.

It was at one of these sing-song nights, coincidentally held at a flat next door to the one I first lived in when I arrived in Glasgow, that I sang my first song in front of my peers. They were totally impressed and I instantly became a member of their elite gang. I started singing at more shows and because of this, I was also becoming a hit with the girls. We started rehearsing for the 1972 *Festival of India* show, which was when I was first introduced to Kuljeet.

I had seen her at shows before but always considered that she was out of my league. For a start, she was four years older than I was. I had just turned eighteen and she was twenty-two – a big gap at that age. She was also a really good singer and all the guys were after her affection. There were guys who were the same age as Kuljeet and I always felt that they would be more attractive for her to be with. I was excited that she had even noticed me; one day she gave me a look that I interpreted as, come and get me. I didn't sleep for days. I couldn't wait for the next Sunday to come around so I could see her at rehearsals.

Every week we seemed to talk more than the week before and by the time the show came round we had become good friends. I even had the honour of taking her to the after-show party. That night I built up enough courage and asked if she would go with me to the movies. I couldn't believe it when she said yes. That was it – it was now official and Kuljeet was my girlfriend. I had achieved the impossible.

Within months she was talking marriage and this got me very confused and slightly worried. I had only known her for a few months and during that time she had done most of the talking and made all the decisions as I was too young and naïve to be able to make any decisions about my future. Although I didn't really know her, I reckoned that part was not too important, because marrying someone you didn't know was a normal situation in my culture. Back then, you didn't get an introduction to the missus until after the wedding ceremony.

I remember my mother once telling me that her mother got married when she was seven years old. She remained at her parents' house until she was fourteen, then moved in with her in-laws. In fact, in Glasgow, my elder brother Iqbal was engaged at fourteen while he was still at school to a girl he didn't even know. The reason for the engagement was that the girl's parents were friendly with my parents, but the families fell out and the wedding never took place.

I knew I wasn't ready but I was so overawed that I could never have said no to Kuljeet. Up until that point I had not considered the consequences; for a start, I had forgotten to consider my mother. There were a number of reasons why my mother would never allow me to marry Kuljeet. First, she was too old for me. Second, I was too young to get married, but that was only because my mother did not approve and the girl was not her choice. I could perhaps have got around this particular objection by reminding her of her mother's age when she had married, or my brother's age when he got engaged. Third, she sang with boys on stage, which meant she was not daughter-in-law material, and, fourth, and most importantly, she was the wrong caste.

Caste, as opposed even to religion, is the biggest barrier when it comes to marriage in Indian culture. It's an irony that the basic principle upon which Sikhism was founded was to try and bring an end to this system where if one was born to a particular caste, that was it for the rest of one's life. It was not possible to work one's way out of one caste into a higher one. If one was born an untouchable, he could work his way up to Prime Minister, but he would still remain an untouchable. My family would never consider Kuljeet as a potential daughter-in-law – she was not good enough to marry into our family because she was of a lower caste and nobody could ever change that situation.

It all came to a head the day I brought Kuljeet back to my house to tell my mother how much I loved her and how much I wanted to marry her. Thinking back, it was not really my idea to take Kuljeet home – it was more Kuljeet's but I just went along with it.

'You are too young to get married,' was my mother's first response.

'What about your mother? You told me she was married by the time she was seven,' I tried to reason, knowing full well it was the most stupid thing I could have said and only added to my mother's ammunition to prove that I was immature. It was the only excuse she could use that wouldn't totally offend Kuljeet. My mother was a tactful woman; she wouldn't go for the caste card unless it became absolutely necessary, and only to me in private. No point in making the poor girl suffer more than required, at least to her face. She told me how she really felt once Kuljeet had left.

'I think you should wait for a while before making any hasty decisions and take time to think things through. Don't rush into something you may regret for the rest of your life.'

A few weeks later my mother suggested that we take a trip back to India to visit my grandfather. 'The break will be good for you and you have not seen your grandfather for ten years.'

The thought of seeing my grandfather again made me so excited – I wanted to go back and see him so much – but the prospect of leaving Kuljeet for two months made me feel sad and Kuljeet warned me that my mother's intentions were dubious.

'She is taking you back to marry you off to someone else,' she warned me, tears streaming down her cheeks. 'I know I will never see you again,' she said, holding on to my hand, unwilling to let go because she knew that if she did, she would never ever get the chance to hold it again. I honestly felt she was being dramatic; I had no intention of getting married to anyone else. In fact, I wasn't even sure if I wanted to marry Kuljeet, and no one could force me to do something I didn't want to.

Back in Yarrow's, I told all my mates I was going on holiday for a couple of months. My leave of absence was organised, as was my going-away night out. At Yarrow's, we had nights out for just about anything in those days; all we needed was half an excuse. A typical Yarrow's night out was, without exception, a Friday night. Fridays were for the boys and Saturdays were for the guys who had regular girlfriends. The Saturday night had to be spent with the 'burds'. Pubs in those days were only licensed to open until ten o'clock so little time was wasted in getting the show on the road. Work would finish at four and everyone would rush home to get cleaned up and meet up again for six. The establishments selected for these events were always in the city centre; they had to be inexpensive, and be the type where the clientele could dance on tables and be as boisterous as they pleased.

A typical night would have between fifteen and thirty noisy guys, all knocking back drinks at a phenomenal speed trying to make sure they got their money's worth from their contribution to the kitty. Things normally went well until about nine o'clock; the subject would then turn to football, religion or something even more personal like who had the ugliest bird or the smallest penis, and you always knew that a fight was just around the corner. Some nights we were lucky, as other works nights out were also being held at the same venue. This meant that it was odds-on the evening's battle would be fought against the other crowd. Either way, it wasn't really important who you fought with, just as long there was someone to pick a fight with.

Since it was my night out, I got grabbed in the toilets and carried into a cubicle. 'You cannae go up the dancin' withoot washin' yir hair, wee man. Here, let's gie you a haun.'

I was held upside down and my head planted firmly into the loo. The toilet was then flushed and my head given a real soaking. 'Nae bother getting a lumber noo – ye smell gorgeous.'

As I walked out of the toilets, I realised I had missed the start of the fight. Chopper Paterson, so called because he was a karate brown belt, was squaring up to wee Willy Ibell, who in turn was being held back by a couple of the more sober blokes.

Within a few minutes, we were out on the street, barred from another Glasgow pub. A lot of noise had been made, with lots of shadow-boxing and flying kicks into the air, but, as usual, no punches actually landed on the opponent.

The standard practice at this point was to break up into smaller groups and try to get into whichever pub was lenient enough to serve us. It wasn't easy as we were barred from most city-centre pubs anyway. The pubs would close at ten o'clock and the only way to get more drink was to go for a curry. Most restaurants had queues outside the doors because everybody was desperate for more drink, but if you wanted booze you just had to wait. Once in, you would realise that everyone in the place was sloshed. It would be difficult to find anyone sober in an Indian restaurant on a Friday night and I don't know how the staff managed to cope. Little did I know that one day I would find out and become a specialist in the field.

After being given the menus, you would place your order and the first thing the waiter would do was total up your bill and present it for payment. It was only after the bill was settled in full that you were offered even a sniff of a spicy onion. The staff in these places knew that there was little chance of getting money once the food had been consumed.

Chapter Seven

SHARAB (ALCOHOL)

I grew up in Glasgow with a fair amount of exposure to alcohol. I am not referring to the people falling out of busy bars but also to my father and his friends. We are Sikhs, and the Sikhs, unless they are very religious and don't drink at all, can be a riotous lot. Especially the Jat Sikhs from the Punjab who love to sing, dance and party. For those of you who are thinking, 'I thought Indians didn't drink,' perhaps there is a little lesson you should learn. Muslims tend not to drink – it's against their religion. Hindus are generally well behaved and gentle and tend to drink in moderation. And my clan, well we just keep going until we are 'Sikh'. The other thing that the Sikhs possess is a sense of humour and the ability to laugh at themselves, I hope.

I did discover in later life that a lot of Muslims drank too. They didn't do it in front of other Muslims but the strange thing was that they were quite comfortable to drink in my company or in the company of other non-Muslims. There have been some quite hilarious times when I have been in the company of two Muslim friends. When it was my turn to go to the bar I would get one of them a vodka and Coke while I got the other one a vodka and fresh orange juice as I knew that is what they both wanted. When I brought the drinks back to the table I would say, 'Right, whose is the Coke and which one of you is drinking the fresh orange?' Without the blink of an eyelid, they would casually take their drinks and sip away quite the thing, both knowing quite well what the other was drinking but never passing comment.

It was not unusual for a number of us to be in a bar and they would all be drinking, and they knew that everyone else was doing the same thing but they just would not admit it to each other. There were times when Muslim couples came into the Ashoka and one of the females would come up and tell me that when she and her friend ordered Cokes, I was to put large gins in them and to make sure when I served the drinks to the table not to get them mixed up. She would then slip me some cash to cover the drink charge so it would not show on the bill. I drank regularly with a friend called Ashraf and he would always drink brandy with warm water. When I asked why he always took his brandy warm he answered, 'When I inevitably face my God, I will say to him that the only time I took alcohol was for medicinal purposes. That is why I never drink cold brandy with ice because then it becomes an alcoholic drink.' Ashraf had obviously found a loophole. These examples are of course the exception and not the rule as most of my Muslim friends are strict when it comes to alcohol and refuse to drink at all.

Although my father and his friends did not squander money in the bars on a Friday night, they were partial to a wee drink now and again. Whenever they had occasion to do so, my father and his friends would get together in one of their houses and drink whisky and eat pakora. Pakora was a tasty Indian snack that in the Punjab was eaten to help a drink slip over. Glaswegians on the other hand didn't really require any help in that department and as I later discovered, pakora found a new role in life as a starter on Indian restaurant menus across the country.

The first time I drank lager was when I was an apprentice at Yarrow's. As I have already mentioned, we would work in the shipyard for three weeks and then go to Anniesland College on the fourth to learn the theory. On one of these college days, two friends, Kevin Dooley and Callum Lavelle, invited me to the pub at lunchtime. I did not realise as we walked to the bar that they had planned to get me drunk and, as soon as we got to the bar, they ordered three pints of lager. I asked them how many of these they would drink on a normal night out and they said dozens; as I discovered later, that was not an exaggeration. They said that since this was lunchtime and we only had fifty minutes it meant that we only had time for one round each. I did not want to be seen as a lightweight and struggled to keep up the pace. Within forty-five minutes I had downed three pints of lager and found myself staggering back towards the college. The whole class, except for the teacher, knew I was drunk and I still can't remember much from that afternoon. I was sixteen and had just had my first drunken experience but as I was to spend another eight years in Yarrow's, many more would follow.

I have always enjoyed a small refreshment throughout my life and it has played a vital social role in most things I have done. From the early days of watching my father and his friends to my wild days in the shipyards where most Friday nights were just a haze, I enjoyed the role it played it my life. I enjoyed the casual nights in the local bar where I would sometimes join my uncle, Amar Dhillon, a man I loved very much, my father and my brothers, Iqbal, Dippal and Binder, for a couple of shandies. Then when I took over at the Ashoka, my visits around all the pubs at ten o'clock to bring all the punters back would not have happened had I not enjoyed my pints of lager. The business deals that were done while downing several jugs of lager would never have been negotiated under more sober circumstances when we would all have got ourselves bogged down in the fine detail.

Yes, I am glad my father chose Scotland, the land where the streams flowed with whisky, as his adopted home as opposed to anywhere else in the world.

Chapter Eight

GOING BACK HOME

It was a huge culture shock for me when we landed in Delhi. The first problems we had to overcome were the corrupt immigration and customs officials. My father had told me to put a ten-pound note in my passport before handing it over to the immigration officer. This, he said, would save me a lot of grief. I immediately recognised less informed travellers who thought by simple reasoning they could get past these Rottweilers. What one has to understand is that these people were totally unscrupulous and would sell their own mothers to make that extra rupee. It was one of the things I always used to dread when visiting India in those days.

Once you got outside the airport, there were crowds of people everywhere. There were hustlers of every shape and form. The biggest hustlers were the taxi drivers and they would rip you off sooner than look at you. If people had nothing to sell, there was nothing to stop them from begging and you would be pestered until you gave them something. The only problem with giving to a beggar in India is that through a sophisticated system of communication they would simply alert fellow beggars to your weakness and before you had time to hide away your wallet you would be surrounded by beggars of every age and deformity, asking for alms.

The worst part of the journey was getting from Delhi back to our house in the village. I could not have imagined making it without my grandfather, although I came to realise in later years that the journey was actually a lot easier without him as he had a habit of trying to do it in the cheapest possible way.

He would barter wildly with taxi drivers. 'You are all thieves!' he would shout, never trying to hide his view from the people he was referring to. Once the taxi was negotiated, it was off to the train station and the cheapest seats available on the train.

My grandfather trusted no one, sometimes not even his own family. He came from a family of four brothers, he would tell me. I knew one to be his real brother and the other two his cousins but he would refer to them all as his brothers whenever he talked about them. He was the only one of his brothers who had got married. It wasn't that the others weren't interested in wedlock, or they weren't desirable: they just couldn't find brides. He explained how at the turn of the twentieth century, it was a well-known and documented fact that baby girls were simply killed at birth. No one wanted the burden of feeding an extra mouth and paying a huge dowry to marry them off. So daughters were just drowned or strangled at birth. This led to a shortage of girls, which in turn led to a shortage of brides. When men started to outnumber women, brides were not easy to come by and, for a long period of time, it became the norm for the boy to pay a dowry to the girl's family. That's if you were lucky enough to find a girl in the first place. My grandfather's brothers were not so lucky. They remained bachelors and, as none of them ever married, they didn't produce any heirs.

'Land is the only way that the people here can survive,' he would say. 'Trust no one because they will stab you in the back and simply take what is yours.'

A lot of people, even close relatives, said he was paranoid. The facts, though, told their own story. His three brothers had disappeared over the years. He said he knew for a fact that people in the village had murdered them and after they were killed wills had been falsified and their lands taken by their murderers.

People now grew fat from the spoil of lands that were actually my grandfather's birthright. He had fought for years through courts to win back lands that he said were not only his, but also the birthright of me and my brothers. He would spend hours talking about the various complications of each court case: what stage each case had reached and who the action was against, and he provided details of the families whom he regarded as his enemies. He would say how at these court sessions, large numbers of family supporters normally turned up to side with the opposition, and how he was just one man, alone, but he never gave up and he was never intimidated by the numbers.

He never ate food given to him by someone he didn't know. He told me never to get too close to people, and if I should ever drink, to do it alone. One of his brothers had been killed while eating and drinking with friends. They had got him drunk and attacked him with swords. He had tried to escape by climbing up a ladder on to the roof and he could have got away if he hadn't been so intoxicated. They grabbed his feet and pulled him back down. They chopped him to little bits, starting with his arms and legs to stop him from escaping. His remains were never found. If my grandfather had to eat out due to some court case running on, and court cases were the only reason he would stay out, he never ate in the same restaurant twice. He trusted no one and, because of his brothers' tragic ends, I didn't blame him for the way he felt.

'I will go the same way,' he often told me. 'They will never find my body. I will be killed by people I trust and all for material goods.'

The irony was that wealth and material goods, which he encouraged me to accumulate, were the very things that he knew would one day bring about his death. 'Totally paranoid' were words often used to describe my grandfather.

'Who would want to kill him?' was the question everyone would ask.

'I will probably be betrayed by someone close. They wouldn't dare try anything while I am awake.' He always pointed to his shotgun as he said this. He didn't go anywhere without his shotgun.

He trusted no one, especially Delhi taxi drivers, who he thought would drive us to a remote place and relieve us of our British possessions. Nor did he trust the coolies at the mobbed railway stations whom he followed closely, knowing that if he lost sight of them for even the briefest of moments, they would magically make at least one of the bags disappear. He stayed right behind them until they had placed our suitcases above the cheap seats in a class C compartment. 'At least you have got seats,' he would say, pointing at people clambering on to the roof of the train, laden with all their worldly possessions.

The train journey from Delhi to Ludhiana, on one of the main railway arteries in the Punjab, took six hours but to me it seemed like six days. This is when you start to make silent promises to never ever again complain about travelling on British Rail. The three-hour delay at Heathrow airport felt like time spent at a holiday resort.

The journey wasn't over yet. A change of train, after a long wait on a crammed platform, and two hours later you were in Moga, almost there now. Suitcases were piled on to a rickshaw, and a thin old man would pedal the two remaining miles to our house at the edge of the village. It was only after this experience that I realised how fortunate I was, though it was good to be back home. I was glad I had the choice of leaving whenever I wished. At least that was what I thought, but my mother had other plans. Sure, I could go back to Glasgow whenever I wanted; I just had to get married first.

Chapter Nine

ARRANGING MY MARRIAGE

'I am not interested in getting married. Anyway, I am too young . . . remember you said it yourself – too young!' I yelled at my mother as she once again made the suggestion.

'Not in India you're not! Remember how young my mother was when she got married. Boys who were in your class at school when you lived here have their own children now.'

I looked at her in disbelief. She looked at me as if I were an idiot.

My grandfather tried the 'good-cop' approach. 'No harm in looking, son – you don't actually have to say yes. Boys in the village don't have the choice that you have. They normally get introduced to their wives at the wedding ceremony and my brothers would have said yes to anything.'

My mother's ploy was to get as many of my relatives and friends as possible to talk to me; they would take turns to try and convince me to change my mind. They genuinely believed that I was being silly.

'Everyone has to get married one day – the sooner the better. I can't wait,' said one of my old friends who was obviously desperate to experience for himself the great night which awaited every young man once he had tied the knot. It's all sixteen-year-old Sikh boys ever talk about. They don't have the option of 'lumbers' after drunken nights out at a nightclub.

The people in the village made it a priority to talk to me at every opportunity to convince me how good an idea marriage was, and for some it became a challenge. My mother even went to the local voodoo man to get some powerful potion which would influence my thinking and make me fall in love. I would find weird things under my bed in the mornings. This could be anything from a few beads to some rice and seemed innocent enough but I knew that these things were left there to influence me through black magic.

Whenever a young boy from Britain came to the village, the matchmakers would go into overdrive. Word spread like wildfire that there was a boy in Landheke village looking for a wife. My mother did all she could to fan the flames and, within days, people started turning up at our door with proposals of marriage.

'Just meet one of the girls,' my mother was now pleading. 'You will have the final say.'

Eventually I decided to compromise and allowed them to set up a meeting with one of the girls. That was my first big mistake because, within twenty-four hours, the matchmakers and my mother had got together and set up a dozen meetings. I went along to a few; I don't really remember much about the actual meetings or what was said. I didn't actually get to talk with any of these girls and to be honest I had no intention of talking to them. I was just going through the motions; most of the talking was done between my mother and the girls' relatives.

They asked what job I did, although I don't know why they bothered. It would have made no difference to them even if I had been unemployed because I am sure that most of them knew about the British welfare system. My mother would ask which class the girl was in at school as most of the girls were either sixteen or seventeen and still studying.

The meetings lasted around half an hour, and we normally left saying we'd let them know. They all said yes. They would have said yes even if I had been fat, bald, had one eye and no legs, and believe me when I tell you that I have seen guys who fit that description who have gone to India and got themselves the most beautiful brides. These girls just wanted to come to Britain, the country where the streets are paved with gold and the trees don't have leaves but ten-pound notes.

'She was nice,' my mother would say each time she introduced me to a new potential bride. 'She's the one, I just know it.' Each time she would look at me hoping I would agree. I don't think there was a single girl she would have said no to. Strange how, in her opinion, all these girls whom she knew nothing about were all so suitable, while Kuljeet didn't even stand an outside chance. Why couldn't she just let me be and marry Kuljeet?

I have little or no recollection of those rendezvous; I remember telling her I didn't want to see any more girls.

'All right, just one more,' she said. 'After that, you must decide.'

'Decide what?' I had no idea what she was talking about.

'You don't think you can just walk away after seeing all these girls. What do you think people will say about our family? They are already saying that we are big-headed and have no respect for tradition. Surely there must have been at least one you liked.' She now had me in a corner.

'I liked them all, Mum. I am sure they are all very nice girls but I just don't want to marry any of them.'

'We will keep the appointment tomorrow. After that, we will see.' With these final words she wandered off to milk the cows.

The next morning, we went along to Moga, to the house of a matchmaker. He had set up a really nice table with sweets of all shapes and colours, a large variety of fruits, and lots of savoury snacks like pakoras and samosas. I could see my mother was quite impressed as none of the other 'candidates' had gone to so much bother. Parminder, the girl I was to be introduced to, and her family also arrived in their own car, and this had a positive effect on my grandfather. These were well-to-do people.

After we had settled down and exchanged the usual pleasantries, my future wife came into the room carrying a tray laden with cups of tea. She served these around the table, starting with my mother, then my grandfather and then she placed a cup in front of me. At no time did she raise her eyes to look at me; she then sat at the far end of the table, never once looking up in my direction. I looked at her a few times, trying not to make it too obvious. The rest of the people in the room continued to talk as if it was a normal afternoon tea and the meeting was over in an hour. The pressure was on as soon as we stepped out of the door.

'Tell me one thing that's wrong with that girl!' My mother had me up against a wall.

'Well, for a start, she's only fifteen, Mum, and don't remind me how old your mother was when she tied the knot. Times have changed and I think you might find it's against the law.'

'Law? What law? No one cares here as long as the families are happy. Anyway, she's only a couple of years younger than you and that makes her the perfect age.'

'I think you have to decide now, son.' My grandfather was about to play the emotional card. 'Make an old man happy. Who knows how many years I have left? I could die happy if I could just see you wed.'

As the weeks went on, I started to relent. The pressure was certainly getting to me and I wanted to come home to Glasgow so badly. I had written to Kuljeet on numerous occasions as I missed her a lot. I knew that if I shared my experiences with her then she would give me the courage and the will to resist and keep saying no. But she had never written back and I felt so isolated. I thought that Kuljeet had forgotten me already. It was only when I arrived back in Glasgow and met up with her for the last time to tell her that I had got married that I discovered she had written to me every day. My mother had bribed the postman and all the letters ended up in the fire. She knew her only hope of getting me to agree to marry was to ensure I had no contact with anyone back in Glasgow. For Kuljeet, it must have been a nightmare.

After a couple of months, I gave in to my family's demands and agreed to marry Parminder. I had only seen her once and Parminder told me later that she had never seen me at all as she had not dared look in my direction when we were introduced. At the time it seemed like the easy option because I wanted to come home. I was engaged on 31 December 1973 and married one week later on 6 January 1974. I had just turned nineteen and my wife had just reached her sixteenth birthday.

Chapter Ten

THE WEDDING

Weddings in India are massive events and tend to go on for many days. Relatives start to gather a week prior to the event and the stragglers can still be found wandering about the village a week after the official celebrations are over. Since my wedding was only one week after my engagement, the functions seemed to go on forever. There are so many formalities and rituals to be fulfilled, from cooking the masses of food to the way the boy has to be bathed and by whom. There is a part to be played by every aunt, uncle, cousin and just about every person who happens to be remotely related.

On the day of the wedding it is tradition that the boy goes to the girl's village accompanied by male relatives. Women from the boy's family don't attend the wedding ceremony. Even the boy's mother is traditionally not present since this is regarded as bad luck, though this practice has become outdated except in rural areas. I have still seen some mothers get up and leave the room during the *pheris*, the wedding ceremony itself.

My mother broke with tradition and decided to attend the wedding. Maybe she just wanted to make sure I went through with it and didn't back out at the last minute. I decided to break with another tradition and, instead of riding to the ceremony on a white horse, I went in a white Ambassador car. I arrived at my wife's village early in the morning, accompanied by about ninety men, most of whom I had never seen before, and we were directed to the village hall for breakfast.

It was common practice in the Punjab for people to carry weapons. Some would carry a sword while others might carry a gun. Weddings were seen as an ideal occasion for people to show off their weapons and hours were spent the night before getting the barrels and blades glistening. During breakfast some of the guys got a bit bored and decided to have a bit of target practice using unsuspecting crows as targets. One of them had been using my grandfather's double-barrelled shotgun and, after use, he had reloaded it but forgotten to put on the safety catch.

The day continued to go to plan and all was well until just after the main ceremony was over. At a wedding everyone sits on the floor and it tends to get quite cramped. Someone accidentally kicked my grandfather's gun and it exploded. When a shotgun goes off pellets scatter in all directions and that is precisely what happened. Everyone panicked. One guy unfortunately had his foot in front of the barrel, but it wasn't there for long: the top of it got blown right off. The top of his foot hit a dozen different people, who all thought it was their own blood and that they had been shot.

It was pandemonium. People ran off in all directions, leaving my wife and me sitting wondering if this was a part of the ceremony. Eventually we were taken to another room and left there while the damage was assessed and the wounded taken to hospital. Even the Yarrow's nights out had not prepared me for this and when I eventually got back to Glasgow and told my mates what had happened, the jokes about my shotgun wedding started to fly all over the place.

Not much celebration was done that day. Suffice to say, the band had to be sent home as no one seemed to be in the mood for dancing, especially the guy who had just lost his foot. I saw him on a couple of occasions after my wedding whenever I went back to India: this poor guy hopping along the street. I would always try to avoid him and would cross the street when

I saw him come towards me. I enquired about him some years later to be told that he was in hospital. Apparently, he had gone to an engagement party and taken a bullet in the stomach. I don't think he was the ideal person to be sitting beside at a party because when he eventually died some years later it was through being shot during a drunken row.

I came back to Glasgow about two weeks after the wedding while Parminder remained in the Punjab to wait for her visa. It was not long before I got the call from Kuljeet. I had been completely cowardly and not called her after getting back. I guess I just didn't know what to say. She was totally distraught and asked to meet me one last time. We met in Kelvingrove Park and she asked me why I hadn't replied to all the letters she had written. I had simply not been aware of those letters. She cried and cursed and got the anger out of her system but she knew that there was nothing that she could do. After she had calmed down, we said our goodbyes. I don't think she wanted to remain in Glasgow and within a few months her parents had arranged for her to be married to some guy from Birmingham and that would be the last time I would see her. I went back to my job in Yarrow's and life got back to normal.

My grandfather disappeared some years later, one week before I was due to visit him. He had fallen out with my father, which was not unusual – my grandfather fell out with a lot of people and made up with them again. He was especially looking forward to me coming back this time.

'Charan is coming soon and I have decided to put the farm into his name,' he had told everyone.

These were just words though and we all knew that he would never have given his beloved land to anyone, not even me. He should have kept his thoughts to himself. Life is inexpensive in the Punjab; a few thousand pounds, and anyone can be made to disappear, witnesses can be bought, police inspectors bribed. If you line enough of the right pockets the case need never even get to court. I was very upset at the disappearance of my grandfather, and I watched helplessly as family friends and close relatives went through the sham of looking for him – pretending they knew nothing of his whereabouts and searching hospitals, temples and other obvious places where missing people end up.

Perhaps they should have searched their consciences, as they knew exactly where he was. I only got to know the truth ten years later. I had heard many rumours over the years, different versions of his death, his murder. Then I came face to face with the man who had played a leading role in the plot to make my grandfather disappear. He was a first cousin who was twenty at the time of my grandfather's murder and I couldn't help feeling that he had been no more than a pawn in the whole scenario. He had been promised a visa to take him to England. His life, he was told, would be full of riches beyond his wildest imagination. The world would be his oyster. When he confessed to his involvement in the murder, I felt no anger. A sense of calm took the place of the turmoil that had been with me for the past decade.

'The old man is totally paranoid,' they had said. 'Who would want to kill him?' They now had their answer. My father got the farm and I decided to let the matter rest as there was no other choice, and nothing would bring back my grandfather.

I decided to busy myself and threw myself into my music and at the same time got together with my university pals for singsongs. Most of these guys had worked in Indian restaurants to get themselves through university and knew the restaurant scene. One of them, while still in his final year, had been given the opportunity to take on the lease of a small restaurant in Argyle Street as he had worked for a few years in one of the landlord's other restaurants. This particular restaurant had been open for two years and it was struggling to get customers through the doors. The landlord had offered it to him for a nominal upfront payment and an affordable rent. The restaurant was called Ashoka and the guy's name was Balbir.

I didn't know Balbir all that well. He was in his final year at university and was about four years my senior. Most of the guys I went around with at the time were in Balbir's age group. He was a bright bloke, possibly because he went to Woodside Secondary School. He had taken a liking to me after he had heard me sing at one of his parties and encouraged me to sing at every opportunity. He was a popular guy at university and was one of the main people when it came to organising social functions and parties. He liked his music and was quite a good singer himself. Everyone liked to hear him sing because he sounded like Mukesh, a popular Bollywood singer renowned for his romantic songs. This also made him extremely popular with the girls. I think most of the girls had a fancy for Balbir and Balbir knew it.

His father, like a lot of immigrants who had come from the villages, was not an educated man and had worked on the underground railway doing manual labour. Balbir was the eldest child, the only son, and had five younger sisters. Feeling a responsibility towards his sisters, he was determined to do well in life. He was one of the people I looked up to and admired in those days. I wanted to be his pal, not knowing at the time that one day we would get together and start a business.

It was also around this time that I was asked to join my first official band and play the dholaks for a guy called Sufder. Though Sufder attended all the rehearsals for *The Festival of India*, he was never considered as a part of the main gang and some people actually tried to dissuade me from playing for him. I saw it as an opportunity to get exposure and would have played with anyone just to get the opportunity to get on to that stage. I ended up playing with every Indian band that came to be formed in Glasgow. These bands were not all around at the same time. Normally one would disband and then I would be asked by someone else to join their band which was just being formed. There was never a time when Glasgow had two official bands because there were never enough musicians to go round. This happened numerous times until years later I ended up joining Bombay Talkie, the band with whom I released two albums and went on many tours, including my favourite one to Malaysia.

The most memorable experience of my singing career was playing twice in the Albert Hall in London in front of capacity crowds back in the late 1970s. I sometimes think it was all a dream but the band assures me that it certainly happened.

The boys in Bombay Talkie never really wanted me in the band because they were all a wee bit younger than I was and they already had a lead singer, Sanjay Majhu. I was only asked to sing with them because they were playing at Sanjay's wedding. Sanjay could not sing at his own wedding, so I was drafted in. The gig went so well that I was asked to become a permanent member of the band. We were together for years and the only time that I could really relax was when I was on the road with Bombay Talkie.

The band members, Binderpal, Rakesh, Kanwaljit, Kamal and Sanjay, were the only guys that I could ever open up to and be myself with. They were the only people who got to see the side of me which was not business. With most other people in my life, business was all they got.

Chapter Eleven

SEIZING OPPORTUNITY

Most things I have done in life have been achieved because I always happen to be at the right place at the right time. People generally put that down to luck but I, for one, don't believe in luck – I believe in fate or *kismet* as my grandfather used to call it. Simply being at the right place at the right time does not mean you are going to be successful in life. I know for a fact that any site I have acquired has probably been on the market for many months and thousands of people have walked past it every day without recognising the opportunity. I think one needs to have the ability to see something that most others can't, to visualise what can be, not what is. One needs to dream and focus, and believe those dreams can be achieved. It is a kind of lateral thinking that makes the difference between success and failure.

After getting married, I came back from India and went back to my job at Yarrow's. I knew even then that one day I would leave and work for myself. I had no idea what type of business I would end up running; I just knew that the opportunity would one day present itself, and that I would seize it.

The world I moved in outside Yarrow's was so different in its approach to life. My Asian friends all talked about opening their own shops or businesses; none of them believed that they weren't going to make it in life. They were all going to be superstars and that enthusiasm rubs off because I, too, was going to be a superstar. Yarrow's was a different world, and in this world people had different priorities.

There was the darts on Monday, there were the boozers to visit on a Friday night and on the Saturday there was the football. Many of these people's lives revolved around football. Monday was spent talking about Saturday's controversies. On Tuesday debate turned to what the outcome of the midweek games would be. Thursday was the time to analyse Wednesday's results and work out which team had to do what on Saturday to remain in a certain position in the league. The target for the majority of these guys was picking up their wages on a Friday night – there was little to motivate them and not much to aim for. Most of the guys in Yarrow's counted the number of years they had to do before they would get their gold watches. Some in their forties started to count the years to retirement. Yet, if you asked any one of them if they thought they were ambitious, the answer was always yes. If you asked whether they would give up their fixed-salaried jobs to work in a job that was commission-based but the earnings potential was phenomenal, they would invariably answer no; and that is when you realise that there are not that many ambitious people out there who are willing to take chances and go for the big rewards. Paying the mortgage each month for most people is all the ambition they need. The balance of the cash gets put aside for an annual fortnight in Benidorm.

I believe that the desire to work hard relates to being an immigrant. That does not mean to say that only immigrants work hard but they do have a different work ethic and making money and achieving status are higher on their agendas than having a good social life. Being an immigrant has nothing to do with colour or creed. I know this to be true because while I was working in Yarrow's some people I knew and worked beside emigrated to countries like Canada and Australia. They would return after a few years and tell former workmates about the success they were having working overseas: the two cars in their driveways and the large houses with swimming pools. These were the same people who never worked overtime while they were at Yarrow's yet, once they went to a foreign land, they worked all the hours they possibly could. Surely they could have achieved in Scotland what they did abroad? The argument that this country doesn't have the same opportunity doesn't hold water. How did people who came to this country achieve the success when all the odds were stacked against them? They did it against all odds.

I know so many stories of early Asian immigrants from the fifties and sixties. Here they were, in a strange land, totally disadvantaged, with no more than a few pennies in their pockets, and if you listen to some of the stories of these imaginative people, you would start to believe that for us it should be easy because we have got it on a plate. The early Asian immigrants couldn't speak English and a lot of them couldn't even read or write their own language. These people had never been to school. You can see their difficulties if you imagine having to go just one week without being able to read your memos, access your computer or check your emails. These guys kept it all in their heads. On top of that was the pain of being separated from their families and loved ones; the isolation and loneliness they experienced would drive most of us crazy. They could not just pick up a phone and dial a number to speak to their kids as there were no phones in the village and the only way to communicate was by letter. I remember that when my grandmother, my father's mother, died in the Punjab, he received a telegram which read, 'Mother expired.'

If all this was not enough, they had to put up with blatant racial and physical abuse and overcome a thousand prejudices that we are protected from today by various laws. These guys still went about their business and overcame every obstacle that was put in their way, like taking an interpreter with them whenever they went to see the bank manager because they could not speak English. Sometimes I think these guys made it in life because the bank manager could never ask them to produce a business plan. In their vocabulary, such things didn't exist. They believed that nothing was impossible and that if they worked hard enough then they could achieve anything.

A lot of them went on to become wealthy men and some even became millionaires. There is nothing mystical about self-made individuals because, generally speaking, they are just normal hardworking people. A lot of them will have left school without any formal qualifications and some would argue that this lack of university conditioning plays a major factor in their success. They are free spirits, who are perhaps so naïve that they think that anything is possible. That is why, so often, a totally dedicated entrepreneur will show the experts that they have got their calculations wrong and that other factors like the human spirit must be considered in any calculations. Because the human spirit is so strong, if one has the will to succeed then they will achieve anything. And how does one allow for fate in any business plan? Because I believe that is what played a major part in my life, more than once.

Chapter Twelve

STARTING AT THE ASHOKA

The first time fate played a hand in my business life was when I got my first job in an Indian restaurant. I was walking along Argyle Street, it was April 1974, I had been married three months and my wife was still in India awaiting her visa to join me. Balbir walked out of the Ashoka and bumped straight into me. A few minutes either way and we would have missed one another and I would never have started working at the Ashoka. After exchanging standard pleasantries, he asked what I got up to at weekends.

'Well, apart from the odd night out, not much,' I answered.

'Why don't you come into the restaurant and help out on Fridays and Saturdays?' he asked. 'I'll pay you quite well if you do.'

I remember hesitating, as I had never given any thought to working in a restaurant. 'What does it involve?' I asked with genuine interest.

'All you have to do is stand behind the bar and pour drinks. It's easy. We'll show you what needs to be done.'

I still wasn't very sure. I didn't know if I would be any use on the wrong side of the bar. The thought of all those drunken punters falling out of the pubs on a Friday night and giving me abuse rushed into my head. I knew how these morons behaved because I had been one of them for years. How the hell would I cope with them? I quickly weighed up the pros and cons and his promise to pay me quite well and decided to take up his offer.

The Ashoka was laid out on two levels: the ground floor had the kitchens, the bar and five tables, which seated twenty-two customers; the basement had a further thirty-eight covers and the toilets. The decor was very standard for Indian restaurants of that period: basic chairs, tables with red paper covers and the usual flock wallpaper with matching carpet. Ventilation systems were never considered a priority when fitting out a restaurant and everything was done on a low budget. After visiting most Indian restaurants, it was considered normal for your weekend clothes to reek of curry until the following weekend, and the Ashoka was no different.

When I turned up for work the next Friday evening, I was handed a black bow tie to put around my neck but it was something that I needed to have some assistance with as I had never worn a dickie bow before. Then I was taken behind the bar and shown how to pour a pint and told which glasses were to be used for the various drinks. There were some drinks that had to be served with ice and others that required lemon. Bharat was Balbir's head waiter and he was a right annoying wee guy who kept tutting and rolling his eyes.

'Take it easy with him, he's never worked in a bar before,' Balbir would tell him every time I messed up an order. I could see he was concerned that I would tell them where to put their bow tie and their lemons and walk out on my first night. Bharat was so particular about everything. Especially the ice and lemon thing, and all drinks had to be served in specific glasses. He would crack up if I didn't polish my glasses.

'Jesus Christ, Bharat,' I would say, 'do you know this is Argyle Street and most of the punters don't care about the glass as long as they get a drink?'

But Bharat was adamant and when I thought back to the way he wanted things done in later years, I felt he was quite right. I always struggled to get the staff to raise the standards when I became manager and I know that I had not made his job easy. At the time, though, this polishing of glasses was all very strange to me, a boy who did most of his drinking straight from the bottle. But I was a fast learner and tried to toe the party line. Bharat always wore a black dinner suit and a bow tie on top of a frilly white shirt while everyone else, including Balbir, wore standard white shirts with curry-stained black trousers.

Everyone was either ma'am or sir to Bharat. I felt I should remind him again that he was in Partick and not Paris, and that when he used words like that in this part of Glasgow, people were liable to think that he might be taking the piss, and he could end up with a sore face. But as I said, I came to realise later that he had been quite right and the people of Partick lapped up the attention. They too wanted to be pampered. In fact, I realised as time went on that all customers loved the attention. If we could just make them feel that little bit more special they would keep coming back for more.

Ashok Varma was a waiter who made 50 per cent of the customers feel special – the female half. The men he left to the other waiters. It never bothered him that they were with their husbands or boyfriends, Ashok chatted to them as if their partners were invisible. God help the ones who came in on their own because Ashok was all over them like a rash. He was not particularly good-looking but he was full of confidence and he had the patter to go with it. He was not proud either and he figured if he asked enough females to join him for a drink then one of them would eventually say yes.

'My name is Ashoka,' would be his opening line, adding an 'a' to his name to give the impression that he owned the restaurant. 'My name is written outside the restaurant,' he would point out as he introduced himself.

He would eventually narrow his prey down to the table he felt was most receptive to his charms, as looks were not high on Ashok's list of priorities. He figured that the ugly ones presented better odds of success as he whittled down the numbers to what would be his next conquest. In fact, more often than not, he avoided the good-looking ones because the chances were they wouldn't deliver the goods.

He was always careful in his approach. The timing had to be perfect because there was no way he wanted to be left to settle their bills, which is what he would have to do if they ever left without paying. Once the bill was settled, he would approach his unsuspecting target again and ask if he could buy them a drink. He had his approach down to a fine art. The drinks he was offering these girls would not be paid for by Ashok, but by the person who would join Ashok and his new friends for the rest of the night.

Ashok was the hunter and there was no shortage of scavengers amongst the rest of the staff to jump on the bandwagon and take whatever had been laid out for them on a plate. Most of the guys were quite happy to pay for drinks while Ashok did most of the hard work. He was fearless in his advances and not fussy about where or when he made love to the many females he had stringing along.

Balbir's father once walked into the emergency exit and caught Ashok with his trousers around his ankles, in a compromising position with a female customer while her husband was upstairs tucking into his chicken biryani.

'Remember and wash your hands after you finish,' was all Balbir's dad could think of saying as he closed the door. Ashok continued with whatever he was doing without losing any of his rhythm, as if nothing had happened. He had no intention of making an emergency exit as Balbir's dad's untimely entry was no emergency as far as Ashok was concerned. His biggest kick was to sit with a customer and his wife and play footsie with her under the table while the husband tucked into his spicy popadoms and jugs of lager.

The working environment in the restaurant was so relaxed and Balbir was a good boss. Everyone who worked there knew each other and were friends as most of them were handpicked or only employed through personal references. Balbir hired staff through his network at Glasgow University; every waiter was a student of some sort. And then there was me.

Although Ashok was a confident person, the one thing that bugged him was that he was going bald. He decided that the best remedy for this would be to buy a wig and he bought one which was actually very good. In fact, around that time quite a few of the guys were starting to go thin including Balbir himself. Nowadays that may not be seen as a big problem and, in fact, it is cool to shave one's head, but back in the seventies when permed hair was all the fashion for men, going bald was not a good thing. I had long flowing hair which was tightly permed and I considered myself as a bit of a trendsetter because I was one of the first guys to go out and get a perm. What a slagging I got when I went into Yarrow's with my long curly locks!

Balbir could do no such thing, and in a desperate attempt to get his hair to grow, he shaved his head and had to make do with a curly wig until it grew back in thicker than before. It was an awful wig as he had only spent about a fiver on it and even back in those days, a fiver did not purchase a very good toupee. He washed it once and put it in front of a gas fire to dry and it just shrivelled up on him. I had to give him a lift into town to buy another fiver's worth before the restaurant opened for business that evening. All the guys were desperate to have a full head of hair and they went to extraordinary lengths to get their hair to grow back. Once there was a doctor friend who had come across an oil which he said guaranteed hair growth and all the guys paid a small fortune to acquire a couple of bottles each. In their haste they did not even stop to wonder why, if this medicine would do what it was supposed to, the doctor who was selling it was going bald himself.

Chapter Thirteen

HAPPY DAYS

There were a number of things I enjoyed about the Ashoka. First there was the pay. At the end of my first two nights, Balbir slipped me my wages. I put the three notes into my pocket without looking, thinking he had given me three quid. At the time, my weekly take-home pay at Yarrow's was under a tenner for forty hours' work, so three quid seemed good, especially as it was my first weekend and I was still to learn my trade. When I checked my wages later on, I was surprised to discover that he had given me seven pounds, which was the equivalent to about four days at the shipyard. On top of this, I enjoyed the company and the atmosphere. I had become good friends with most of the staff and after a few months I was enjoying it even more because I was now a dab hand at serving tables. It didn't seem like work, more like a night spent with friends socialising.

I would finish my full-time job at four-thirty on Friday afternoon, get a bus home, get cleaned up, and be in the restaurant by six. The last tables usually left at around midnight. Then the guys would all sit and have a few drinks. Sometimes the few drinks turned into all-night sessions, especially when the musical instruments came out and the sing-song started. A lot of times we were joined by friends who worked in other restaurants and the Ashoka got itself a reputation as the place to be for a late night lock-in. Often, the sun would be well out by the time we left the premises and I remember coming out on one occasion to find that the cars which had been left on Argyle Street had all been booked as they had not been moved prior to eight a.m.

I was now living a bit of a double life. By day, I was Wee Singhy at the shipyard and, by night, I was a chic waiter at the Ashoka with my dickie bow and my boyish grin. I was known locally as Kid Curry. I used to live in fear of the boys from Yarrow's nipping in and catching me in action. After all, dickie bows were for poofters, not macho shipyard workers.

The licensing hours for public houses were different then, not as liberal as they are nowadays, and all the pubs closed at ten. We would find that between six o'clock and ten o'clock the restaurant would be dead. Most days, we only had a few tables to serve, and time was passed playing cards or generally sitting around sipping pints of lager. At ten o'clock, the punters started to arrive and there was usually a queue fifteen minutes later.

Most nights would pass without any incidents, but there would also be the nights when the fights would start. These fights were usually amongst drunken friends and contained to one table; other times they would spill over and a couple of tables would start taunting each other. The taunts would become arguments and before you knew it, the pakora and the chapattis would develop wings and start to fly. I remember on many occasions walking into the basement part of the restaurant and diving for cover to avoid an airborne pint tumbler. I would look around, and who would be right in the thick of it trying to get people apart? Balbir! I realised now why the wages were so generous: danger money!

We would all have to wade in and pull everyone apart. The women were the worst to deal with. If they had a fork in their hand, you had to take great care in how to handle them. If you hit a 'burd', even if she was beating the shit out of you, the bears would stop fighting amongst themselves and turn on you. 'No, sir, ye cannae punch a woman in Partick!'

I guess that's one way to bring things under control, but it usually meant you were off work for a week recovering from your injuries.

The other thing you had to watch out for were the runners. These were the people who would bolt out of the door once you had cleared away their plates and they had sent you to the kitchen to make them a complicated sweet, normally a banana fritter, that they knew would take you ages to make. And they weren't always guys. Girls were just as liable to dash out the door as guys were. For most people, it was the challenge of sneaking out without paying that was exciting, and once they were stopped, either at the door or a couple of hundred yards down the street, they apologised and blamed each other for the obvious misunderstanding, dipped into their pockets and the waiter was usually left with a huge tip.

Sometimes they didn't have the cash and you were given a watch or some other form of security. You just had to take whatever they were willing to leave as you can't get blood out of a stone. If they didn't have any jewellery, it would be clothing, perhaps a jacket or a jumper. They would come back the next day, sober and embarrassed, and exchange whatever they had left as a guarantee for cash. The odd one would argue that there was no way the bill could have been so high and after much debate would pay it anyway while threatening never to come back for a meal ever again. As if we would want him back in the first place! The funny thing is that most of them did return for meals and once they were caught, didn't do a runner again and actually became good customers. One guy even left his shoes, but, needless to say, we never saw him again. Only in Glasgow!

I now understood why we were always asked for money up front whenever I went for a meal after a night out with my mates from Yarrow's. Balbir once chased two huge guys who had done a runner down Argyle Street. The reaction to chase punters down the street was impulsive and little thought was given to the consequences. About five hundred yards down the road, they stopped and turned round to size up the pursuer.

When they saw it was Balbir, all five feet nine inches and weighing about ten and a half stones, they chased him back to the restaurant.

'Did you get the cash?' I asked him as he came flying through the door.

'No, the bastards were too fast for me.' Saying this, he straightened up his dickie bow and continued as if nothing had happened.

The funniest runner story happened to a couple of waiters at the Maharaja in Gibson Street. The restaurant had about thirty punters in, and there were only two waiters on. When a table of three guys dashed out the door, the waiters reacted instinctively and chased them into Kelvingrove Park. Unfortunately, these guys had been too fast and the poor waiters returned after five minutes to an empty restaurant. While they had been out, the remaining punters had grabbed their jackets and also disappeared without paying their bills!

Then there was the guy who came in and asked if we had space for twelve children. He explained that it was his son's thirteenth birthday and he was playing football with his friends in the park around the corner. He asked if he could bring them in for a slap-up meal and collect them later on. This was not unusual and we were delighted to get the business on a quiet Saturday afternoon. He returned about half an hour later with a bunch of hungry and wide-eyed teenagers and we were to look after them with no expense spared. The man said he would return in an hour to take them home.

We let the kids choose anything they wanted. The Cokes and Irn-Brus were guzzled down as if there was no tomorrow and the sweet menu took a massive pounding. They were eating so much I was sure that at least a couple of them would explode. As the clock ticked by and almost two hours had passed, I asked the 'birthday boy' when his daddy would be coming back to get them and square up the bill.

'That wasn't my daddy,' said the wee boy. 'In fact, I don't even know him. We were playing football in the park and he asked us if we were hungry and, when we all told him that we were, he brought us all in for this meal.'

At this point they all left and we all just stood and looked at each other in absolute amazement. Though we were mad at being scammed, we all had a good laugh at the story for years to come. Yes, you know what I think! Only in Glasgow!

We were always happy to hear anything negative about Gibson Street restaurants because we really hated them with a vengeance. Perhaps I should provide a history lesson for those who don't remember Gibson Street. It is a street very close to Glasgow University, which housed numerous Indian restaurants. In fact, it had so many restaurants that it was nicknamed 'Gandhi's Revenge' by curryholics. The reason we didn't like Gibson Street restaurants was because they were all busier than we were, especially the Shish Mahal, and the Koh-I-Noor.

Two cousins operated these restaurants, but there was little love lost between them and they competed furiously for the same business. They had queues at their doors seven days a week, and the proprietors always had these cheesy grins on their faces. They didn't measure their business success by the numbers of customers dining at tables but by the length of the queues outside their doors. During the early evenings when the Ashoka only had a few customers, Balbir would get depressed and go out for a drive. He would head for Gibson Street to see how the competition was doing. I never asked why he did that because we all knew they would be mobbed and that he would come back suicidal. We weren't regarded as competition by the Gibson Street restaurants because they were the big boys. They were established and doing a roaring trade; we were just novices. He would return from his drive twenty minutes later, even more depressed.

'The Shish and the Koh-I-Noor are mobbed. People are queuing in the rain to get into those bloody places and they are not even that good.'

'Well, they must be better than us, boss, because we're fricking empty.' I knew this always wound him up.

'Well, it's only a matter of time. We will have our day,' Balbir would say and, from the commitment in the tone of his voice, I knew that one day he would.

We all need to chase a dream, even if sometimes the dream seems impossible to achieve. Balbir had a dream to own a restaurant that would be busier than the Shish Mahal. It was a tall order, but we knew it wasn't impossible, because anything can be achieved. You just have to want it bad enough. I learned later in life that success does not come to those who are best at what they do but to those who want it bad enough. The Gibson Street guys were too smug; they thought they were so far ahead of the rest that no one would ever catch up. But in any line of business, you must never underestimate the competition. And you must pioneer changes in your market. Otherwise, you will become dated and people with fresher ideas will take your market share.

That was exactly what would happen to Gibson Street!

Business at the Ashoka gradually improved and it was getting busier by the month. In my opinion, Balbir was not running it like a business but it was his laid-back style and informal and unconventional business methods that actually made the difference and drew the punters through the doors. The employees were his friends and his management style was very relaxed. It could be argued that it was this style and the relaxed working environment that made the Ashoka unique, thereby contributing to the success of the place. We were all allowed to have tabs and to have a few beers during work. At the end of the week, the tabs were cleared and deducted from the wages. I remember when I became manager, and the practice was allowed to continue. One of the waiters had drunk and smoked all his wages during the week and I paid off his week's hard graft with a packet of Benson and Hedges.

Those years were full of good times, with sing-songs into the early hours of the morning, and lots of free booze for most of the staff. Balbir was never a scrooge and what he had, he didn't mind sharing. Whether it was for his friends in the restaurant or when walking into a bar and buying all the punters a round of drinks, he always saw this as an investment and it was one of the valuable lessons that I learnt: keep your customers sweet.

At that time I lived in Argyle Street, across from a pub called the Park Bar, and each morning my bus to Yarrow's would take its route past the Ashoka. One Monday morning I saw three fire engines parked outside and smoke billowing out through the windows. It looked pretty bad. When I went to the restaurant that evening to see if I could help tidy the place up, I realised just how bad it was.

Chapter Fourteen

ALWAYS LEARNING

Balbir was sifting through the rubble, trying to salvage whatever he could. There wasn't much to salvage and, as he walked around picking up unrecognisable objects, I realised for the first time how much it had all meant to him. Balbir was raw and naïve at the time. He had signed a lease which had been prepared by the landlord, a man we all called 'Uncle'. His name was Mr Binning and he had properties all over Glasgow. Mr Binning was a wealthy man. He was one of the early immigrants who had worked hard to build up his empire and he wasn't about to give it away by giving tenants easy leases. Balbir didn't want to waste money on lawyers and, anyway, he wanted the restaurant so badly that he would have signed any lease.

The insurance money would be paid to the landlord, who, when he had the time to get around to it, would fix up the restaurant for his tenant. Balbir's fate was in Binning's hands. Mr Binning was in no hurry; he was doing nothing until he got the insurance money and Balbir signed on the 'buroo' – shortened from bureau, this is the Glaswegian name for signing the dole or claiming unemployment benefit. The next year was a terrible struggle for Balbir and I witnessed at first hand the stress he went through due to lack of money. Once you get used to a steady cash flow, it is very difficult to adjust when, suddenly, the tap gets turned off and you can't even afford to go to the pub for a single beer. He managed to reopen about a year later, with most of the fitting-out work done by one Indian joiner, who also managed to do a bit of plumbing and electrics. Balbir was there every day, sometimes working as a labourer, but mostly as an adviser to the joiner, who we reckoned had lied when he told us he was a master tradesman. Balbir was glad just to get the place trading again. After this experience, Balbir was a lot more careful with his money. I had subconsciously learnt my own lesson: never leave yourself underinsured and always get a lawyer to check out leases drawn up by men calling themselves 'Uncle'.

I suppose for me the timing of the fire was quite good as that was when my wife arrived from the Punjab to join me. It had taken almost a year to cut through the bureaucracy and get her visa but she had eventually managed through patience and perseverance. I went to Heathrow airport by train to meet her and when she walked through the gates I hardly recognised her. This was my wife, and she would be my wife for the rest of my life, yet she looked nothing like the girl I had married. It was not that she had changed, it was just that I had hardly got to know her in the few weeks that I had spent with her after we had wed. Once I was married, my grandfather suggested that I leave as soon as possible for Glasgow and start earning money again.

'There is no point in you hanging around here,' he told me. 'Don't forget that you now have responsibilities and you have a wife to support.'

I was living in a three-bedroom tenement flat with my parents, four brothers and one sister. When my wife arrived, we were given our own bedroom. My wife immediately became a part of my family and she took on household duties, helping my mother with the cooking and cleaning. After a few months, she was fixed up with a job working in a sweatshop environment as a machinist. She would get paid on the Friday and dutifully give her unopened wage packet to my mother.

That is how things are in an extended family. My mother was in charge. A similar matriarchal situation seems to exist throughout the Mediterranean world and points east. It's only the Anglo-Saxon countries where this tradition has essentially faded away. We all went to work and brought the wages home and gave them to my mother. We would then be given spending money to keep us going for the rest of the week. If we ran short, we would simply ask for more. The positive side to this arrangement was that I never had the worry of paying any bills. Although I was married, my wife and I were never allowed to go out with each other. Pubs were a definite no-go area – only bad women went to pubs, according to most of the first-generation Punjabis who had come to Glasgow from small villages. There was no way my wife would be allowed to drink or smoke and eating out in restaurants was also forbidden.

Even the men did not eat out in restaurants as they were considered too expensive. Why pay so much money in a restaurant when they could make it at home a lot cheaper, and so much tastier? And what is the point of getting married and having a wife if you weren't going to make her cook? These were not just our house rules: they were the same in most households at that time and they were pretty simple. The sons' wives went to work and they came home and cooked for the family. They went to the Sikh temple with the mother-in-law on a Sunday.

If they wanted to go anywhere else they would normally be chaperoned by the mother-in-law. I remember once taking my wife out for a drive and on the way back we popped into the Ashoka for some pakora. I still don't know to this day how my mother found out, but a few minutes after we had sat down, my dad came into the restaurant to check if we were there. What a row my mother gave Parminder that day! After this, Parminder decided it was less hassle if she just stayed at home and we rarely went out as a couple unless it was to a wedding or other family function. This only changed once we moved out on our own.

The main event for Asian families was the Indian movies on Sundays. My wife usually went with my mother and I normally went with my mates whose wives were also there with their mums. It seems like such a strange arrangement but the wives just became a part of the whole family and accepted this as the norm.

It was at this time that my family acquired their first business. A couple of boys who played in my band at the time were looking to buy a shop for themselves. They had seen a newsagent in Argyle Street which was on the market. It was not the type of shop they wanted but still considered it a decent deal. The seller, Mr Malhotra, was looking for three and a half thousand pounds for it.

'If we give him a thousand pounds up front, we can pay the balance in monthly instalments with no interest,' I told my dad as soon as I got home from the band rehearsal.

This was how business was done amongst the Asian community. Even if you were buying a house there were no such things as mortgages. Once the two parties had agreed a price there was usually a down payment of around 20 per cent, and the balance would be paid over a couple of years. No one ever charged interest because they themselves didn't pay any interest on their debt either. It was a great way of doing business; there were never any complications as everybody paid their debts or ran the risk of getting a bad name in the community.

My father was not keen to invest money into a business, as he was concerned that none of his sons were capable of running one.

'And who is going to work in the shop?' he asked.

As far as he was concerned, we all had good jobs and were bringing home decent pay packets. Why risk going into business? My father was still driving the buses. My elder brother was a motor mechanic, working as a patrolman with the AA. I was at

Yarrow's. I had three other brothers. The younger one, Dippal, was doing well at school and was regarded as university material and my father didn't want him to take his focus off his studies. The two younger than him were fifteen and ten and still at school and obviously too young.

After some discussion and persistence on my part, along with the support of my brothers, it was decided that we would all just muck in and make sure the shop was manned. Our parents eventually relented and we were in business. How's that for a business plan? One of my young brothers, Binder, eventually left school and worked full-time in the shop, with the rest of the family helping when they had the time. Over the years, the shop became a success and made a lot of money for my family and made them think more about business. They eventually sold the business but kept the property and it still provided them with a very good annual income for many years.

Chapter Fifteen

TOURING INDIA

Back in Yarrow's I was now itching to leave. I still wasn't sure what I wanted to do with my life but I was feeling the frustration. It was now 1978 and I was twenty-three years old. I felt I had to get out of Yarrow's as soon as possible. I was involved at the time with the Asian Arts Centre, which had been established to promote Asian dance and music. The man in charge of the centre was called Mr Sewa Singh Kolhi.

I had known Mr Kolhi most of my life, and had grown to admire him a great deal. He was an excellent organiser and coordinator. He had set up the centre and was making it into a great success and I used to spend time there teaching young kids how to dance bhangra as well as playing the dholaks for a girls' dance troupe. I was a sort of a jack of all trades at the Arts Centre and Mr Kolhi valued having me around and listened to my input. He called me to tell me that he had managed to organise a trip to India for a troupe of dancers from the Arts Centre. We would be hiring musicians in India but he asked if I would like to go along as the singer. All I had to do was about five numbers in between the dances to allow the girls time for their costume changes.

My parents were keen for one of my brothers to go and stay in India for a while and do a bit of work around the family home but they were surprised when I volunteered. It was only a short while before I got on the plane that I told them of my two-week tour commitment. I went to Yarrow's and asked for a six-month leave of absence, but after a bit of deliberation by my manager, going on a singing tour with a band was not considered adequate reason for such a long leave and my request was refused. I was told I would have to quit and reapply for my job when I got back. I was assured my job would be pretty safe. They knew that by not allowing me the leave and making me resign they would create a break in my length of service and if they ever had to make me redundant then my payoff would not be so high. Well, they needn't have worried because once I had left I knew I would never work in Yarrow's again. Refusing me leave was probably the best thing to happen to me.

I didn't have to think about it: I handed in my notice without hesitation and left the following week. Before I left, the boys organised another night out to see me off, and that was a night out I will never forget. It was a leaving party and stag night rolled into one and, believe me, the stag nights back in the seventies were just as eventful as they are now. Instead of going to Prague we went to Paisley and although the ladies did not have exotic-sounding names they were certainly not shy.

I remember my days at Yarrow's with great fondness. I was free from stress and I worked with some great guys who taught me many things about life in general. As I walked out of the gates for the last time my thoughts went back to the day I had started working in the machine shop and had been introduced to my first tradesman, Andy Coia. The first thing he did was to send me to the store for 'a long weight'. I was left standing for ages while everyone else got served until eventually, after about an hour, the storeman said to me, 'You can go back now, son, because I think you have waited long enough.'

I also thought of some other things that Andy had told me and taught me. Once when I was upset because someone had referred to me as 'the wee darkie boy', Andy said, 'It's not as bad as you think. People will look at you and pick out your most distinguishing feature and then they will slag it off, just like a caricature.' He reminded me that he got called 'a big-nosed bastard' all the time, apart from the times he was called an 'Eyetie'. This was a reference to his Italian origin, even though he was born and bred in Glasgow. He reasoned that if I were fat, then I would be a fat bastard, if I were bald then I would be called a baldy bastard.

'The only thing that they can see about you that is different is your colour, so they will call you a black bastard. Don't let it bring you down because it means nothing.'

After that day, I did not let it get me down when I got called names. What annoyed me after that was not what I was called but the tone in which the offensive words were used. That told me how racist the person was, if indeed at all.

We were in Delhi in January 1978 and the tour would last two weeks. Parminder accompanied me to India and was met at Delhi airport by my father who took her straight to the village. I promised to see her in two weeks' time. We did a few gigs in Delhi and then moved through to the Punjab and performed in all of the major cities. The whole trip had been organised through the Government of India so we were looked after really well. The highlight of the trip for most of the troupe was when we were invited by Morarji Desai, the then Prime Minister, for tea. I was feeling a bit edgy because I had read somewhere that the Prime Minster was a great believer in the medicinal powers of drinking urine so decided to give the tea a miss.

Harnek Singh was a guy from Glasgow who thought of himself as a great bhangra dancer. He had been to university in the Punjab and had also been involved in the university dance group. This in his opinion made him an authority in the arts and he was taken along as a stage choreographer. It was Harnek who introduced me to the movers and shakers in the Delhi arts scene. We had a free night in Delhi, which was our second night in India, and Harnek asked if I would like to accompany him to a party he had been invited to. The party was thrown by a lady called Ajit Caur at her home in an exclusive suburb in New Delhi. When we arrived, the main room was full of people reciting poetry or singing *kafees* and *ghazals*. These were usually love songs and poems recited by trained singers who were serious about their music.

We were handed some Black Label and took our places on rugs on the floor. Harnek pointed out a few of the celebrities in the room, prominent poets whose names I was familiar with, and we joined in the applause given to each of them as they recited their most famous works. As the evening wore on and the drink started to work its magic, the music got louder in volume and lighter in content. Harnek picked his moment and announced that they were just about to witness a singing sensation from Scotland.

I felt some uneasy shuffling around the room, and could hear people ask one another if I would be singing in English. The majority of people were shrugging shoulders as they braced themselves for my performance. 'Must be courteous and not laugh at our guest,' seemed to be the thought going through most people's minds. I could also sense that some of the prima donna performers in the room couldn't wait to see me make a fool of myself. I loved to entertain, I loved the applause and that night my audience loved me. I was different from what these people had heard in Delhi before. I was young, full of vigour and energy, I always believed in singing from the heart and getting engrossed in every lyric, and that night I felt on top of the world. As a young man I was at my peak in every way.

'He is a breath of fresh air.' Ajit Caur turned to Harnek. 'He is going to be a star.'

Harnek was getting more acknowledgement for bringing me to the party than I was getting for being there. By the time we eventually left to return to our hotel he was feeling so high that he thought he had been the life and soul of the party.

'You did well tonight, mate – I think they liked you,' he said, putting his arm around my shoulder and giving me a hug as we walked out into Ajit's garden. I took in a deep breath to fill my lungs with the cool night air and felt on top of the world.

We were due to stay in Delhi for about five days and Harnek told me the next day that Ajit Caur had phoned to ask him if we would go round to her place again before I went away. 'She wants to show you off to her high-society friends because, if you ever make it as a singer, she wants people to know that she saw you first.'

We went back to her place a couple of days later. This time, there were even more people there than before. You could see by the way these people carried themselves, the way they talked, how the ladies in their expensive silk saris and twenty-two-carat gold jewellery sipped fine wine or Black Label and soda water, that these people were Delhi's finest. I knew that Harnek and I had not been invited to this do because we shared the same upbringing and finesse as these people. We were the entertainment but I didn't mind that one bit.

I didn't share my thoughts with Harnek, as I was sure I would have seriously hurt his feelings. He thought he fitted right in. Nothing would be achieved by my shattering his illusion. The night was another great success for Ajit Caur. She had scored brownie points over her adversaries and she was proud as Punch. I was pleased as I thought I had sung really well. It was great to be appreciated back in my motherland, by people who took their music seriously. I promised Ajit Caur that since I was going to remain in India for at least six months, I would come back to see her.

'Let me know when you can stay with me for a few weeks. I'll get you on the radio and we can organise a show for you. I will make sure all the media attend. It will be high profile. This show will launch your career,' she told me as I bade her farewell. She was so confident that she had made a major discovery.

The rest of the troupe returned to Glasgow and I went home to my village to spend time with my wife. I stayed at home for a month and then decided to head back to the bright lights of Delhi. I first went to Aligarh, a large industrial city a couple of hours from Delhi, home of the boys who had been my backing band during the tour. I asked if they would support me for my big gig in Delhi and the guys all said they would be pleased to help. Ajit Caur lived up to her end of the bargain. She wasn't looking for any financial gain from this project; it just fed her ego and her vanity, and I had to entertain her friends for the two weeks that I was there. The night before the big show, my backing band had their own wedding gig in Delhi and we all thought it would be a good idea if I went along with them and did some of my numbers.

'We will treat it like a dress rehearsal and get the timing spot on,' said Anil, the band's keyboard player.

It was a big wedding, with hundreds of people and lots of pretty girls shouting for encores and flirting with their eyes as they danced to our rhythm. We were invited to a party afterwards and there was no way we were not going. The cheap local brew flowed like water, and the singing continued into the early hours. I still don't remember what time I got home. The one thing I won't forget for the rest of my life is waking up the next day, the most important day in my singing career, without a voice. I was completely hoarse.

Ajit Caur had done a terrific PR job. There were posters and banners everywhere. I was given top billing and Ajit Caur had managed to get some big names to be supporting acts to pull in the crowds. My heroes were my support bands; it was a dream come true. I had been looking forward to this day all my life and now it was down to me.

For me, though, the day started as a nightmare. It was the first time in my life that I had ever lost my voice and I had no idea what to do about it. Over the years I had used and abused my voice on many occasions but it was always good the next day. This time it was different. All day was spent inhaling an assortment of menthols and aromatic spices but the voice was not coming back. I even thought of ways I could get out without losing face and found myself wandering around the corridor looking for a fire alarm that I could set off. It happened in Glasgow all the time but, alas, the hall didn't have a fire alarm system. I would just have to go on and hope for the best.

We decided to lower the key for all my numbers to see if that would help on the night. The MC announced my name with great zest, and in his introduction piled on the praise, telling the audience what a terrific singer I was and what a brilliant voice I had. I found myself cringing for the first time in my life. The curtain opened and the band burst into the intro of the first song. I danced on to the stage from the side, weaving my way through the band, all of them smiling and nodding in my direction to give me prominence and importance. I worked my way to the front of the stage and grabbed my microphone in a similar style I had seen used by Mick Jagger and waited for my cue. The audience were anticipating something mega and I felt the electricity in the atmosphere. Most of them were now on their feet, clapping and stamping to the rhythm. I held the mic close to my mouth, closed my eyes, filled my lungs with air and tried to hit the opening C sharp.

Whichever note it was I hit, it wasn't a C sharp, and even the tone-deaf in the audience cringed with pain. I continued singing as if everything was fine but wishing to myself that the stage would open up and I could just disappear. I contemplated fainting but reckoned that was too cowardly. If the devil had appeared at that moment and offered me a deal, I would have sold my soul that evening. After the third song I decided I couldn't continue; my audience had suffered enough and I signalled to the MC to come and rescue me. He walked on and took the mic and heaped on more praise, having obviously taken his tea break while I was on. I left the hall by the rear entrance within minutes of coming off.

Later that night I returned to Ajit Caur's house, where she had brought a few people back from the show. I offered my apologies for letting her down but she told me not to worry and that I should learn from the experience. She said that she still believed in me and offered to do it all again in two months if I wanted, but I felt tired and my heart was not in it any more. I wanted to go back to my village. I missed my wife.

'No thanks, Ajit,' I said with sincerity, as I appreciated what she had done for me, 'I don't feel like singing. I think I'll go home to the Punjab.'

Chapter Sixteen

OUR FIRST BABY

When I got back to the village, Parminder said there was something that she wanted to tell me. She put her hand over her stomach and asked, 'Do you know what I am going to say?'

It had been five years since Parminder and I had got married and there was talk in the Sikh temple about the reasons for us not yet having a child. The fact that Parminder was still only twenty-one was somehow overlooked but the aunties were having a good time discussing the issue. Some of them had even suggested that we should send Parminder back to her village and I should get another wife who would bear me many children. I don't think any of them even considered the possibility that the fault could lie with me.

Parminder had not had an easy time when she arrived from India and she had also had the misfortune of having contracted tuberculosis. A short while after she had arrived, she had been taken into Ruchill Hospital and kept in an isolation unit for three months. She was totally distraught as this was not what she had envisaged when she left her parents to join me. She could not speak much English and she struggled to cope at the hospital. I would go and see her every night and after a few weeks decided that a wee trip to the chip shop would do her good. I told her to go to the toilet and then climb out of the window on to the roof of my car and she was more than happy to cooperate. This became a regular occurrence and it helped her to cope with being in hospital. We would go for a drive and after half an hour I would sneak her back into her ward. I am not sure if the nurses ever found out but if they did they had turned a blind eye.

We stayed on in the village for seven months and I enjoyed my time with my grandfather. We would have stayed longer but our first baby was due in September and we both decided to come back and have the baby in Scotland. I agreed with her view that it was safer and she had more confidence in the NHS.

'They can't be that bad in India at delivering babies,' I said. 'They get plenty of practice – just look at the population.'

But deep down, I too wanted the baby to be Scottish. Just in case it was a wee boy who would, one day, be good enough to turn out for his country at football. As it turned out, there was no wee boy and on 10 September, my wife gave birth to our first daughter. I went home and broke the news to my mother and I recall she turned pale. It was not the news she had been waiting for, as she had prayed for the past six months for her first grandson. She herself had given birth to five sons so it couldn't be such a hard thing to do.

'How is this possible?' she quizzed.

'It's possible, Mum, no mistake,' I assured her. 'I was there and saw it coming out.'

She was silent for many hours. I went out with my mates and we all got completely sloshed. I named our daughter Ceetl, meaning cool, as in a cool breeze, and when my mother held her in her arms for the first time she forgot whether it was a boy or a girl. We moved back into my parents' house along with the rest of the Gill clan and I went off to look for a job.

I had two choices – I could go back to Yarrow's or I could work in the Ashoka for Balbir. I chose the restaurant for two reasons: first, it was more fun than Yarrow's could ever be; second, I knew if I went back to Yarrow's I would end up in a rut and get used to the monthly pay cheque. I was worried that if I went back I might never leave. The restaurant was not so permanent and it would be no problem to move from that job and start working for myself at any time. After all, it wasn't a real job, according to my father.

It was hard work, the hours were long and the pay wasn't all that good when you had to do it full-time. The part-timers' wages were so much better. I didn't see it as a real job either, but the main thing was that I really enjoyed it. I was the only full-time waiter along with Balbir as all the others were part-time. This was good because I learnt to do everything that I would ever need to know. It didn't bother me what I had to do; I was given no job specification and I never asked for one. I took pride in everything I did. For instance, the toilets would be spotless when I cleaned them and I could vacuum the whole restaurant in ten minutes with a Hoover that spat out more than it sucked in.

Within a few weeks I was officially the manager, which felt great even though I had no one to manage. I was on the same wages as before and still the only full-time employee, but at least I was moving up the managerial ladder. A few weeks later, I was mopping the toilets when Balbir came in with his accountant, Riaz Ahmed. He had a really superior attitude but I always thought of him as one of those guys who felt that he was better than everyone else just because he was an accountant and, because of this, felt superior to those who were in manual jobs. As he pissed away in my clean urinals still smelling of disinfectant, he turned to Balbir and said, 'Your manager sahib is working very hard.'

'It has to be done,' I said, disguising my gritted teeth with a polite smile.

Years later, when I bought out Balbir, the first thing I did was sack Riaz Ahmed.

Chapter Seventeen

DO I BELIEVE IN KISMET?

I often wonder how life would have turned out for me had the bulb above table eight not fused that Friday night and, also, had I been too lazy to replace it. I had gone round the restaurant and cleaned every corner and when checking the lights discovered a couple had fused. It was Friday and all the tables would be getting used so I knew I would have to replace the bulbs before opening the restaurant. There were none left in stock, so I walked down Argyle Street to the gift centre to buy a couple of sixty-watt bulbs from the wee shop that sold everything. It was in the gift centre that I met the man who offered me the opportunity to change my life in yet another direction.

Mr Gurcharan Singh Shan was a flamboyant man. He was always dressed in smart suits and loved his gold. He was always dripping in it. He loved showing it off too, quite often holding out his gold Rolex in front of you to tell you the time, even though you never asked for it in the first place. He wore really smart starched turbans which were always in loud colours – no danger of him getting run over on a dark night – and his beard was immaculate, held in place with large amounts of Brylcreem, the moustache twirled up and round like a bull's horns. I had met him on a number of occasions before. He was always around when we did our shows and fancied himself as a bit of a singer and performer. Sometimes he would come backstage to give me a couple of last-minute tips, such as how to shake my hips to get the girls excited as I was about to walk on stage.

'Do it like Elvis Presley,' he would say, demonstrating the move with a pelvic thrust.

I greeted him with a respectful dip of the head and a traditional Sikh greeting. '*Sat Sri Akal*, Mr Shan!' I shouted as I entered the shop. One always tends to do that when meeting someone wearing a turban, even if they do from time to time do Elvis Presley impersonations.

'*Sat Sri Akal*,' he returned the greeting, holding out his hand and showing off his massive gold cuff links. 'Where are you working?' he asked.

I told him that I was working in the restaurant down the street and he said, 'Why don't you come and work for me?' I didn't have to ask what he did for a living because Mr Shan was legendary in the Indian community. He was known as 'Mr Shan, the Insurance Man'.

'What would I do?' I asked with genuine curiosity.

'Sell life insurance,' he said. 'I think you would make a great salesman. You would make a lot of money.' As he finished the money sentence, his right eyebrow rose and he gave a greedy type of smile. I was almost blinded by the gold cap on one of his teeth. I don't know if he was sincere in his praise because after I had joined the company I realised that he had told all the other numpties that he employed the same thing.

'Come and see me at my office,' he said, pulling out a card from a huge black leather wallet, intentionally showing off a wad of twenty-pound notes as he did so. 'Call me next week and we can meet for a chat.'

He picked up his alligator-skin briefcase, shook hands with the shopkeeper and danced out of the shop. As I left the gift centre clutching a carrier bag filled with half a dozen bulbs, I saw Mr Shan get into his huge blue Mercedes and accelerate up Argyle Street. As I watched him screech round the corner and out of sight, I knew it was time for a change of career. I wanted a blue Mercedes too.

I discussed my chance meeting with Mr Shan with Balbir that weekend and asked him if he thought I should do it. 'No harm in going along to see him,' encouraged Balbir.

I didn't waste any time in making the phone call because I have always believed in striking while the iron is hot, and the interview was set up within a couple of days. It was not an interview as such, more a convincing exercise by Mr Shan to recruit me on to his sales team. It was all a numbers game to him. The quality of recruits didn't matter; he figured that if he employed enough people then he was bound to find a couple of nuggets in amongst all the rubble. He would recruit anyone who was able to go and sell a few insurance policies, even if it was to family and friends. For this they would be paid commission and Mr Shan would also be paid overrider commission on any policies sold by his team.

It was very much a pyramid type of arrangement. There was Mr Shan at the top and below him were two assistant managers who were also recruiting and training their own teams. When an agent sold a policy, he or she would get commission, his assistant manager would get commission and, of course, Mr Shan would get commission. This was an industry norm and all insurance companies worked in the same way. On most types of policies, the first two years' contributions made by a client were used up in costs and that is why the commission rates were so good and paid up front.

'If you sell a policy for twenty pounds a month,' started Mr Shan as soon as I took my seat opposite him at his large mahogany desk, 'we multiply the monthly premium by twelve to give us an annual figure, and pay you 70 per cent of that as soon as the policy gets issued. That means on one twenty-pound policy, you would earn one hundred and seventy pounds. What do you think of that? Just one policy a week and you would make almost a thousand pounds per month.'

I didn't realise that four times £170 was not £1,000 but the numbers sounded so huge that it didn't matter. I was also busy reading the various invitations that Mr Shan had received to numerous society parties, including one to the Queen's garden party at the Palace of Holyroodhouse. Also, at the time, I was working six days a week, ten hours a day and earning £130. He didn't have to convince me too much. I was in and told him there and then that I would take the job.

'Why don't you do the insurance thing during the week and work at the Ashoka at the weekends?' suggested Parminder. 'That way you would still have some money if you didn't sell any policies and also, if things didn't work out, you could always go back to the Ashoka.'

What she said would make sense to most people because it was the sensible thing to do. I thought about it briefly but decided to burn my bridges. I knew selling insurance would not be easy and the last thing I wanted was the easy option out. I knew that if I worked weekends then the pressure to sell would not be as severe and that if I went a few weeks without selling, the chances were that I would just do more shifts at the Ashoka and eventually end up doing six nights a week again. If I was to have any chance of success, the safety net would have to go. It had to be 'do or die'. I told myself that I should just jump into the deep end and knew I would learn to swim before I drowned.

When I started at the office, I realised that more than 75 per cent of the associates had other forms of income and that this job was seen as extra money. They were just playing at it. During my three years at Credit and Commerce Insurance Company, I would see dozens of them come and disappear after selling a few policies to their family and friends.

It was the spring of 1981 and Parminder was almost eight months pregnant with our second baby. I was sent to

Birmingham on a week's training which would make me a professional insurance adviser and give me the credentials to advise people on their insurance needs. It was nothing complicated; there were only two types of policy we would be focusing on selling initially. The type of people I would be dealing with for the first year or so of my career only had two needs. One was a straight life insurance policy, where the main purpose was to provide a lump sum of cash for the family in case the breadwinner snuffed it. The second was an investment policy which would give you back zillions of pounds after ten years if you contributed only twenty pounds a month. You could retire to the Bahamas and never have to work again. 'Just sell the dream' was the main message of the training session.

Halfway through the week I called home to see if everything was all right.

'Everything is fine,' said my mother, but I could tell by her voice that all was not well.

'What's the matter?' I asked. 'Is Parminder all right?'

There was a pause and a heavy sigh before she answered. 'It's another girl,' she let out finally.

The tone was not one of joy but of bereavement. Girls were not popular things to have in Asian families. Along with them they brought responsibilities. They had to be married off eventually and that is not cheap. A boy would grow up and work alongside his father and look after his parents in their old age. A girl would have to be brought up, educated and well groomed – all that investment just so that someone else can take them away after you have spent all that money.

'They are both fine so don't worry,' she said.

I told my mother that I was fine and that she should not worry either. 'It is God's will,' I said with a sigh.

Inside, my heart was dancing. I wanted to run back and see my beautiful new baby and hold her. She was four weeks premature so she was a lot smaller than Ceetl had been but she was fine. I didn't want to let on to my mother that I was happy as that would just have upset her more.

'Do you think I should come home?' I asked.

'No need – it is only a girl. Finish what you are doing and we will see you in a couple of days.'

I went to the bar and celebrated the birth of Basant by myself. I would hold her in a few days but, for the next two days, I had to focus on my training. She was born when the flowers were in full bloom and that is why I would name her Basant, as it meant springtime.

I sold my first policy to myself because I had never bothered to take any life insurance. I reckoned that things were different now as I had responsibilities. Then I sold to a couple of other people I knew. The first few months were relatively easy as I was approaching people that I knew. It was amazing how, during that period, a large number of friends started to avoid me and stopped taking my calls.

Chapter Eighteen

GOING OUT ON MY OWN

I had been in the job only a few months when my mother called me into the kitchen and dropped the bombshell that would change my life forever. 'I think it is time that you and Parminder found your own place to live,' she said coldly.

To most people in the western world, that may not be a strange request. After all, I was a twenty-six-year-old man with two kids of my own. What the hell was I doing staying with my parents in the first place? The Indian tradition of the extended family system is completely different to the way we live our lives in western society. Parents do not want their sons to leave home, even when there are five sons and they may all be married with numerous kids of their own. We should all grow old together and live as a tight unit. Parents who held together a large extended family were the envy of the whole community and commanded great respect. This was a bolt out of the blue.

'Why me?' I asked meekly. 'I don't want to leave.'

I couldn't understand what had brought this on and the thought of going into the big bad world on my own terrified me, even though I was a grown man with two children. Normally, a son would say to his mother that he was moving out and she would plead with him stay, to think of the family's good name and not bring shame upon it by moving out. Why would she do this to me?

When I was a twelve-year-old kid, I used to think I had been switched at birth. A lot of kids go through this phase because they think that there must be a fairytale life out there and that they were surely destined to be royalty. All that now came flooding back. Was I really adopted? No amount of pleading would budge her; she said that her mind was made up. I would have to go and fend for myself. She accused me of not pulling my weight in the family. 'All you do is go around singing and playing your music. I will see what you do when you have to pay your own bills. You are not going to make it because you just don't have it in you.'

According to my mother, I was not earning enough money for the family kitty; my contribution was pitiful. I could not understand what she was saying. I had worked since I was thirteen. The only thing in my name was a deposit bank account in which I had managed to save £150. Parminder had worked for the past six years, religiously bringing home a weekly pay packet and handing it unopened to her mother-in-law who would give her back a couple of pounds for her bus fares for work the next week. We had never been out to a restaurant for a meal or a bar for a drink as a couple. Parminder didn't drink, didn't smoke and only wore the clothes that were bought for her by her mother-in-law. We owned no property either in Scotland or in India and I didn't have a car.

On reflection, she just wanted me out. She told me to rent somewhere until I could afford to buy some place to stay. At first I was disillusioned and very hurt and thought about leaving right away, but once I had a chance to think things through, I was angry.

'If she thinks that she can kick me out of the house with nothing, she has got another think coming,' I said to Parminder. 'Our money has gone to help build everything that this family has. The shop is paid off, this house is paid off, we have other property that was paid off. Where the hell do they think the money came to pay for all that? We made a contribution. I am not leaving with nothing. I will go but I want what is due to me.'

Parminder wanted no confrontation. 'Please don't cause any trouble,' she said. 'Let us just go. We can rent a room somewhere and we will work hard and everything will be fine.'

We had a family meeting where my mother cried loudly when I told her that the only way I would leave is if they gave me one of the flats the family owned. She accused me of greed and could not believe I had the audacity to make such demands. I tried to reason that the fair thing to do was add up all the family assets in Glasgow, total them up and divide them by four as that had been the number of family members responsible for building up those assets in the first place. I counted Parminder and myself as one. My mother is not very educated but it didn't take her long to calculate that we could be talking a large sum of money. She could accuse me of being greedy all she wanted but anyone brought in as an adjudicator would come to the same sensible conclusion as myself. We were due a share of the assets.

The next few weeks were hellish. The only times we talked as a family ended up as arguments, my mother always taking the lead, my father meekly nodding his agreement in support of my mother, and my brothers not wanting to get involved. How I wished my father was a stronger character and able to make a sensible contribution to this awkward debate. He could be firm and make a decision and we could all be happy. Every night, Parminder would plead with me to back down, her resolve to fight for what was rightfully ours diminishing by the day. My mother's ploy was working on my wife but as the days went on I was just as determined not to leave empty-handed. I knew if I gave up the fight now that I would never survive, and my mother would never thank me for it anyway. Whether I left with something or nothing, I would still be the baddy so I might as well take what was due to me.

Eventually, after much debate and no real calculation of assets, I was given a ground-floor, one-bedroom flat in the south side of Glasgow. Parminder and I did not view it. We were just given the keys and told to move out within the next few weeks. We went to see the flat the next day and it was not pretty. It was completely empty, just floorboards and bare walls. It reeked of dampness, there was mould in the bathroom and there was no kitchen as such, just a sink and a cooker that had been disconnected. There was no gas or electricity as these had been disconnected, so we just went around it with a torch.

One week later we were all packed and ready to leave for our new flat. We were allowed to take the bed. My friend Surjit and his wife turned up with his Transit van. There were six of us in the van when we flitted and although we had all our personal possessions with us that day, the van didn't seem full at all. All our stuff fitted into a few black bags. Surjit dropped us at our new residence and as he left he handed me £200 and said, 'Just give it back whenever you can.' He knew I didn't have any money and he also knew I was too proud to ask. I took the money and thanked him and made a mental note to repay him in a similar fashion some time in the future, God willing.

As there was still no power in the house, and there wouldn't be for another week, our meals consisted of mainly rolls and fritters. There was a newsagent's shop across the street and the owner allowed me to go in and use his cooker to heat up Basant's milk because she was only five months old and not yet old enough for a chippy. I lay in bed one night looking at the shapes on the ceiling made by the two flickering candles, Parminder and me at each end of the bed with Ceetl and Basant in the middle, and I contemplated my future. At that time it didn't look too bright. I watched my family sleep as if they didn't have a care in the world and decided that if I could help it, they would want for nothing.

I knew it would not be easy as I analysed my situation – I was in a commission-only job with no guarantee of income, I had no money, two young kids and nothing in the house. But I also knew that there were twenty-four hours in every day and, if necessary, I would work every one of them to make sure my family would have everything in life. I decided that I would start the next morning.

The next year was the toughest in my life. Although the commission paid out in advance was great, the downside was that if the client stopped paying their premium within the first year, the commission which had been paid to you, and which you had already spent, was deducted from the next pay cheque. The net result of this was that there were some months that you would hardly have anything in your pay packet.

Parminder was also doing her part. Prior to giving birth to Basant, she had worked as a machinist for two different companies, one of which was called Jacob's and Turner. She enjoyed working for them because her experience with her first employers had not been good. Contrary to how the name sounded, Jacob's and Turner were actually owned by a Pakistani family by the name of Khushi, and she called them to see if she could do some work from home. They supplied her with a commercial sewing machine at home and gave her a couple of large black bags with cloth which Parminder would spend the day sewing into anoraks. Sometimes, when I came home from work in the evening, we would sit and I would help her put the labels and tags on to the zips. I would then have to take the black bags full of anoraks back to the factory, walking past a million machinists. For me it was embarrassing but I guess they didn't give me a second glance because for them it was a common sight. I would put the anoraks on a desk to be counted by one of the Khushi sons who would give me some cash and another black bag full of cloth for the whole cycle to be repeated. The Khushis were another example of a hard-working Asian family doing well and the two sons, Akmal and Afzal, went on to own a company called Trespass which became a well-known brand all over the world. Later in life, I became good friends with Afzal and Akmal Khushi and the days when I took up the black bags full of anoraks often came up in our conversations.

After selling life insurance to my friends over the first few months, I was now running out of contacts. There were only so many friends that you could sell to and they were now finished. It got to the stage that I was becoming the party bore. I was the guy that nobody wanted to sit next to at a dinner. I sat up late one night pondering my next move. I almost phoned the Ashoka and asked for my old job back but decided against it. I told myself that I had the opportunity to earn good money and I should not blow it. I would go out the next day and cold-call customers by knocking on their doors to find new business.

It took me a while to master the art of cold canvassing. At the start, I would just drive to an area and park my car where no one would see it. I reasoned that nobody would take financial advice from a guy driving a rusty old banger so I would make sure that the car was well hidden. It was all I could afford and I had bought it for £300 by asking Mr Shan for an advance out of my future commissions, saying that he could deduct this over a three-month period. I convinced him by saying that it would enable me to sell more insurance policies and that we would both make more money if I had a set of wheels.

I didn't have a coat, so I had to make do with just a shirt, tie and blazer, even though it was a freezing cold, slushy February. The slush would seep through my cheap shoes and my socks were soon soaking wet and my feet absolutely frozen. After a while they were so cold that I could no longer feel the pain. I was not concerned about selling insurance policies; it was just nice to be invited in out of the cold and offered a cup of tea, which did not happen too often. I remember being in one garage talking to the owner and the icicles must have been hanging from my nose.

'Jesus! Are you not cold? You should put a coat on before you catch pneumonia,' he said, showing genuine concern.

'I know,' I said. 'I didn't realise it was so cold and I left my coat in the car.'

I was too embarrassed to admit that I didn't own a coat and that I was too broke to buy one. I also never used to have any money to buy lunch. Sometimes Parminder would make me sandwiches to take to work and other times I would just make do until I got home in the evening.

It was then that a guy called Steve Konzan joined the company. Steve talked a great game and told me that he was well experienced in the insurance industry. He claimed to have worked for numerous companies and to have been headhunted by Mr Shan to come and work for him. I felt that Steve was exaggerating because if he was half as good as he claimed to be he would not be working for Mr Shan. When Steve suggested that we canvass together as a team, and said he would show me how to do it as it was his speciality, I could not say no because I was not doing well at all on my own.

We opted to go for a particular type of client and decided that the people we were comfortable talking to were restaurant and bar managers. We developed a presentation that we practised on each other until we were able to answer every conceivable question and overcome almost any objection. We would walk into the bar, ask to speak with the manager and then introduce ourselves and tell them that we were working in the area and would like to discuss with them a scheme, which would set them off on the road to owning their own pub. This always caught their attention because I knew from personal experience that all managers wanted to open their own pubs one day.

The hardest part of any sale is getting the opportunity to sit across the table from a prospective buyer. Once you have their interest, the rest is relatively easy. When we had them sitting down with a cup of tea, we would do our presentation. I would never refer to the product I was selling as life insurance but as a means of saving money to open their own business. We were selling the dream. By saving £50 every month, in ten years' time they would have £10,000 in the scheme. They could then use this as a deposit to open their own pub. I started to close the sales and for the first time felt that I was on the road to success.

After a while I realised that the same approach could be used when approaching other businesses and I started pitching to hairdressers and shop managers. I always approached the manager and never the owner because that was my niche and I was selling the dream for them to be in the same position as their boss one day. Things were going well for me and within one year I was promoted to assistant manager, which meant I could recruit my own team, train them to sell and get commission on their sales as well as mine. The other handy thing that Steve taught me was a way to get free lunch. When I told him one day that I was hungry but had no money, he took me down to a casino where he knew we would get served with as many free sandwiches we could eat. Steve was thick-skinned but I think that to get on in this world, sometimes one has to be.

Parminder and I managed to do up the flat to a reasonable standard. Although we had a decent income coming into the house, it was only just enough to make ends meet as I was paying up everything I owned in instalments. Every piece of furniture in the house had been bought on HP, so things were quite tight and it did not take long for that monthly cheque to disappear. It had now been almost two years since my mother had asked me to move out and, of course, it had also been almost two years since our last baby. Right on cue, in February

1983, Parminder once again went into labour and had to be rushed into hospital. This time I was at her side holding her hand and telling her to breathe and push at the same time.

I then had the task to call my mother and tell her that she had become a grandmother again and that it was another girl. She was stunned. 'Where are all these girls coming from?' she wanted to know.

'I don't know, Mum, but she is very beautiful.'

'It doesn't matter how beautiful she is – it is a son you need, even if he is ugly!'

There was no point in arguing with her. I went back to the Ashoka and celebrated the birth of my daughter Preetpal with my friend Balbir. I had wanted to call her Preet because the word meant love. Parminder thought that the name was too short so we decided to add 'pal' as this was common practice with Indian names. I don't think that Preet has ever forgiven us for that. I didn't give Preet's name the same thought as the first two and I am still not sure if I was finding it a challenge to keep coming up with innovative names.

I had a few agents working under me by now and I was always on the lookout to recruit more. I always believed that there were a few guys that I had worked beside in Yarrow's who could do well if they came into the insurance industry. I approached them and suggested that they should chuck their jobs at Yarrow's and come out into the big world as it was full of opportunities for those who were willing to work at it. Only one guy took up my offer and that was Kevin Dooley, the guy who along with Callum Lavelle had got me drunk when I was at college with them. It must have taken a lot of balls for Kevin to leave his regular job and come into a job that was commission-based. Although he was nervous at first, he stuck in and many years later, when Mr Shan moved on, Kevin became branch manager. To this day he still advises me on my financial matters and his story should serve as great motivation for those who are thinking about working for themselves but are just too frightened to take the plunge. My most successful recruit was a Chinese girl called Solin Lee. She specialised in selling to the Chinese community and all her policies were for at least £100 per month. Due to this, my commission cheques got larger and larger and I felt I could now afford a slightly better house.

By the time our fourth child arrived, we had moved to a semi-detached house in the Bishopbriggs area of Glasgow and this time, when Parminder went into labour, we decided to try a change of hospital to see if they could do something different in the gender department. The first three had been born in the Queen Mother's Maternity and this time we decided that the baby should be born in Stobhill Hospital. I was never the superstitious type but I guessed it was worth a try. Once again my mother had been praying for months and I felt that this time all the bases had been covered. The strange thing about my mother was that the only time I really saw her was when Parminder was about to give birth. In between times, I would hardly hear from her.

'It has to be a boy this time,' Parminder said as she started to push for the fourth time in about six years. 'What does it look like?' she asked anxiously as the head popped out.

'It's only the head. Come on, a big push – one last time. Just think, you are never going to have to do this ever again.'

With the next and final push, the baby was in the midwife's hands. 'It's a beautiful healthy girl!' she shouted with glee as she grabbed the scissors to cut the umbilical cord.

Parminder looked disappointed at first but, when the nurse handed the baby to Parminder for her to hold in her arms, she turned to me and said, '*Bohut soni hai, henna?*' ('She is beautiful, isn't she?') Then she turned to me again and said, 'I think you should go and tell your mother.' I always felt that Jaspreet would have to be a fighter and being the youngest girl with three big sisters would be challenging. I knew she would be a winner and I named her Jaspreet, which means 'love of glory'.

I was never ever disappointed that we were having girls all the time. When friends phoned to commiserate, I would tell them that I was very happy that my children were all healthy and that I wouldn't change them for the world. They didn't believe me.

'Well, I guess you have to say that,' they would say.

My mother would scold me for celebrating. 'No wonder you keep getting girls,' she would say. 'How can you celebrate like that?'

She was in tears when she went to see Jaspreet in hospital and after she left all the women in the ward asked Parminder why she had been crying. Parminder had to tell them that she had been overcome by happiness and could not hold back the tears of joy.

Chapter Nineteen

FIRST VENTURE

Just after my third daughter had been born, I met Balbir for a drink. He told me that he was thinking of buying another place and was looking at the best way to fund it. It was a restaurant called the Shah Jahan in Elderslie Street near the city centre in Glasgow.

'It is a really nice restaurant but it's doing crap business. I think we could turn it around. How would you like to be a part of the new set-up?' he asked.

We had been in the bar for a good few hours and downed numerous pints of lager. If he had suggested a trip to the moon in an air balloon I would have said it was a fantastic idea. 'Let's do it!' I said, not even asking how much money was involved. Perhaps I was thinking that this was just another drunken idea, which Balbir would have from time to time but forget about the following morning.

We needed £30,000 to buy the lease and budgeted another £6,000 for some signage and a paint job. Balbir would also get a small overdraft to help with the minor refurbishment. We got hold of a paper napkin and started to work up the business plan. Many a major deal has been struck on the strength of a paper napkin and a jug of lager. I am a Sikh and we Sikhs, as you know, are very fond of a small refreshment . . . now and again. I think it's a pastime that many Glaswegians are quite familiar with. A recent curry survey carried out by our call-centre staff revealed that 50 per cent of the people had eaten a curry in the past seven days and 25 per cent had not. The remaining 25 per cent thought they had but couldn't remember!

Balbir suggested that we bring in other investors and give them shares in the business. It was the best way to fund the deal without getting in over our heads. The banks would have been no use as they would not have loaned money on a lease. We decided to have a consortium of six people who would not only bring in £6,000 each but, if the business were to take off, would also be able to come on board and get involved as operators. We came up with a list of around eight or nine possible names and then whittled them down to four others plus myself and Balbir. Three of them were Balbir's cousins. Two were brought in because we knew they had cash and one because he was a chef in the Ashoka. The last and final person was Gurmail Dhillon, my cousin, who would one day go on to become a director at Harlequin. We knew that he could get money together and he was also a chef working for one of our competitors. We knew he could be brought in to work when we needed him once business could afford to pay his wages.

All I needed now was £6,000. No problem to a man of my means, you would think. Well, I had no means. I was broke. Most of my wages were still going towards paying our debts and there was still no money in the bank. So off I went to see my bank manager, Alan Johnstone at the Bank of Scotland. I had no collateral because the flat I was living in had already failed a survey and the surveyor made his point clear when he wrote in his report that he did not consider the property suitable for lending purposes. Alan was keen for me to get the funds that I needed and tried to be helpful.

'Why don't you ask your father to be a guarantor?' he suggested. 'I don't see how else I can lend you that amount of cash.'

I went straight over to my parents and explained what I was about to do and I could tell that my request for help was making them feel uncomfortable.

'We will speak to the rest of the family and we will let you know,' they replied in unison.

I was a wee bit disappointed because I thought they would say yes. After all, I wasn't asking for cash and I knew that I would pay off the debt even if it took me all my working life. A few days passed and no one called to say that my dad would sign as guarantor so I decided to go and see my family once again.

'I am sorry we can't help,' said my dad, 'but we need to keep all our assets free because your brothers will need them when they go and borrow from the bank one day.'

I tried to put up a case and assured him that if and when that day came I would clear the debt. But they had made up their minds and nothing was going to change their decision. I left the house with a heavy heart but a renewed sense of determination. The next day I went back to the bank and explained my plight.

'All right, let's do this,' Alan suggested, 'if you can go out and raise three thousand, then I will give you three thousand as a personal loan.'

I was excited again; I was halfway there. I don't remember asking about bank charges or interest rates; my focus was on raising my half of the money. So out I went with my begging bowl to the people I thought might help, and that was another great learning experience for me, because help came from people I least expected and the ones I had down as certain backers made the most imaginative excuses.

My biggest helper was my mother's brother, to whom she had not spoken for some time. He didn't even ask what the money was for or when he could expect it back. He gave me the cash unconditionally, only telling me when I gave it back to him that the day he had given me the money he had written it off and did not expect it back. I also approached my cousin and close friend, Sadhu. He was Gurmail's brother and I don't think he was too pleased that we had not chosen him as a partner but had gone for his brother instead. He gave me a thousand pounds but his wife made it clear that they would need it back within a month. I gladly took the money, at least it would buy me time. Within a week, I had managed to get my three grand and with the balance coming as promised from Alan Johnstone, my first deal was done.

Balbir then took the bold step of changing the original Ashoka to a vegetarian restaurant and all his clientele followed him to the new Ashoka at Elderslie Street. Business was soon booming and within six months we also managed to open a small takeaway unit in the west end of the city. After about ten months Balbir started to feel the pressure. He felt that he was doing most of the work so he gave all the partners an ultimatum: we were all to give up our jobs and his cousins would have to sell up their shops and work full-time for the restaurant business. He felt that we all had to commit ourselves to growing the business or leave.

The only two people who decided to leave were his two cousins, who were not willing to sell their shops and come and work on a meagre wage. Both Gurmail and I said that we were quite happy to give up our jobs and commit full-time to growing the business. Balbir then suggested that we should all go our own ways and said he was happy to keep his cousin Jagtar, who was also his chef, on as a partner and that perhaps Gurmail and I should form a new partnership. We sat down and valued the business, because in order to keep the Ashoka in Elderslie Street Balbir was happy to throw the original Ashoka into the pot. Gurmail and I would keep the original Ashoka and the takeaway and for this we would have to pay his two cousins £12,000 each for their initial investment of £6,000. The last year had been quite good and I had managed to save a couple of thousand pounds. We negotiated with Balbir's cousins and they agreed to wait for the money in order for us to get the business rolling. I managed to pay them out of our cash flow within the next twelve months.

Chapter Twenty

BACK TO WHERE I BELONGED

My first day back at the Ashoka was quite confusing. There were guys wandering in off the street, pissed, stinking of drink and being abusive. I didn't realise until they had stuck the dickie bows on that they were the waiters! Our staff at that time wasn't that well trained! For instance, wee Chick Young, a well-known sports presenter, was a regular customer. He was in all the time and he would order things like one pakora, one lamb bhoona, one nan bread, at other times having a set meal for one or a 'Teatime Special' for one.

So a waiter said to him one day, 'Mr Young, you live on your own, don't you?'

'How do you know that?' enquired Chick.

'Because you are an ugly wee bastard!' came the reply.

But I loved running a restaurant in Glasgow, and I loved how much Glaswegians loved their curries. For instance, we had this regular customer who loved the Ashoka so much that he decided he was going to name all his kids after his favourite dishes. His wife, of course, wasn't very pleased. But their first-born was a wee girl and he called her Patty because he liked patia. He liked some raita with it so he called the second one Rita and the third one just had to be Nan. By this time, his wife thought this was a good idea and decided to name the next child after her favourite dish. So if you are ever in a bar and bump into a sad-looking guy called Chicken Tikka McAllister, you'll know he doesn't love his mother. OK, those stories are not entirely true but it would not surprise me if they were. Stranger things than that have happened.

The Ashoka West End, as it now came to be called to differentiate it from the one in Elderslie Street, had been operating as a vegetarian restaurant for some time. It had not worked because the carnivorous Glaswegians didn't think eating vegetables was the way to live. 'If God had intended for man to be a vegetarian he wouldn't have created the chicken,' was one customer's comment.

After about six months it was changed back to a normal restaurant, but the damage to business had been done. Most of the business had been transferred to the restaurant in Elderslie Street and in our first week of trading we took £1,500. I was not worried because I knew with hard work, and having Gurmail in the kitchen, I would have the turnover up to where it was before, over £4,000 a week.

As it turned out, it was harder than I thought, but very enjoyable. We were working long hours as we not only opened the restaurant ourselves but also stayed until the very last customer had left and the staff had been fed. Sometimes we were in the restaurant until four in the morning. When I would eventually get to bed I would be so tired, but I would be very happy. It was not a problem for me to work every available hour because I loved my job. I always tell people that unless they actually enjoy what they do, they will never do it well. If you don't look forward to getting up in the morning and doing something you enjoy, then change what you do. You only get one shot at life and there is no point in wasting it.

So, what did I do differently at the Ashoka West End from our colleagues in Gibson Street? We had started with a restaurant which turned over £1,500 in its first week and we grafted hard. There were two of us, myself and my partner-cum-chef, Gurmail Dhillon. Having a partner in the kitchen was tremendous: no temperamental chefs, no blackmailing or extortion when the restaurant had busy nights. Good chefs back in those days were few and far between. Wages were extortionate, as the chefs knew that their demands would have to be met. If you wanted to hire someone to work for you in the kitchen they were the ones who interviewed you, as opposed to the other way round. They were doing you a favour by working for you and it would have to be on their terms. A typical interview would only last a few minutes and there was never any mention of qualifications, experience or menu design.

It was a small industry and the main workers were all known. They would start by negotiating their wage and this was always net of tax. The restaurant owner was expected to pay the tax, PAYE and any other standard deductions that would normally be paid for by an employee. Due to these demands it was not uncommon for restaurateurs to under-declare chefs' wages to avoid paying too much tax. The downside to this was that cash had to be extracted from the business to cover the shortfall in wages and this led to the owners having to fiddle their tills in order to pay their chefs. The vatman and the taxman soon became wise to this and a lot of restaurateurs ended up in bother. This was not only a problem with Indian restaurants and I would guess that the practice was widespread in every business which handles cash, including bars, takeaways and most restaurants, be they Italian, Chinese or Scottish. It took a long time to overcome this problem and now chefs do take responsibility for their own deductions.

Holidays and working hours were rarely discussed as these were standard throughout the trade and accepted by both sides. The deal breaker was always the alcohol, as the chef would ask how many pints of lager he was allowed free of charge on his working days. About three pints a night was normal, after which he would agree to pay a reduced fixed price. There were rarely limits put on to how much they were allowed to consume any given day and it was quite common for the kitchen staff to be totally pished out of their heads by ten o'clock at night. I tried to put an end to this by negotiating a no-drink policy before ten o'clock to at least get the best part of the evening out of the way, and hoped that they would still be sober by the end of the evening. I knew that it would be difficult to implement this as the staff were set in their ways, but I was determined to make the changes. I knew that it was important to raise the standards in order to be a success and slowly managed to change a lot of habits which I thought were bad.

Later in life, Harlequin would buck the trend and introduce a total no-drinking policy by staff during working hours and, in fact, there came a time when they were not allowed to drink on the premises. It was also common back then for chefs to smoke while working in the kitchen. I would not even blink if I walked into a kitchen and saw a chef cooking away at the stove with a cigarette hanging from the side of his mouth. Nowadays a chef wouldn't even dream of doing such a thing or he would end up being fired. I didn't know it then but Harlequin would one day become the first Indian restaurant chain to introduce a non-smoking policy in most of their restaurants for customers as well as staff.

My focus was to build my business, and for the first four years that focus was complete in every sense. The Ashoka West End was my life and I was always in the restaurant working the tables and charming the customers. At ten o'clock every night I would take a working break and would go round the local pubs to show my face, say hello, buy a couple of drinks, and invite everyone back. It became a ritual – every night was the same. I have always believed that one must stay close to a business as one tries to develop it but I have seen people take this to the extreme and stand at their tills all night. The only way to get new customers through the door without spending a fortune on advertising is to go to where they are and drag them back in. I know that a lot of my competitors would have said at the time that I was spending too much time in the pub and that this would be my eventual downfall. I never went out and got drunk and I went to the bars with one thought in mind: bring in more customers.

Within a few years we'd taken our turnover from £1,500 to £15,000 a week. It wasn't easy – seven days a week, fourteen hours a day – but as I keep telling my managers, there are no short cuts to success and there is no substitute for hard work; not in the restaurant business.

The Ashoka West End started getting the queues that Balbir had craved when he was the boss. Now both the Ashokas were turning away customers at the door. The queues would start at seven p.m. and not disappear until ten p.m. Then there would be a lull for one hour, which allowed me to nip around all the bars to meet some of my regulars. When the pubs closed at eleven p.m. the queue would form once again and we would have people waiting for tables well after midnight. Those were the days when customers were happy to sit anywhere just to get a meal.

I was always looking for small ways in which to improve the service or the product and one day I decided to up the ante and improve the standard of coffee that I was serving. I also bought a cup stacker which was heated and this allowed me to serve the coffee in hot cups. The coffee now went out piping hot and it remained warm for ages. After the first busy night I realised that this was not good as the customers seemed to be taking forever to finish their coffees, which meant I was losing business at the door as I could not turn the tables fast enough. The next night, the cup warmer was left switched off and it was only used on very quiet nights. What is good for one restaurant is not necessarily good for another.

Getting punters out of the restaurant fast was very important – especially at the weekends. I discovered that, if I played faster music, then the customers would consume their food more quickly than if I played ballads or love songs and I had special tapes made up just for this purpose.

It was normal practice for punters to share tables. If there was a couple sitting at a table set out for four people we would just put another couple next to them, and most of the time we didn't even ask if they minded. Nobody ever had a problem with this arrangement and people were quite happy to share tables with total strangers. Even when it was Valentine's Day, you would have a guy just about to propose to his girlfriend and we would just plonk another couple right next to them. It didn't stop anyone from proposing and would often end up with all the customers having a celebration.

We invested in our restaurants, raised the standards of our kitchens and trained the chefs ourselves. We put in place in-house training programmes for our waiters. Food safety was important and I became a stickler for hygiene standards. I believe good chefs have been the major factor in the success of Harlequin Restaurants. I get really concerned about health and hygiene in our kitchens, and when I saw a kitchen porter scratching himself and handling food, I reprimanded him. I bought him some stainless steel tongs for handling the chicken tikka, and told him the importance of washing hands after going to the loo. I went into the kitchen a few days later, and noticed a piece of string hanging out of his fly and, when I asked him what this was for, he gave me an explanation I was not prepared for. 'Ah've been giving this health and hygiene a lot of thought, boss, so I decided to tie a piece of string to my willie. Now, when I go to the toilet, I use the string to take it out so, if I don't touch it, I save time 'cos I don't have to wash my hands. And it saves you a lot of hot water.'

I didn't know whether to laugh or cry, whether to pat him on the back for showing initiative or grab that piece of string and drag him across the kitchen with it! But I kept my cool. 'But how do you put it back in?' I calmly enquired.

'Oh! That's the easy part!' he said. 'I just use these stainless steel tongs that you gave me.'

Now I know that some of you are wondering if that really happened or is it just something I made up. Well, I will let you decide.

Business was good and I was enjoying running the restaurant, I was feeling no pressure of any sort and I thought that nothing could go wrong. It was around this time that the building, which housed the Ashoka West End, became due to be refurbished. We got notice that the entire building would be covered in scaffolding for a whole year. I dreaded the effect this would have on business. I also knew that when scaffolding is put up for one year, there is a strong possibility that it may still be there two years later.

There is a positive in every negative situation and one has to look for opportunities. I decided that this could be the right time to approach my landlord, Mr Binning, to see if he would be willing to sell me the property. It was better to buy it now before the building got refurbished rather than later because even although I was paying for the refurbishment, it was Mr Binning's property which was being enhanced. Knowing 'Uncle Binning', he would want more money once the work had been done.

I told him of the potential problem and how concerned I was that business would suffer and that I would struggle to pay my rent if there was any downturn in the turnover. I asked if he would sell me the property and after some time thinking about it he said that he would. I asked him how much he wanted for it and he said £70,000. I knew it was too much but as far as he was concerned it was a 'take-it-or-leave-it' situation. I went to see Alan Johnstone and asked if he would provide a £50,000 loan as I could come up with £20,000 from the Ashoka profits. We got the place valued by a surveyor and the value came in at £35,000.

'How can you pay seventy thousand for a place which is only worth half that?' said Alan. 'Surely, you are not serious.'

But I was serious and I knew that I had to own the bricks and mortar. I had to buy the property. We managed the get the loan based on the strength of our trading figures and I bought my first business freehold. It felt good. I met Mr Binning a few months later and he said, 'You have a bit to learn about the art of negotiation; I would have taken less.'

'So do you,' I replied, 'because I would have paid you much more.'

Chapter Twenty-One

EXPANDING THE BUSINESS

Balbir came to me with a new proposition. There was a site in York Street, near the city centre, that two of his staff had an option to lease. All the planning permissions were in place to open a bar and restaurant, and it was ready to be refurbished. The two boys had no means to fund it and just wanted to get out of the lease. It was too much for Balbir to take on himself and he asked if Gurmail and I would take a 50 per cent stake in the new venture. By the end of the night and a few pints of lager later we were partners once again.

It took about nine months to develop the restaurant and bar in York Street. It was my first experience of building a restaurant from scratch and what an experience it was. I worked with an architect who was pretty incompetent and the squad that we worked with were the tradesmen that we used to do minor refurbishments in our existing restaurants. I also brought in a friend to do the joinery work and my uncle became the labourer. Although we had a set of drawings to work to these were not detailed and a lot of the detail was just made up as we went along. Balbir was quite happy to leave the refurbishment to me but he was always on hand to make decisions when it came to the design aspects as he had experience of that and I was just learning.

None of us knew about building regulations and we learnt them together. One day we decided to knock down a wall, which we didn't realise was supporting the whole building. We had just started to make a hole when the wall started to crumble and to this day I don't know how we managed to get a lintel in the hole fast enough to stop the whole building from collapsing on top of us. Those months were the hardest I have ever physically worked. I was down on site every morning at eight a.m. and stayed until five p.m. The rest of the guys would go home to put their feet up in front of the television and sip a cold beer and I would go home for a shower and a shave and head into the Ashoka to serve table until midnight. It was a very tough time for me and I hardly saw Parminder and the kids but these were the sacrifices that I had to make in order for me to reach my goals.

We decided to call the restaurant the Spice of Life because I had seen the name used before and had always liked it; the bar we called the Harlequin. The reason for the name was that a friend of one of the staff was a starving artist called Janice whose speciality was painting harlequins. Although she agreed to do the murals very cheaply I told her that even that was too expensive. I decided to show her an old card trick that Andy Coia had taught me while I was working at Yarrow's. It was a clever trick where the hand is faster than the eye and involved sleight of hand to produce an illusion. Janice fell for the trick, believing she would make ten times her money as she thought I had messed it up. But giving the impression of messing up was a part of the trick and I ended up getting the murals for free, leaving Janice even hungrier. I had no idea at the time that the name would become so massive in the catering industry.

The restaurant and bar opened eventually and it did not perform well. We had done the fit-out on a tight budget and the finishes in particular were quite cheap.

'I think it's in the wrong part of town,' Balbir suggested.

'Aye, now he tells me, after all the time and money we've spent doing the place up,' I said to Gurmail.

We traded the site for a year, continually having to put money into the bank account from our own pockets to keep the bank manager happy. If it was not for the fact that none of us had to depend on this business to pay our mortgages we would have gone bust within six months. We had Monir Mohammed as manager of the restaurant. He had worked for us for a number of years and he was not only a decent waiter but could also do a shift in the kitchen if he had to. This was important, as it was common for chefs to go AWOL for days due to binge drinking. Monir did his best but it was a real struggle trying to get punters to come in through the door. Monir continued to work for me for a number of years and eventually went on to open his own restaurant called Mother India. He now has three restaurants and is doing really good things within the industry.

Teresa Doherty, who had worked for a while in the Ashoka West End, moved to York Street to manage the Harlequin bar. She stayed on with me until I sold my business and was one of the key people in the group's success due to her versatility. She could cook in the kitchen, serve in the bar, wait at the tables and she could also do accounts and manage the office. There was not much that Teresa could not turn her hand to and her input was invaluable. But even her versatility could not pull in the punters and we were struggling to keep our heads above water.

We still felt that the site would come good one day and decided to buy the freehold from our landlord, Mike Shrigley, at a price of £110,000.

'You cannot go wrong with property,' my grandfather had always said.

I wondered if he would have been of the same opinion if he had seen the location of the restaurant in York Street. But once again my grandfather would have been proved right. The ink on the deal had not even dried when I got a telephone call from a consortium that were buying up all the property in York Street because they had plans to redevelop the whole area. They offered £180,000 and we could have sold up, made up all our losses and still be left with a wee profit.

'I think we will easily get two hundred and fifty thousand for it,' said Balbir.

'You must be off your head, talking stupid numbers like that,' I said. 'I am going to ask for half a million pounds.'

He thought I was crazy and said so too. 'You will never get that much and probably blow the deal,' was his opinion.

I asked if he would take the £250,000 and let me keep the balance as a thank you for all the hard work I had put in over the past three years. He told me to eff off but said he was quite happy to let me negotiate the deal. Eventually, after much negotiation between me and the prospective buyers and with help and advice from Mike Shrigley and some sleepless nights, they paid us £460,000 and we were so pleased that we all went out and got drunk. For the first time in my life, I actually had a bit of cash in the bank.

I think we were still drunk when we decided to put most of that money into a frozen food wholesale business and bought a company called Union Frozen Foods. Two brothers who owned the Koh-I-Noor restaurant, which back in the sixties and seventies was one of the busiest restaurants in Glasgow, also owned this company. I had learnt a lot from the way the brothers had run their restaurant, especially what not to do, because, along with a lot of restaurants at the time, they were under-declaring sales and avoiding the payment of VAT. I think that the vatman decided to take a high-profile case and set an example so one of the guys actually ended up in jail. I learned an early lesson from their misfortune and that was to keep a clean set of accounts.

Union Frozen Foods had two parts to its business. It supplied a lot of the Indian restaurants in Scotland with meat and chickens, and it also manufactured curries and sold them into cash and carries and a couple of small retail chains. We knew nothing about the business; we had never done any wholesaling and we knew nothing about manufacturing. Balbir had always felt that it was a natural progression for us to expand our business through retail, as the curries sold by supermarkets were 'shite'. We didn't realise that the market was so price-driven and the supermarket buyers were looking to buy curries in for pennies. At the prices they wanted to pay, producing 'shite' was an achievement in itself.

Another part of the business we acquired was a contract that was in place to supply halal cooked meals to a few schools in the Glasgow area for Muslim children. Abdul Gaffur, the brother responsible for running the business, discussed the contract with me and I asked where the halal meat came from for these meals. I was surprised to find that the supplier was not a halal butcher but one that I had never even heard of. Abdul was comfortable with this as he felt that all you needed to satisfy the schools was a certificate of authenticity from the supplier and the one he used supplied the certificate and he had no reason to doubt their integrity. 'Once you have the paperwork, then you have shown due diligence. If you go to the local halal butcher, you will not make any money from this contract.' Although his supplier could have been totally kosher (for want of a better word), this comment made me feel very uncomfortable.

I don't regard myself as a deeply religious person. A lot of the time I find religion to be very contradictory, especially when it comes to food and meat and the importance of how an animal is killed before it can be eaten. Although I don't believe in a lot of things, I do believe that if someone else wishes to live in a certain way and their belief is that they will only eat halal meat, then if I am to supply them with their food, I have to be certain that the meat I supply is to their standard. My conscience will allow nothing less. After we took over the company, one of the first things we did was to change our meat supplier for the kids' meals. Although the supplier seemed 'kosher' my instincts told me that the meat may not have been halal. I could never be sure otherwise and I would want to be one hundred per cent certain.

It was not a large order and I took the decision to buy the meat from a local halal butcher. The authenticity was now assured, and I felt much better within myself for doing this even if the change meant that we were now making very little money from the contract. A few months later, when some of the Muslim parents got to know that the company had been taken over by Sikhs, the contract was cancelled and given to another Muslim supplier. I wonder what those kids are eating just now. This was just another kick in the goolies one gets from the human race as one goes through life.

Why we got ourselves into this situation by buying Union Frozen Foods I will never know but, once we had made the commitment and paid the money, we knew we would have to make a go of it. We knew we needed another partner who could help run the new company as we had no time to do it ourselves, and we brought in Paramjit Samra to do the job. His only credentials were that at one time, prior to buying his own corner shop, he had worked in the manufacturing unit for Union Frozen Foods. None of us really knew him that well and we were not sure how good he was, but we didn't even interview him. The fact that he was related to Gurmail, as their wives happened to be sisters, was good enough for us. We asked Gurmail what he thought and he shrugged his shoulders and said he thought it was all right, which is what Gurmail did a lot of the times when he wanted to disagree. I think in this case he had been put into a situation that if he had said no he would have had problems from his relatives for obstructing what would have been an opportunity for Paramjit. So even if he had wanted to say no, he found it hard to do so and he made the decision which would make his life easy at home.

'That's all right then,' I said, 'no need for an in-depth interview. Let's get him in.'

We changed the name of the company to Spice of Life Foods Ltd, again, I still don't know why. We didn't do the things a lot of people nowadays would do, such as bringing in a marketing company. We just felt that we wanted to change the name and we went ahead and did it. Over the next few years we left the day-to-day operations to Paramjit Samra and the company traded away without making too much money. It was never stressful. I didn't know it at the time, but this would be the venture that would almost put me out of business.

During this period we expanded our business at a good rate. It was easier to expand having Balbir as a partner and the sites that we opened traded reasonably well. First we felt that we needed a presence in the south side of Glasgow and decided to open the Ashoka South Side in the Clarkston area. The opening of the Ashoka in Johnstone followed this very quickly afterwards. For the Johnstone restaurant, we decided to bring in another partner, namely my youngest brother, Sukhdev. He had told me that he was working long hard hours in the family shop and was not very happy. Bored out of his skull standing behind a shop counter, he said that the bar counter sounded more glamorous. He managed to lever some money out of the family business and came with us to run the Ashoka in Johnstone. We were on a roll and we were the leaders in our industry. We felt invincible and thought that we could do no wrong. All we had to do was to buy a struggling site, change it to an Ashoka and the punters would pour in but we were to be brought down to earth with a thud.

This was the time when we bought a restaurant which went on to become a nightmare for anyone who tried to trade it. We bought the property in Paisley because Paramjit supplied the owners through Spice of Life Foods and reckoned it could be a very good restaurant under our management. I had my doubts about the site but I was also told by Jarnail Singh, who was Gurmail's brother-in-law, that, if we took it on, then he would also come into the business and work as a chef. Another guy, Ashraf Mohamed, who worked with Paramjit as a sales manager and whose job it was to sell poultry and meat into the

Asian restaurants, also said that the restaurant was a sure bet and that he would also invest.

I reckoned that all these guys couldn't be wrong and we decided to go ahead and buy it for almost £400,000. The market was at its peak with Indian restaurants changing hands at crazy prices and the price we paid was the going rate. We then spent £200,000 on the refurbishment, but when we opened for business hardly anyone came in. It traded miserably. No matter how hard we tried it just wasn't working and we were trading every week at a loss. Jarnail and Ashraf could not go on taking the continuous losses and we eventually let them out and allowed them to salvage most of their initial outlay. Gurmail, Paramjit and I were left holding the baby.

Over the next fifteen years, the Ashoka Paisley would have many tenants under many different guises doing all varieties of food in an effort to make a success of that wretched place. They would inevitably all fail and I would always be left holding the keys. So many times I tried to sell the property but never had any takers. I don't know how much money that place has swallowed up, I eventually sold it for the princely price of £100,000. I had lost a lot of money on that site but I was just happy to see it go.

By this time Balbir and I were involved in a number of joint ventures. We had the frozen food business, the Ashoka South Side and the Ashoka in Johnstone. On top of this, Balbir had his own two restaurants, the Ashoka on Elderslie Street and Balbir's Brasserie, which was located a hundred yards down the street from his Ashoka. As time went on, I started to get a bit disillusioned by the way things were going. I felt that I was everywhere trying to build the various businesses and thought that I wasn't getting the support from Balbir. He was only spending time in his own restaurants and neglecting the jointly owned ones. At least this was my perception. I discussed this with him on a number of occasions but he said that he was not willing or able to commit any more time. I then asked him to appoint me as managing director and that way he didn't have to do anything. He could remain a shareholder and just pay me a decent wage for running and growing the business.

'All you have to do', I reasoned, 'is acknowledge the work that I am doing.'

For reasons known only to himself, Balbir was not willing to do this and cracks in our relationship started to appear. He did not want to be a part of Spice of Life Foods any more either because he didn't want to work with Paramjit. He was not pleased with the way he kept the books and ran the business so Balbir wanted out. We discussed terms and we came to a price that he was happy to accept. He accepted my offer without too much debate and, in later life, I wondered if he should have asked for more. I knew that was not his style as he always admitted that he paid too much for things when he bought them and always sold them too cheap. I paid him his money to relinquish his shares and knew that was the last time I would work with my mentor. It was time for me to move onwards and upwards.

I sometimes wonder if breaking my business ties with Balbir to the detriment of our long friendship was the right thing for me to do. We had been together for so many years and we had been successful. A lot of people would have advised me differently. If I could turn the clock back, I would make the same decision today as I did at that time, even with the benefit of hindsight and many more years of experience. I believe that there comes a time in every man's life when he has to move to new levels in his quest to achieve what others see as unachievable. Not everyone will share your ambition, so sometimes friends and associates who don't have the same goals and the same vision can and will become your limiting factor. There can be no half measures, there can be no shirking of the responsibility to make the tough decisions. You cannot let emotions get in the way and allow the heart to rule the head when it comes to business. So, if others cannot keep up or their agendas are different from your own, then they have to be left to follow their own objectives. These are the tough decisions successful people have to make in their lives time and time again. I was so driven at the time that nothing else mattered because I wanted to climb the ladder of success. Alas, as Stephen Fry once said, 'It is only when you get to the top that you get to know if the ladder has been leaning against the right wall.'

This single-mindedness can then be seen by colleagues as ruthless and insensitive, but I would argue that you cannot grow a business which is formidable without making decisions that are going to upset people. If you choose to follow your heart and leave a legacy, then don't be upset when people don't understand your motives, your will and your determination to succeed, and refer to you as 'that ruthless bastard businessman'. People adopt different styles and methods to reach an end result. Sometimes that end result is the same but it can be acquired in a variety of ways.

Paramjit Samra, on the other hand, has always been a law unto himself. Spice of Life Foods was a really tough business to operate and his continual hard work saved the company. I have to confess that I made some blunders in the enterprise, the worst of which was to seriously underestimate our relocation costs which put tremendous pressure on the company's cash flow, but Paramjit worked really hard to make it work. His management style has always been very hands-on, he will not delegate even the most menial of tasks and he is in the loading bay most days, driving a forklift. This was invaluable when we were trying to save the business and his hard-working approach has helped him to build a turnover of around £5 million. It has also allowed him to make continuous profits and have a good income for himself and his family but his turnover has been pretty stagnant over the last ten years. I think this is a pity because, ever since the early days at Spice of Life, I really believed that if someone could stabilise the business there was the potential to build a £50 million turnover company and make some serious profits. Having overcome the first hurdle with the business, I do now feel that Paramjit has missed a major opportunity to grow the business to this level.

Throughout the years I have been asked one particular question on so many occasions. That question is what my opinion is of the way that certain people run their organisations. I would always give the same answer and that is that my way is not the only way. There are numerous examples of people running their businesses in unorthodox ways and becoming so immensely successful that you have to admire their gall and their nerve. Just because it is not right for me does not mean that it is wrong. Don't believe that there is a textbook method of running a successful business because it simply does not exist.

That is not to say that one should discard the basic rules that apply to everyday business such as setting goals, having strict financial controls, building teams, staff motivation and training, to mention just a few. No matter how you are seen to run your business by others, you still need to know exactly how your business is performing and be in complete control of every situation. If you don't do that you will not last long.

I guess the way that Balbir and I eventually separated and went our own ways was not pleasant for either of us. We had been friends for many years and had worked together for so long. We both knew that this was the end of an era and that we would never work together again. The challenge of choosing partners is a difficult one; it is always one of business's dilemmas and most people get it wrong time and time again. I believe that business partnerships are not for life and a successful partnership is one where both parties have had some benefit when the association is brought to an end. It is important for everyone to benefit.

There is nothing wrong with having a series of partnerships which can be dissolved when the opportunity arises to make a profit or when things don't go according to plan. It is true that not everyone will make equal gains and some people will come out of a particular deal better than others but this is usually determined by input into the venture and should be recognised by all parties. My association with Gurmail Dhillon has lasted the best part of twenty-five years and one of the reasons for this is that we are completely opposite personalities. We don't even share the same interests and I don't think I have ever been out with him for a beer in a bar without someone else being present. Our interests and hobbies are completely different and I think that this has been a good thing. In business, we had different areas of control and while Gurmail was happy in the kitchen playing a supporting role and making sure things were OK behind the scenes, I was happy posing for the cameras, holding platters of food that he had cooked.

It was also at this time that I came up with a concept that radically changed the way that I ran my restaurants and it is something I would advice anyone running multiple outlets or branches to consider doing. When I first discussed the concept with some advisors, they thought I was mad because it meant that I would be handing restaurants that were worth millions of pounds to my staff without any money changing hands. They had never heard of such a concept. I believed that I was doing the right thing and decided to go ahead with my idea. I knew that the best way to make profits was to ensure that each unit was profitable and that could only be done if the costs could be controlled. The best way to control the costs was to empower the managers and let them share in my savings. I would put their earning potential in their own hands.

I realised that most of my key managers and chefs had been with me for many years and they were all good at what they were doing. I decided to give the manager and the chef of each restaurant the freedom to run their own restaurants. This was done by looking at the accounts for the past two years and agreeing an adjusted profit with them that we all knew could be generated. I then signed a management agreement with them to pay me a fixed amount every month and, if they made any more money, they could keep it for themselves. They would be responsible for all the bills, including staff PAYE, VAT, rates and all the normal operating costs.

The difference could be seen immediately, staff costs decreased overnight and, instead of calling a plumber every time they had a blocked toilet, the managers were soon putting their hands down the pans to save themselves the callout charges. Instead of calling an electrician every time a bulb fused, they were now changing that bulb themselves. The change was superb and some of the guys trebled their incomes in the first year. I was happy too because my workload had now been spread and I was getting a fixed income coming in every month. I channelled my energies into making sure that standards were not compromised and that customers were still getting the service to which they had become accustomed. We also helped the managers to manage their businesses by providing them with admin support including monthly management accounts. This not only helped them to control costs but also allowed me to keep an eye on my assets.

Chapter Twenty-Two

ANOTHER WEDDING

At home, things were also going well and we moved into a house in Bearsden, one of the more affluent suburbs of Glasgow. There was a big difference between our new home and the one we had left in Bishopbriggs. The house was set high on a hill and looked in towards the city. The main living room had a large balcony and as I surveyed the scene on the day we moved in, I felt that I had finally arrived.

The girls were all at the local primary school and business was ticking over nicely. Parminder had sent for her youngest sister to come and visit her from India and had then decided that she didn't want her to go back. She spoke to a few of her friends and they all gave her the same advice.

'The only way she can get to stay here legally is for her to get married. You are going to have to find her a man.'

I told her that I was not happy with the plan as I had promised as her sister's sponsor to make sure that she left the country before her visa expired. Parminder took the advice of her friends seriously and decided to talk to the local matchmakers. Her argument was that we were not breaking any laws by taking this route and, in fact, were actually helping Scotland solve its shrinking population problem.

The next weekend, we all went to a local wedding where someone attending from America noticed Parminder's sister. The next morning, I received a call from Mr Sewa Singh Kolhi. 'Does your sister-in-law want to get married?' he asked, getting right to the point.

I covered the mouthpiece and shouted to Parminder, 'Does your sister want to get married?'

'Of course she does,' said Parminder without hesitation and without even asking her sister who was sitting next to her.

'Mr Kolhi . . .' I began.

'It's OK,' said Mr Kolhi, 'I heard. In fact,' he continued, 'I thought you might say that so I took the liberty of inviting the boy and his family around to your house for dinner tomorrow evening. The boy is here from America for yesterday's wedding and does not have much time. If you want a wedding to take place then we have to pull out all the stops.'

I was thinking that this was good news for me, because if she married this bloke then as far as I was concerned I would have kept my word as a sponsor when I eventually shipped her off to America. I went through to the lounge and told Parminder the news. Without saying a thing, she headed straight into the kitchen and started cooking a meal for fifteen people.

The meeting the next evening went very well and we let the boy and girl spend an hour alone while the rest of us chatted about the wedding. As far as the whole room was concerned, it was as good as on and the boy and girl hadn't even come through to tell us what they thought. In fact, by they time they came in and said that they were happy, we had already set the date and discussed the dowry.

'It is normal,' I said, 'in this situation to look into the background of each other's families to ensure that they are happy with whom they are marrying into. Would you like me to give you the details?'

Mr Kolhi was as sharp as usual in his observation and said, 'We take it that you looked at your wife's family before you married her. As her sister's family is the same, you have already done the due diligence. If it's good enough for you, then it is good enough for us.'

I could see the logic and why waste time? We all congratulated one another by passing around sweetmeats and the wedding was set for fifteen days' time.

The next morning, Parminder and Gurmail left for London to buy clothes, jewellery, gifts and various other outfits and returned with a packed car boot two days later. While she was away, I had my own duties to carry out in preparation for the big day. I had to book the hall, book the Sikh Temple, print the invitations, book the photographer, get a wedding cake and send invitations out to all the guests. I also had to sort out the catering and the drinks. It was a lot to get done in a fortnight but the wedding day arrived and went off without a hitch. It is another example of what can be achieved if you set your mind on it and that nothing is impossible.

My son told me recently that he had heard that in some parts of Asia a man doesn't know his wife until he marries her – he asked me if this was true. I told him it was and that it was the same the whole world over. He's fascinated by marriage and he asked me how much it costs to get married.

'I don't know, son,' I said, 'I'm still paying!'

He said, 'Mum said you're a millionaire because of her.'

I replied, 'Yes, if it wasn't for her I'd be a billionaire!'

I am pleased to say that Parminder's sister's marriage to Rajah from Houston, Texas, turned out to be a happy one and as they got to know one another they also started to love each other. They went on to have three great kids and this year they celebrated their twentieth anniversary. My thoughts turned briefly to my own daughters' futures as I watched them have a good time at their aunt's wedding. I wondered what fate had in store for them and if Mr Kolhi would also be involved when they got married. Or would they just go out and organise their own weddings? Only time would tell.

Chapter Twenty-Three

THE BARRELHOUSE

David Murphy came into my life when he bought the Dukes Bar in Old Dumbarton Road. It was a busy wee bar situated about a hundred yards from the Ashoka West End. He had traded Dukes very successfully before buying larger premises a couple of hundred yards away and selling Dukes. David ran a really great bar and although a lot of his punters often said that he was a difficult character to get on with – 'fucking weirdo' were words used when some people described him – they would still flock to his bar and he had the place doing exceptionally well. I have often come across people who are described as weirdos and I think that it is a word used to describe complex characters. Very few of us have the time to get to know other people and look into what makes different individuals tick. I usually find that if we cannot fit people's personalities into a box with which we ourselves are comfortable, it is easier for us to class them as weirdos.

I liked David a lot and we got on very well. Quite often, I would go round to his new pub, Murph's Barrelhouse, and we would sit in long after the punters had left and chat about life. On one of these visits, just before Christmas one year, David said that he was pissed off and would really like to go away on a long break after the busy spell was over at the bar.

'I know,' I said, 'let's go to India. We will do a three-week tour of Delhi, Agra, Jaipur, Mumbai and Goa and then I will take you to the village to meet my mother-in-law.' The last sentence was added to dissuade him in case he took me seriously.

'Great idea! It's just the type of break I need.' His speech was slurred and as we hugged each other outside the bar and staggered off in opposite directions, anyone listening would have thought that our conversation was pure fantasy – just the kind of conversation one would expect from two drunken guys at two o'clock in the morning.

I called David the next day and asked if he remembered our conversation of the previous night. He said that he did and that he was still up for it if I was. We spent twenty-one days touring India. David had a mixed experience, including the dreaded Delhi belly, and vowed never to eat curry again . . . until he got back to Glasgow. When he was not well we went to my home in the Punjab and David made a remarkable recovery eating fresh vegetables picked from the fields outside the house. His recovery was so remarkable that within a day he was up and about.

One day he went wandering off into the village with his camera to get some pictures of the locals and after a few hours he had still not returned. As it started to get dark I decided to go and find him. Finding a white man in a Punjabi village is as hard as finding a drunk in Sauchiehall Street at eleven o'clock on a Friday night. Piss easy. People kept pointing me towards the middle of the village and saying, 'He went that way!'

I eventually tracked him to a house where a wedding had just taken place and David was sitting in the middle of the courtyard like a guest of honour with a table full of food and drink in front of him. He was smiling from cheek to cheek and enjoying every minute.

'This is not all, Charan,' he said with a wink, 'the groom just came up to me a few minutes ago and said that his wife is in the bedroom and that I should go to her. Is this some kind of tradition?'

I had to bring him back down to earth and tell him that he was not the 'white god' he thought himself to be, and that all that the groom wanted was to introduce the bride. Also that, for the privilege, David would be expected to give the girl some cash as a gift, as was tradition.

It was also on that visit to India that I realised that you could purchase anything in most counties of the world if you had the money to do so. One night in Mumbai, we were walking back to the hotel after a few drinks when we were approached by a dodgy-looking character who came close to my ear and asked if the 'sahib' would like some marijuana. It was strange that he didn't ask *me* if I wanted any and I wasn't quite sure if I should be offended or not – he probably saw me as the white man's lackey. I told him that the sahib was not interested in any form of drugs. Unwilling to take no for an answer the greasy little salesman pressed on with his sales pitch. 'I could get a beautiful girl for the sahib. All the girls were very beautiful and very clean.' The very fact he had to say that they were clean had me doubting his honesty. It is the same as someone starting a sentence saying, 'I tell you this without a word of a lie.'

'Look here,' I said, trying to bring the conversation to an end, 'the sahib is not interested in girls. The sahib prefers boys.'

Turning to David I said, 'That should get rid of him.'

The guy kept up his pace and without the slightest hesitation and without breaking his stride said, 'No problem. What age would the sahib like the boy to be?'

During our time in India David confided in me and told me of the problems he was having with his business. It was a mixture of financial mismanagement and personal problems including a pending divorce to which he and his wife had mutually agreed. David had cash-flow problems and asked if I would be interested in taking a stake in his bar. As soon as we arrived back in Glasgow, I found myself an 80 per cent shareholder in Murph's Barrelhouse. I didn't have to put in any cash as all that was required was some refinancing. We remained partners for two years and I eventually bought David's stake and he went off in search of new horizons in the Middle East.

Chapter Twenty-Four

MURPHY'S PAKORA BAR

The bar across the road from the Ashoka West End, called the Exchequer, had been a thriving pub run by a guy called Jack Connell. Jack had bought this run-down, drinking man's, spit and sawdust bar and refurbished it very tastefully. His next challenge was to get rid of the old clientele so that the ones that he was trying to attract would not get verbally abused by being called toffs, faggots or poofters, or, even worse, end up getting chibbed. He got into so many scuffles that, more often than not, his shirt would be ripped and hanging around his neck, and a lot of the punters referred to him as the Incredible Hulk. He cleaned the place up and got it so busy that it was almost impossible to get in after nine o'clock in the evening. He then sold it to a guy called John Dorward who was totally incompetent at running the business and, over a couple of years, ran it into the ground. It had been placed on the market and Dorward had been trying to get rid of it for months with no takers.

One quiet Tuesday evening, I went over to the Exchequer at ten p.m. to see if I could drum up some business. I ordered my usual pint of lager and started to chat to the regulars. I noticed three Asian guys sitting in a corner in deep discussion with the owner. Although they were strangers, I knew they were in the restaurant trade. Two of them wore white shirts and black trousers – a dead giveaway – and I knew that the third guy was probably a chef because he sat back and I could tell by his little involvement that he could probably not speak English. I started to get concerned. The reputation of the Ashoka West End had spread amongst the restaurant fraternity and everyone knew that we were bursting at the seams. These guys could only be here for one thing. There was no other reason for John Dorward to be entertaining three Asian guys because John was not known for his hospitality. That's why business was so bad in the first place. I finished my beer and went back across to the Ashoka.

'The bastards are moving in on our territory!' I said to Gurmail as I kicked open the kitchen door. 'They will be opening a spanking brand-new place while we have bloody scaffolding covering up our frontage again.'

Gurmail shrugged his shoulders as if to say 'that's business' as he stuck a large piece of tandoori chicken into his mouth. 'Jesus Christ!' I thought. 'How can he eat at a time like this?'

I wasn't in a good mood so the customers that came in that night were not met with the customary peck on the cheek, and the girls didn't get a kiss either. I was worried. Eventually, I could take no more as the curiosity was killing me. There was no point in me going home to bed that night because I would never be able to sleep, so I went back across the road to see John Dorward.

'Aye,' he said with a smile as he poured me a pint of lager, 'they have offered me a hundred and eighty thousand and I am going to take it.'

Without thinking too much and before he had a chance to hand me my drink I asked, 'What if I were to offer you a hundred and eighty thousand, John? Would you sell it to me instead?'

John told me that he would rather do business with me than the three guys that were in earlier. 'I don't know any of them,' he confirmed. 'And I don't like Pakis anyway.'

For once I wasn't going to argue that his comment was racist and found myself nodding in agreement.

'I will take your offer,' he said and stuck out his hand to close the deal.

I took his hand and said, 'Yes, John, it's a deal.'

I don't think he saw me swallow. All I needed now, I thought, was £180,000. I downed the pint in one and went back across the road to break the news to Gurmail.

The next morning I found myself in familiar surroundings: sitting across the desk from my prematurely ageing bank manager.

'How much is the property?' asked Alan Johnstone, as I shuffled nervously in my chair.

'I am going to pay a hundred and eighty thousand for it,' I said.

'How much do you need to borrow?' he asked, hoping that I would ask for the standard 70 per cent of the valuation.

'I need a hundred and eighty thousand,' I said, trying to look bold and confident.

I told him that if he gave me the money to buy the place then I would come up with the money to refurbish it. I said that I would spend £100,000 on refurbishment and that would be my contribution to the deal. I knew as I told him this that I would have to talk to all my suppliers and try and extend credit terms with them. I knew I could also get money from the brewers to help with the refurb. Without too much bother, he agreed to give me the money.

A couple of weeks later, while the lawyers were still trying to resolve various issues, John Dorward came into the Ashoka and handed me the keys to the bar. He owed the bank and brewers a lot more than the money that I was paying and, even if he were to hang around for the handover, there was nothing in the deal for him so he decided to disappear and leave everyone else to sort out the mess.

The bank and brewers both had a security over the property and would have been within their rights to remarket the pub and try to achieve a better price. I was not sure if they would accept my offer. Those were the days that I took chances that I would never advise anyone to take now. In fact, I would say that they would be mad to even consider such things. I decided to refurbish the bar before it was legally mine and moved in with my tradesmen. We ripped the place apart and threw out all the fittings and furniture. My lawyer told me to stop vandalising the property as it didn't belong to me and that I was committing an offence and would end up in jail. I told him I would stop but when he left I continued to throw things into the skip.

I started my fit-out and spent £100,000 of borrowed money on new fixtures, fittings and lighting. The refurbishment took six weeks and as opening day approached, the deal had still not been done. I removed the old ventilation duct at the back of the building and put up a bigger one overnight before anyone noticed. That way I would not have to wait weeks or months for planning permission and get permission from the residents above as I was fixing the duct on to their properties. I kept my fingers crossed that no one would notice and decided I would apply for all the permissions retrospectively.

The invitations went out and it was my big opening night. There was only one problem: I still had no right to be in the property, never mind trade from it. I was expecting the bank or the brewers to walk in and ask me to leave and thank me for doing the place up for them. Had they done that, I would have had no option but to leave the bar. There was no sign of either the bank or the brewer but I did get a visit from the planning department who asked me to remove the flue and reinstate the original one. An argument followed and I told the planner to 'fuck off'. The strange thing is that he did and I never saw him again until I applied for my retrospective permissions. He turned out to be a really nice guy. That night I opened for business in premises that I did not legally own and I had not paid any money for. That situation remained for another four weeks until the deal was officially done, and I could trade Murphy's Pakora Bar without being afraid of being chucked out.

Having a bar across from the Ashoka was fantastic because instead of the customers having to queue outside in all sorts of weather I could now send them across the street and they could have a couple of drinks as they waited. Ten minutes before their allocated table became available, I would run across to the pub and tell them that their table was now ready. It worked a treat. I was now making money from my queue and they were thanking me for it. The only downside was the traffic that I would have to dodge every five minutes to get across a busy road. On a number of occasions irate drivers had to apply emergency brakes and show me two fingers or make gestures with clenched fists which they moved in an up-and-down motion as I tried to waltz my way through the traffic. Murphy's Pakora Bar traded for many years until I sold the business on to Sanjay Majhu and retained the property. It has since had a couple of different tenants and been through hard times, but it is now trading well once again as The Goat.

The concept of the Pakora Bar had been simple: I did not want a restaurant competing with the Ashoka West End and, knowing how popular the various varieties of pakora were, I decided to combine the two great Glasgow passions and give punters a chance to have their pakora and pints under the one roof. The Pakora Bar traded well from its first day of opening.

Things had certainly moved on from the days when you got a bunch of guys all trying to outdo each other in how hot a curry they could eat. In those days, they would be on vindaloos with extra chillies and jugs of lager and the perspiration would be pouring down their faces. It was lager in, sweat out, lager in, sweat out. I would get really concerned because, lets face it, it's not natural. I never met an Asian who ate curry like that. And I'd say to these fellas, 'C'mon, lads, calm down! You'll do yourselves an injury, burn your spleen out or something.' But then, as I got more experienced, I got wise and just let them get

145

on with it. In fact I encouraged them! And all the time I was buying shares in Andrex toilet paper.

So where did I get my business acumen? Well, I think it came from my father. When we first arrived from the Punjab, Glasgow was pretty rough and we used to get bricks put in through the window all the time. When it happened my dad would just say, 'Don't worry, don't worry.' But we were terrified. When it happened again, he would just say, 'Don't worry, don't worry.'

A few months on, we got two bricks through the window. We said, 'Look, Dad, this has got to stop. You have to tell the police.'

He said, 'Don't worry, son. Just a few more weeks and we can build that extension!'

It's really interesting though. It raises the age-old question that no one seems able to answer: are entrepreneurs born or bred?

My paternal grandfather, Sajjan Gill

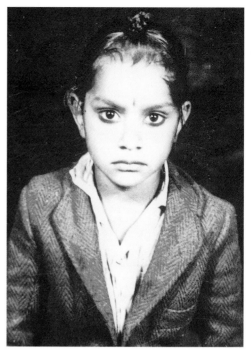

This is me as a wee boy before the haircut

Here I am wearing my first suit

The men of the family – my father Mehar, on the left, my uncle Amar and me, in the middle, with my brothers

A typical Yarrows night out with me getting stripped yet again!

This is me with my first car . . .
and my second suit

Here, I'm trying to look sophisticated in my
pin-stripe suit – sadly, the modelling agency
never did ring back

My grandfather and Parminder's grandfather
negotiate the wedding terms

Just married – Parminder and I are flanked by my grandfather, Sajjan, and my mother, Bhajan

This is me and Parminder's brother Dayal pictured just before I was married – Dayal has a shotgun just in case I change my mind!

The happy newly-weds . . . but maybe the hair was a bit of a mistake

Derek Johnstone pours me a celebratory glass of wine just after the deal for Ashoka to sponsor Partick Thistle was done

Sanjay Majhu with his sitar and me with my dhol brightening up Argyle Street

This is me with my first mentor, Uncle Kolhi

My cousin Gurmail and I doing a bit of trendsetting

Here I am at the charity do, the Hottest Night of the Year – on the left is the football pundit Chick Young and on the right is the radio presenter and comic Fred MacAulay

Another snap from the Hottest Night of the Year event and this time I'm with two of Scotland's top entrepreneurs – Sir Tom Hunter and Michelle Mone

Gurmail and me at an Indian market looking for some menu ideas

And here I'm with the mobile Medicare unit for HelpAge India

I was delighted to receive my MBE from Her Majesty the Queen for services to the catering industry

My dad, Mehar, proudly admiring my MBE

The family celebrating the award – what a fantastic day!

The Ashoka West End – it all started from here

The family – behind, Sampuran, Preetpal, Jaspreet and Ceetl's husband Chan; in front, Basant, me, Parminder and Ceetl

Chapter Twenty-Five

ENTREPRENEURS – BORN OR BRED?

Well, I'm afraid I don't have the answer to that question either, but I really believe that certain things that happen during childhood lodge somewhere in the back of the mind and do come back in later life to influence important business-life-changing decisions. There's nothing mystical about self-made people. Generally speaking, they are normal, hardworking individuals, just like some of the guys who came to this country at the same time as my father. Educationally, a lot of them would have left school without any formal qualifications. Some would say that the lack of university conditioning was a major factor in their success, because they had no preset parameters to work to. They were free spirits, who were perhaps so naïve that they believed anything was possible.

The key to their success was hard work and long hours. They wanted to lay a foundation on which the next generation could build and they did this with a little bit of inspiration and gallons and gallons of perspiration. They hoped their offspring would have a similar work ethic to themselves and work the hours that they worked themselves. They had very little time to be with their children and then could not understand why the kids were against following in their footsteps. Perhaps, if they had led more balanced lives, then the children would have been more inclined to take over but watching their parents slave away day and night had the opposite effect, which was that there was no way that the kids wanted to work in shops.

There was one such guy who ran a grocery shop in Old Dumbarton Road. The locals knew him fondly as Black John but to this day I have never been able to suss out why they gave him that name: he wasn't black and his real name sounded nothing like John. I would sometimes go into his shop if we ran out of teabags or needed change for the till late at night. He was open seven days a week from six-thirty in the morning until eleven o'clock at night. He did not have a driving licence or a car so he would have to walk to and from his shop, which took almost half an hour each way. It was not much of a life but he felt that he was making a real difference to the lives of his children.

'Of course you are making a real difference,' I would taunt him, 'they never see you so it is bound to have an effect on their lives.'

One night he told me that he had taken stock of his life and decided to make big changes. 'The kids are not interested in taking over the shop,' he said, his voice shaking with emotion as if the shop had been his ashes and bones and his kids were not willing to look after them.

'I have decided that I am not going to kill myself working these long hours and decided I am going to take life easier. If the children don't care then why should I?'

I told him I totally agreed and asked what changes he had made.

'Well, now I have decided to open at seven-thirty in the morning and close at ten.' He really believed that this was a major change and I guess that for him it was.

'What are you going to do with all your free time?' I asked.

He looked me square in the eye and without a hint of humour he said, 'I don't know. Maybe you can give me a part-time job.'

I decided that I would not end up like Black John – though, if I had taken a good look in the mirror and been honest with myself, I would have seen the reflection of old Black John looking back at me on numerous occasions. I realised that, although I was a little bit more educated and my outlook was more modern, I was really no different from him.

Still, I didn't dwell on other people's problems for too long because I had enough of my own. One of them was to keep out the competition once and for all, and I was able to do this when the bar next door to Murphy's Pakora Bar came on the market. Again, it was a distress sale because once more the place was not trading well. One of the reasons for this was because of the size and shape of it. It was too small and the shape was not easy to work with. I could foresee that one day this chap was going to end up in trouble and that I would get the opportunity to buy the site. In anticipation of that day, I had bought the empty shop next to it about a year before and decided to sit on it. I was ready for my checkmate move as soon as the guy declared that he was in trouble.

That day came just as I had predicted and I bought him out for £80,000. I then knocked into the shop next door and got myself a spanking new restaurant which I called the Spice of Life and which started to take the entire overflow from the Ashoka West End. I was prepared for a 15 per cent decrease at the Ashoka when the Spice of Life opened its doors but no such thing happened. If anything, the Ashoka got busier because now we had more people coming into the area knowing that, if they could not get a table in the Ashoka, then they would be able to get into the Spice of Life or Murphy's Pakora Bar and these two places started making money too.

Chapter Twenty-Six

MINTING IT IN ASHTON LANE

Business, to me, is all about timing, recognising opportunity and making quick decisions. All of these things, along with paper napkins and jugs of lager, featured strongly when I bought the Ashoka in Ashton Lane, my most successful restaurant and one that made me pots of money.

I remember it was just before Christmas and I'd finished a murderous shift in the restaurant. As my chefs well know, there's nothing I like better after a hard night's graft in the restaurant than my favourite meal . . . a Chinese takeaway! So I drove down to a place called the Gourmet House, in Ashton Lane, to see my wee friend Henry Lee. I had got to know Henry as I used the restaurant on a number of occasions and we had become reasonably friendly. Henry was having a bad Christmas, because business had been poor. His chef had just walked out, his wife had been giving him grief about not spending enough time with his children and his manager had timed his move to perfection and asked for *that* pay rise. As I walked through the doors, Henry must've thought it was Santa Singh himself!

He sat me down at a table and, reaching for a pen with one hand and a paper napkin with the other, he said, 'Gill, we must talk . . . you must buy my restaurant!'

'Well, actually, Henry, I was only looking for lemon chicken.' I was totally surprised by his approach.

'If you buy my restaurant,' he said, 'you could have all the lemon chicken you want – free!' And he started furiously scribbling some figures on to a paper napkin. When his waiter appeared with a large jug of lager and two empty glasses I knew we were in for some heavy negotiations.

I knew it was a great deal for me and that wee Henry was selling out too cheap as he was under pressure. He didn't see the potential of being in Ashton Lane, an upcoming area. I think the problem was that he was there too early; his timing was just a wee bit out and now I was being offered the site on a plate. It was a couple of days before Christmas and I was due to go on holiday on Boxing Day. I had to close the deal before Henry changed his mind. If he had put it on the market there would have been numerous takers at twice the price. I needed a carrot to close the deal. I knew that Henry was doing very little table business and that most of his sales came from takeaway and home delivery. On top of the cash, I offered him my takeaway premises at Partick Cross free as a part of the deal. 'All you have to do, Henry, is to transfer your telephone number to our takeaway unit and you would be able to keep 75 per cent of your business.'

This was just perfect for Henry. He sold me his restaurant, took over my takeaway which was half a mile down the road, and by transferring his business he kept most of his goodwill and was also able to keep himself in a job. The flip side was that I was also able to transfer the takeaway phone number to my new restaurant and keep my takeaway business as well. It was a sweet deal for all concerned and when a deal gets done where everyone feels that they came out the best, it is fantastic. I took Henry down to the lawyer the next morning and got him to do a letter transferring the lease on to my company. Before I left for India three days later, I had a letter from Henry saying that he was relinquishing his interest in the lease to me.

As soon as I got back from holiday I started to refurbish the Ashton Lane restaurant. It was a similar scenario to the Pakora Bar, because although Henry had allowed me to take over his existing lease, the landlord had still not consented so the deal was still not done. Once again, I found myself spending money on premises that I had no legal right to enter and hoped that all would turn out well in the end. Luckily for me, it did and I had the place open and trading within three months. To emphasise the timing of the deal, as soon as I had started to refurbish the restaurant, workers from the city council arrived and re-cobbled the whole lane. Henry popped by to visit and said, 'Gill, you lucky bastard, I have been waiting for that to be done for years!'

It was certainly good timing because within a year of my opening, another few bars opened in the Lane and the place was buzzing with nightlife. The clientele were amazing, there was always a fantastic atmosphere and the Ashoka in Ashton Lane was minting money. This was just as well because some of my bad decisions were now beginning to come back and haunt me and it was costing me a fortune. Gurmail had suggested that I stop going to bars or restaurants because I ended up buying them and he said that this was not always good.

Chapter Twenty-Seven

MORE PROBLEMS

I was glad that Ashton Lane and the Ashoka West End were making the money that they were because I also had places that were losing it and the profits from these sites had to be pumped into those loss-making units on a regular basis. One of the limp sites was the Ashoka in Paisley and the other was our wholesale and manufacturing unit, Spice of Life Foods. Although Paisley was losing money, it was not as bad as the factory, which was a bottomless hole needing cash input every week.

When we had originally bought the wholesale unit it was located in an old converted church. There was no way we could have grown our business from the church premises because they were not up to standard. If we wanted to supply the larger multinationals then we needed a purpose-built unit. I knew it would cost us a lot of money to move but if we stayed on at the church then it was just a matter of time before the environmental health department shut us down.

I found a site in Whiteinch, not far from the west end of Glasgow, an old factory that had been used to pack butter but had been shut down for a few years. It was a huge space, 36,000 square feet with a large loading bay and yard. I paid £250,000 for the freehold. I bought it from an Orthodox Jewish guy from London who couldn't believe that we were only willing to pay a measly £250k for such a vast building. In his opinion that should be the annual rent because that was the kind of figure he was getting in the London Docklands. He had obviously never been to Whiteinch and insisted on coming up to see the building for himself. He took one look at the area and within minutes he turned to me and said, 'You have a deal, my friend.' It was just what we needed to expand.

Once again my inexperience in the manufacturing side showed and I didn't do my sums properly. I failed to do a proper business plan, which in all my years in the restaurants I had felt was a waste of time. This was OK because when it came to restaurants the business plan could be formulated overnight in my head and I would know exactly what I had to do. But this project was not a restaurant and I failed badly to do proper cash flows and look at a worst-case scenario. I also stuck with the architects I had been using for a number of years refurbishing restaurants, which was a massive mistake, as they had never designed a food factory either. I really think they should have pointed me to someone else who specialised in that field but they didn't. They decided to keep the job and we all sort of learnt together. I also used the wrong tradesmen, who I thought would save me money but also ended up botching up a lot of things. I had budgeted to get the whole thing set up with £500,000 but that money soon got used up and I went back to the bank for more. The bank pushed out the boat and lent me enough cash to finish the job but only after they had taken cross-company guarantees for every business I had.

The problems did not end once the manufacturing unit was open as we were unable to increase our turnover to cover the extra overheads of the larger unit and pay back the interest on the borrowing. Twice weekly I received the expected call from Alan Johnstone who would ask the all-too-familiar question, 'How much will you be banking today?' I was juggling funds from one account to another and meeting with suppliers to extend credit terms but eventually things began to settle down as we started to get orders through from

Farmfoods, Asda, Iceland and Makro. Once again, Paramjit played his part and helped to make sure that the increase in business was being serviced and orders were met. There was no question of his dedication when it came to putting in the extra hours.

Chapter Twenty-Eight

THE RICKSHAW

Once again I was allowed to venture into bars for a beer but the habit of buying the local pub in which I drank was a compulsion. It was a different kind of addiction to the one suffered by the rest of the clientele. I had bought up most of the block across the road from the Ashoka West End and the only pub left to buy was a bar called the Roadhouse. The pub had been there for a hundred years and was used by the locals and it was extremely busy when it came to the Orange Walk season. When a couple of guys took it over and gave it a complete facelift, spending vast amounts of money, the locals abandoned it. I think the new owners were pleased that they had managed to get rid of some of the local riffraff but the problem was that they were unable to replace it with new clientele. The bar was great but I think once again the timing was out because it was too modern for an area that was very traditional at that time.

The guys struggled for a couple of years but the writing was on the wall and on one of my visits I bought the freehold for £110,000, which was far less than they had spent on the refurbishment. It was a bargain. It was like picking up Park Lane on the Monopoly board for a couple of hundred quid. I didn't know what I was going to do with the place but eventually decided to open a pizzeria. I brought in an ex-manager from the Ashoka West End called Din and his wife Naz to run it but it didn't perform too well and I eventually sold the business for almost the same price that I had paid for the freehold and kept the freehold as an investment.

Naz was an exceptional girl and I had employed her when she was just sixteen years old. She was a real grafter and, no matter what problems she had in her personal life, she left them outside the door when she entered the place where she worked. She is now one of Sanjay's key franchisees and is still serving all those tables with a perfect smile. Din went on to do an MBA at the University of Strathclyde and then opened a teeth-whitening clinic at Partick Cross. I asked him if he had done his research prior to selecting that particular site and if he had considered the fact that very few people in Partick actually had any teeth. Din had the last laugh because his business took off and he started to expand his concept across the country.

Like I have always said, business is all about timing, but then I guess that could be said for a lot of things that we do in life. I have always had a knack for seeing opportunities that others walk past every day. A lot of ideas came to me from everyday conversations with customers or friends. For them, it would be a normal topic but I would always be thinking whether whatever was being discussed could be applied to the way that I work and if it could improve the way I did business. When I was thinking about launching my home delivery service, I discussed the idea with Chick Young, the journalist who, after the initial misunderstanding with my waiter, had become an even more regular customer and was now a good friend. Chick worked as a sports journalist with the Glasgow *Evening Times* newspaper but, more importantly, he also did a restaurant critic column under the guise of the 'Diner Tec'. Due to this, he was well aware of what was going on in the Glasgow restaurant scene and it was good to have him around to bounce my ideas off.

We were talking about the launch when Chick jokingly said that I should do my deliveries on a rickshaw. Practically, it was a stupid idea but, from a PR point of view, it was fantastic.

I was on the phone the very next day, sourcing a rickshaw from Mumbai. The rickshaw itself cost only a few hundred pounds and if I wanted it sent by sea, then the transport cost would be negligible too. I did not have time to mess around as the home delivery service was due to launch within a fortnight and the mail shots had all been arranged. I paid over £1,000 to have it flown over to Glasgow. The next thing I had to do was to utilise it in my launch but I needed an angle for the press to write the story. They were not interested in a rickshaw home delivery service. The tabloids told me it was not corny enough. I needed to offer the papers something a wee bit more interesting.

I decided that the guy who would pull my rickshaw had to be called Rick Shaw and surely there had to be one in Glasgow. I opened up the Glasgow telephone directory and sure enough, there were a couple of Richard Shaws listed in the phone book. I called the first number and asked if I was speaking with Ricky Shaw and he confirmed I was. 'How would you like it if I were to get your picture in the papers?' I asked.

Ricky was cautious and asked me to get to the point, telling me in the same sentence that he didn't need double-glazing. I explained that I wanted him to pose next to my rickshaw and pretend that he would be driving it to launch my home delivery service.

Ricky was not convinced. 'You are winding me up, mate, aren't you?' He thought I was one of his friends trying to play a joke on him and asked, 'Did Wee Benny put you up to this?'

I assured him that I did not know Wee Benny, there was no wind-up and that I was genuine.

Then Ricky's entrepreneurial side kicked in. 'So what's in it for me then? A picture in the paper must be worth a few quid.'

Rick told me that he was an electrician and that, if he posed for me, then he would expect to do some of the electrical work in my restaurants. The deal was done and Rick was happy to have his name associated with my launch.

The thing that bothered me for a long time about wee Chick Young and the 'Diner Tec' column was the fact that he ate in the Ashoka West End at least three times a week yet he had never written about it in his column. The style of the column was that the critic was a sleuth who went around with his moll and they both commented on the meal that they had. Sometimes the restaurants got great write-ups but other times they got roasted. The column was extremely popular and it made a real difference to turnover if one were to get a favourable report. There were times when his moll had fallen out with him at the last minute and I would get a call from Chick to ask if I would go along and be his moll for the evening. When I went with him, I was always fair in my comments and I suppose that is one of the reasons that he took me along. I told him that I preferred not to do Indian restaurants because there was a conflict of interest so, when I went with him, we stuck to Chinese or Italian.

'Why have you never done the Ashoka West End?' I asked as we chomped our way through one of the worst Chinese meals I had ever had. He looked at me blankly and confessed that he had actually never thought about it. I reasoned that the fact that he was always in there meant he must think it was good and, therefore, I should get a good write-up.

He agreed to do a 'Diner Tec' on the Ashoka West End but that it would have to be fair and honest. He suggested that he would come in one night and not tell me that he was in on official business and I would stand or fall by the standard of food and service that evening. I agreed to his proposal and said that I looked forward to his incognito visit. The next week when he came in with his girlfriend he was wearing a tie, which was something that he rarely did when dining at the Ashoka. 'Table for two, please,' he said with a wink, at the same time pointing to his *Evening Times* tie.

He refused to tell me what he was going to print and said I would just have to wait and see. It was an agonising wait because the column was so important to me. I needn't have worried, it was one of the best write-ups that had ever appeared in the column and the result was an even busier Ashoka West End.

Chapter Twenty-Nine

PARTICK THISTLE

I was always looking for ways to get my mug into the newspapers as I felt it was the cheapest way to advertise the business. There was one time when four of my regular customers decided to walk the West Highland Way, a tough trek which starts in Glasgow and ends some ninety-six miles away in Fort William. I decided that I would walk with them and also promised them a wee surprise along the way. I wanted to make sure that we all got our weekly curry and phoned up Captain George who hired out helicopters and asked if he would be willing to fly a curry fifty miles up the road. He said it would not be a problem and said that the charge would be around £300. I said that I would pay his price but asked if he would do it for free if I managed to get the picture of him delivering the curry into the *Daily Record* as this would be good PR for his company. We agreed that if the picture of him and his helicopter appeared in the press, then there would be no hire charge for the chopper.

When we had walked for three days I phoned the *Daily Record* and told them that I was walking the West Highland Way and that I had a craving for a curry. I told them that I had just placed an order at the Ashoka and they were going to deliver it to me up in the hills in a helicopter. I asked if they wanted to send up a photographer with the curry. The next day, a large colour picture appeared of Captain George serving my friends and myself a curry with the chopper parked in the background. I was pleased and so was Captain George.

The best piece of PR that I have ever done came through Chick Young. One evening I was in the restaurant when Chick came in for a takeaway meal. He had just been to Firhill, the home ground of Partick Thistle, to report on the match. Thistle's normal strip was red and yellow stripes but on this occasion they had played in an all-white strip and Chick commented how strange they had looked. He also remarked that he had never realised, due to the loud colours of the normal strip, that they didn't have a shirt sponsor. I could not believe it. 'How can they not have a shirt sponsor?' I asked. 'Even the local Boys' Brigade team get their shirts sponsored!'

We discussed the possibility of the Ashoka becoming the shirt sponsor for Partick Thistle.

'Do you think they will go for it?' I asked, thinking about the mouth-watering prospect of Partick Thistle playing against one of the Old Firm wearing Ashoka West End shirts. He told me that he had already run the idea past big Derek Johnstone, the Thistle manager, and he did not seem against the idea. I asked Chick to try and tie down a deal for me. He came back the next night and told me that he had negotiated a deal for me that he thought I would be happy with.

'There are eight games left to play this season, plus a cup game against Celtic. They are happy if you pay them eight hundred pounds to sponsor the shirts.'

'Don't you think eight hundred a game is a bit steep?' I asked, feigning shock but delighted that he had got such a good result.

'Don't be stupid,' he replied, 'we are talking Partick Thistle here – not Juventus! It's not eight hundred a game – it's eight hundred for the remainder of the season. That makes it a hundred a game.'

I told him that I still thought it was expensive but since he had been so helpful in pulling the deal together I would not let him down and would go ahead with the shirt sponsorship. I couldn't understand why he got upset when I charged him for his takeaway that night.

The press coverage we got was phenomenal and I got to see Partick Thistle play against the mighty Celtic wearing Ashoka West End football strips. What a thrill that was! Before the start of the next season, the marketing people at Thistle got wise and asked for a huge sum of money to continue the sponsorship into the next season. I decided against it because there was little mileage in continuing with the deal. I was happy that I had made history by becoming the first Indian restaurant in the UK to sponsor the strips of a major league side. To my knowledge, I don't think any other restaurant in the land has repeated that achievement.

That was not the only time that I hit the headlines in my association with Partick Thistle. This club had always played a part in my life since I was a wee boy. Quite often I was saved a hiding from the supporters of one of the Old Firm sides when I told them that I was a Thistle fan as opposed to a Rangers or Celtic one. Once you confessed to this they would usually laugh in your face and walk away. Firhill stadium, in Maryhill, was only a short walk from my secondary school and, on a number of occasions, I found myself on the terraces shouting on the 'Jags'.

In 1995, I was at a sports dinner that was attended mostly by people from within the Asian community. Asians were not well represented in the sports arena in this country and an association (of which Mr Bassi was chairman) had been set up to try to encourage young Asian kids to participate more in local sports, as well as introducing them to some of the more traditional sports that were played back in India so that a sense of culture could be maintained. During the dinner, George Galloway, who at that time was a Labour MP, walked into the restaurant followed by a television news crew and announced that he was representing a group of Asian businessmen who were ready to table a bid for Partick Thistle. He indicated that he was pleased that they had thought he was worthy to be their spokesman and was proud to represent them.

It was a bolt out of the blue and the whole room was taken aback. It left us all wondering who was in the consortium and we all looked at each other with suspicion. A few guys at my table asked me if I knew anything about this and I told them honestly that I didn't have a clue. During the dinner, George came to speak to me and asked if I would be interested to know more about the Thistle takeover bid and would I consider being a part of the consortium. To me, it was no different from being approached any other day of the week with a business proposition. My normal reaction to a business proposal is that, if it looks interesting, then I want to know more about it. I didn't realise at the time that even considering taking over a football club like Partick Thistle would attract more media attention than taking over Harrods. The news of the takeover was released on the television in the morning news and after that the story started to grow arms and legs.

The media began to draw their own conclusions as to who the consortium were but, as far as they were concerned, it didn't really matter because it was a cracking story and would go on to fill not only the back pages but also the front ones as the takeover rumours gathered momentum. George Galloway didn't name anyone he was representing and the press were left to speculate on who these mysterious people could be. If the press phoned anyone prominent within the community to ask if they were involved, they would be met by the usual 'no comment' stance that Asian people tend to take when finding themselves bombarded with question from reporters. This was taken as a yes by reporters looking to fill another few columns on the back pages during a close season when there was little else to report. When I was asked the question, I confirmed that I was interested in negotiation but maintained that I had no idea about the identity of others who may be involved.

A few days later, Galloway came to see me at the Ashoka in Ashton Lane and asked if I would want to have a look at the

Partick Thistle accounts to see if a takeover was viable. I told him that that would be the normal route to take in any business transaction. I also asked him who the consortium were and he told me that he had met individually with a number of people who had shown interest. The only name to come up in the conversation was that of Mac Rasool, a man who had made his fortune from the video rental industry.

The next day, George told me that the consortium was now wishing to examine Thistle's books. At the time, I believed that Oliver was a willing seller but soon realised after press reports that this was not the case. This made me feel uneasy as I thought that the situation might turn hostile. The *Sun* newspaper quoted Oliver as saying that Partick Thistle had been hijacked by Galloway, that the MP's actions were designed to win the Asian vote and suggested that it was cynical self-interest. Galloway denied this.

I was now hitting the headlines as the leader of a consortium that I had never met and was getting phone calls from every newspaper and radio station on an hourly basis. I told them all the same thing which was that I had been asked by George Galloway if I was interested in knowing more about the Thistle takeover and I had told him that, if the numbers stacked up, then I would be interested in any business proposal that was put on my desk.

The Thistle fans got caught up in the controversy. Like most football fans, they believed that their board had not been delivering the goods and that Thistle, with the right investment and chairman, was a club that should be playing in Europe. They saw what was in the press and thought about the millions that the wealthy Asians would pour into their beloved team. They turned against the board and started to ask for the head of Jim Oliver, the Thistle chairman.

The Thistle board didn't know what had hit them or which way to turn because it seemed they were being asked to sell their shares even though there had been no official approach by any member of any consortium. I read in the press that Galloway had met Oliver at a golf club and Oliver had agreed to sell a 51 per cent stake but I had no knowledge of these negotiations and, as far as I am aware, no one from any consortium was at the meeting. As I read the news and listened on the radio to the booing that Jim Oliver was receiving on the terraces, I promised myself never to get involved with a football team.

I imagined what it would be like if paying customers who came into my restaurants behaved in a similar fashion to the punters who go and watch their favourite teams on a Saturday afternoon. I could just see them shouting for their waiter to be substituted if the poor guy was having an off day. Or shouting through the kitchen door and telling the chef that his curries were shite or that he was illegitimate just because the nan bread was cold. Would they kick the chairs in disgust when they were presented with the bill and ask me to sell the restaurant to someone else if the service, in their opinion, was not up to scratch? Somehow, I could not imagine it happening in business – alas, only in football.

I suppose football is an integral part of life for lots of people – for many, perhaps even life itself. It is certainly what a lot of die-hard fans live for on a week-to-week basis. I knew so many guys in Yarrow's who had nothing to talk about during the close season but, once the season started, you couldn't shut them up. When there was no football being played, they would actually get withdrawal symptoms.

The press love giving people a hiding when they are down, and, on this occasion, they decided to kick the shit out of Jim Oliver. Everything that Jim said was misinterpreted and taken out of context. He spoke about the takeover bid and referred to me as 'some Indian with a curry shop'. I was asked to comment on Oliver's remark and I reminded them that my company turnover was many times that of Partick Thistle and told them that, although I was not pleased, I didn't think that Oliver was being racist when he made the remark but he should have chosen his words more carefully. I didn't want the story to take another twist. My attempt to cool the situation took a battering when a frustrated Jim told the press that he was happy to negotiate with anyone, be they Asians, Eskimos or one-eyed black lesbian saxophone players. There was a media frenzy and accusations of racism flew. I was feeling bad at this point not only for Jim Oliver but also for the fans. The media circus had been performing now for over a week, people were getting hurt and genuine fans were having their hopes falsely raised. I decided to bring the matter to a head.

I called Mac Rasool and asked him about his interest in Partick Thistle. This was my first contact with him and, during that discussion, I realised that Mac had been told the same story as myself and it seemed to me that there was no real consortium. George had, of course, had individual meetings with a number of people and asked them if they wished to know more about the possibility of taking over Partick Thistle. As far as I could see, they had simply expressed an interest to know more and that was the 'consortium'.

George had organised a press conference for the next morning at which I guessed his intention was to put pressure on the beleaguered Thistle board and I decided that enough was enough. I called George and told him that, when he held his next press conference, he should come clean and name the consortium. If he didn't, I told him, then I would call my own press conference and tell my side of the story. I told him that, if the consortium was not named, then I was unwilling to continue. At the end of the discussion, George promised to clear up any misunderstandings.

The press conference was held in an Indian restaurant and the press reported that no members of the consortium were present. The next morning's headlines were not quite what I expected but the press did learn that there would be no takeover of Partick Thistle by Asian businessmen. It was reported that Galloway had branded Oliver a racist and he announced that he would be withdrawing as consortium spokesman because the Jags supremo had refused to meet them. He refused to reveal the consortium members' names.

I later confirmed that, at some time in the future, when things settled down, I may still talk with Oliver about the Jags and said that any discussion would be businesslike and conducted directly with the chairman and not through a middleman.

Exit George Galloway and, soon afterwards, exit poor Jim Oliver too.

Chapter Thirty

ANOTHER BABY

Around this time, I had also managed to move home once again and we bought a really nice town house in the west end of Glasgow. It was one of the most desirable addresses to live in and things were certainly looking up. I also upgraded my wee Porsche 944 to a monster Porsche 928 which was sold to me by a wee guy called Ian Johnston. He had called me the night before to say that he had the very car for me and he would bring it to my house and show it to me in the morning. When I went to view it outside my house the next morning, the sneaky bastard had already put my private registration plates on the vehicle and I had to admit the car really suited those plates. I still think it was a great sales strategy by Ian to put those plates on the car because it certainly helped to close the deal and I bought the car straight away. I started to think that I had everything a man could ever want.

'What about an heir? You still don't have a son,' people would remind my wife constantly.

When Parminder and I sat and counted our blessings, we both knew that we had all we needed. We had four beautiful daughters and lacked nothing materially. The problem was that every time Parminder went to a social function and got herself surrounded with all the old 'auntie-jis', she would come home depressed. 'Everyone is saying that we should be trying for a son,' she would say whenever she got home from wherever she had been.

'I think I can only do girls,' I would reply jokingly.

Our youngest daughter Jaspreet was now five years old and at nursery. I think Parminder had gotten so used to having a kid hanging on to her apron that she was struggling with the idea of being home alone with all the girls at school. The girls needed a brother, she argued, and she also pointed out that we had one spare bedroom with a blue carpet just going to waste.

It didn't take long for Parminder to get pregnant once our minds had been made up. After all, I had always argued that curry was one of the greatest aphrodisiacs known to man and I was getting plenty of curry. If Parminder wanted to try for another 'wean' I was up for it. I had read somewhere that colleges around the world had spent vast sums of money doing surveys with volunteers about the effects curry had on their libido, and they all came to the same conclusion: curry had aphrodisiac qualities. Surely, they could have saved themselves a lot of time and money by taking a look at the population of India. Or just visit my house in Glasgow's west end. I was living proof. We had four girls in five years. There were times when she had to fight me off at night when I came home from the restaurant. I would quite often find her hiding under the bed, trembling with fear. The problem was that Parminder didn't drink so I couldn't even slip her a couple of gins to loosen her inhibitions, and believe me, it is no easy task trying to spike a Coca-Cola with a chicken breast curry.

Once the community got wind of the fact that Parminder was pregnant, we got numerous calls from people wishing us well and telling us that they would pray that our next-born would be a boy. The old aunties would offer Parminder advice on what to eat and what not to eat. Most of the advisers contradicted each other and had Parminder totally confused. It reminded me of the story of the man who was asked by the taxman to explain his tax returns. The man was petrified just thinking about the meeting and he asked his accountant how he should dress for it. The accountant was very cautious and advised him not to drive but to take a bus. He also told him not to shave for a few days to look dishevelled. He reminded him to wear an old shabby suit, remove the Rolex and just go and plead poverty and hope the taxman takes pity on him. The man then asked his lawyer what he should wear to the meeting and the lawyer was much more bullish. 'Spruce yourself right up,' he advised, 'take the Bentley and get yourself a designer suit and walk in full of confidence because you have done nothing wrong.' The day before the meeting the man told his priest of his dilemma and the conflicting advice that his professional advisors had given him. 'Let me tell you a story, my son,' started the priest. 'Some time ago, I married a couple in my chapel and the bride was very confused as to what she should wear on her wedding night. She asked her mother who advised her to wear the cotton pyjamas, with the buttons up to the chin and tie cords around the wrists, the ankles and the waist that she had given her. The bride then asked her best friend who told her to wear a sexy silk nightie that would fall off at the subtlest touch.' The man was now even more confused and asked the priest what that story had to do with his predicament. 'Well, son, the moral of the story is the same – it doesn't matter what you wear, you are going to get fucked anyway.'

Parminder was certainly confused – they even advised her on what I should be eating, as if that was going to make a difference three months into her pregnancy. One of her friends turned up to the house about a month before Parminder was due to give birth and handed her some herbal medicine that she had picked up on her recent travel to India. 'Take this even now and you will be guaranteed a boy,' she insisted.

To this day, that woman believes that Sampuran was born due to her input and we let her believe it. We didn't have the heart to tell her that we binned the stuff as soon as she had left our house.

This time, when Parminder went into labour, we went back to the hospital which had given us our first three girls. We decided that the hospital didn't really have any influence when it came to what sex a baby would be and that we were just being superstitious, and stupid.

'We don't want another sister!' shouted the girls in perfect harmony as I helped my pregnant wife into the front seat of my Porsche.

'Why can't you grow up and buy a decent car?' she screamed as another contraction racked her body.

Fourteen hours later, Parminder gave birth to a bouncing baby boy and the celebrations that followed lasted many weeks. I went to visit Parminder the day after our son was born and she said, 'How was Victoria's nightclub last night? Was it busy?' As I sat there nursing the mother of all hangovers and trying to figure out how the news had reached her so quickly, she continued, 'I hear you were dancing on the stage without your shirt. What kind of way is that to celebrate?'

I was struggling to come up with an excuse when my mother danced into the room, followed by my father. I had never been so glad to see them in my life. I made a mental note to try and slip away before my parents and hoped that, by the time I came back in the evening, Parminder's mind would have turned to other things.

When she came out of hospital we had to take our new baby to the Sikh Temple so that he could be blessed and also to give him a name. It is normal practice for the priest to read a chapter from the *Siri Guru Granth Sahib*, which is the holy book of the Sikhs, and, depending on how the verse starts, a letter is given with which the child's name should begin. The letter we were given was 'S'. We decided to name our new baby Sampuran, which means 'complete'. We felt that this name was most appropriate as it summed up our lives at that particular moment. Parminder took the meaning quite literally and decided that she would have no more children in this life. Within a week she had me visiting my GP to organise a vasectomy before I could do any more damage.

'There are two ways to do this,' said Barry Glekin, my GP. 'You could go through the family planning clinic where there is a waiting list of three months or I could refer you to Nuffield Hospital and you could go private. That way it will be done and dusted within a fortnight but it will cost you a few bob.'

I didn't have to think too hard. 'I will go private,' I said. 'God knows what will happen in three months now that I am back on the production line.'

Doctor Barry referred me to a private clinic in Glasgow and within a few days I was sitting in front of a prominent consultant who also happened to be a regular customer at the Ashoka. He counselled me on the pros and cons of what I was about to do and went into great detail of how he would render me useless; all this in exchange for a recipe for spiced onion. He then went on to discuss charges that included an anaesthetist, theatre time, his time and a few odds and ends. He said that the main charges were for the use of the hospital and then, as he wrote down and began to add up the fees, he must have started feeling guilty.

'What are you doing on Thursday at lunchtime?' he enquired, looking up from his note pad.

I told him that my timetable was flexible and for this important operation I would make time whenever.

'Well, I will be working at the Western Infirmary that day so if you come along at one o'clock, I will do it for you free during my lunch break.'

It was an offer that was too good to refuse. I told him that I would see him on Thursday and rushed off to prepare myself mentally for what lay ahead. That Thursday I went to the appointed floor at the given time to be met by the surgeon. I was expecting the usual hustle and bustle of an operating theatre but, to my surprise, the place was deserted. He handed me a gown and told me to strip off and put it on and then make my way to the theatre room. As I lay on the operating table I felt a sharp pain in my groin as he inserted a needle to numb my testicles, As he did this, he told me how well the spiced onion had turned out from the recipe I had given him.

He then went on to discuss the previous night's football results. It was the day after an important Old Firm Scottish Cup semi-final in which his team had just taken a hammering. He blamed everything from the weather, the team selection and the referee for his team's exit from the competition. I had watched the game myself on television and his team had been trashed. They were rank rotten. I lay back and agreed with his analysis of the match because there was no way I was going to contradict a man talking football while he held my balls in one hand and a scalpel in the other! He was finished in ten minutes and suggested that I go home and rest because, once the anaesthetic wore off, I would feel 'considerable discomfort'.

I went back to the office to finish off a few things before heading home to bed and switching on some old John Wayne videos I had hired in preparation of this day. I had chosen the movies with great care as I didn't want anything raunchy which might have an effect on my manhood and cause me any discomfort that would be more than considerable. There was very little reaction to the operation and I felt no pain the next day. By Saturday evening, I was back at the Ashoka West End, serving tables as if nothing had happened. My surgeon came in for a takeaway on his way home from the hospital and was surprised to see me up and around so soon. I returned the favour he had done me and didn't charge him for his 'Teatime Special'.

Chapter Thirty-One

FROZEN ASSETS

I was back looking at the business at Spice of Life Foods. We had lost a major client and another big account had gone into receivership owing us a lot of money. Our lack of experience in a credit business was now beginning to show because our credit controls were abysmal. Paramjit was still unwilling to use computers because he didn't trust them to keep proper records and he still preferred to use his manual ledgers. I found it so frustrating working with him but he always insisted that his way was best. There was so much bad debt in our books that even I was shocked. We had given so much credit to other restaurateurs whom we supplied and they were now letting us down.

When I asked Paramjit about the bad debt he failed to acknowledge it and always maintained that he would get the money. He would not write it off the books. Whether it came in or not, only Paramjit knows but it was still outstanding according to our accounts and eventually we had to write off hundreds of thousands of pounds. The most disappointing thing for me personally was that people whom I had admired in the industry were now bouncing cheques on me. These were the guys I had looked up to and wanted to emulate when I opened my first restaurant and here they were, bouncing cheques on me left, right and centre. I just could not believe it. The pressure with the cash flow was back on and I found myself once again having to support the wholesale business out of the restaurant profits.

I thought that the only way to solve the problem was to try and trade out of it and we had to increase the sales of our pre-packed frozen curries. I decided to invest more money and bring in a sales manager to handle the 'Maharani' brand as well as trying to get new accounts with some of the bigger supermarkets. I hired a guy called John Savage for that job. He believed we had a good product and the price and the packaging was right and he promised to deliver big-time. As the year wore on, the orders were still not coming in at the level required and I felt that I would have to concoct another plan or contemplate the scenario of going out of business.

The world of business can be very lonely because people close to you seldom understand your motive to stay on the move and keep yourself under pressure at all times. If you try to discuss your problems with those who are closest to you, the easy answer for them is to tell you to stop doing what you do and start to take life easy. They reckon that it's all your fault in the first place and the problems are easy to resolve by just stopping to grow your business. They don't understand the kind of maniac who will risk all he has, time and time again, when he has all the material things he needs. They don't realise that asking you to stop being what you are is like asking a fish to stop swimming or the grass to stop growing. It is a natural impossibility to change because such is the make-up of an entrepreneur.

The most difficult time for an entrepreneur is when things start to go pear shaped, because they have to continue to put on a brave face for the sake of staff morale and there is no way that they want to send out the wrong signals to business associates and competitors. When in public they will continue to tell everyone that things are going well or at worst they will say that the year has not been as good as the one before. They don't seek advice because they think that no one will give them the proper advice and that most people would be happy to see them going down anyway. They hope that even if they do go bankrupt then a lot of people will not get to hear about it and they can just go into hibernation until things are forgotten. The stigma of failure is so bad in this country that no one wants to discuss it in front of the person who has been through the ordeal. But behind their backs it is discussed with zest and humour.

For this reason, by the time they seek help it is usually too late and it is left to the receivers to sell any worthwhile remains to the vultures. I know it is difficult but I believe that before it is too late one should try and seek help and that way try and salvage whatever possible. I decided that was precisely what I would do and I started to plan to save what I could from my business.

John Savage was keen to do a management buyout for the Maharani brand and Paramjit Samra was keen to take on the wholesale side, as he was confident that if he did not have the baggage of Maharani he would have no problem in trading his side of the business profitably. John decided to take on Richard Beattie as a partner in the new venture and together they managed to put together some funding for the buyout. I engineered the deal, and to get the funding for their venture they both had to give personal guarantees and put their houses on the line, which they were happy to do. If they had asked me my true opinion of their chances of success, I would have said very low. As it was, they didn't ask me as they thought they knew better. After all, Richard was the accountant and he knew the financial problems of the business more than any other person. John Savage had been with us now for almost two years and reckoned that he knew how to run the Maharani brand better than all of us put together.

To be honest, right from the start I had my doubts as to them pulling it off and when John Savage pulled up in his new company car, a nippy wee BMW, just a few days after becoming managing director, I knew they were doomed to failure. As he walked me around the gleaming new car, showing off the gadgets that my old Porsche did not possess, my thoughts went back to my first years in business and my first car. I drove around in a clapped-out old Renault, which I had to park on a hill at nights so that I could roll it down in the morning; it would never start otherwise. I also thought back to how Gurmail did not buy a car for three years after starting work at the Ashoka West End because we reckoned that the business just could not afford it. I congratulated John but inside I was saying to myself, enjoy it while you can, because you won't have it for long. Within a year, they had lost their business, their cars and their houses and the Maharani brand was sold off to a company in Dundee called Top Hat Foods.

Samra took the wholesale division and ran a very tight ship. He managed to trade the business into profit and, to this day, Spice of Life Foods continues to maintain its turnover. Due to his continued contribution, the debts were repaid and, without his hard slog, that would not have been possible. So often I have seen businesses going down due to the greed and the naivety of the directors who see a limited company as something that is there to be continuously milked and pay themselves unaffordable salaries and expenses. They will often stay in top hotels, eat in designer restaurants and drink expensive champagne when a Travel Lodge and a Big Mac would easily do the same job. It is the directors who see the company purse and their own pocket as one, and believe in leaving assets in a company as opposed to stripping them out, who are the ones who go on to build successful companies. After selling off all the bits and pieces of the Maharani brand and the wholesale distribution to Paramjit, I was left with the freehold property that I decided to retain. It resulted in a debt of around £1.7 million. This was secured against all the assets and properties that we owned. I swallowed the debt by refinancing and put it into my new company, Harlequin Leisure Group Ltd. The rent from Paramjit helped to pay off the debt and, as I said before, the debt could not have been repaid if Paramjit had not worked 24–7 for the next few years.

It was a time of recession and of soaring interest rates. That was probably the one time that I felt the whole thing could go belly up. I received a call from Alan Johnstone and he told me that the head office wallahs at the Bank of Scotland wanted a meeting. I was not too worried as the bank had always been supportive and I had delivered every time. We were partners, is what they had always told me.

I went to the head office the following week accompanied by Alan Johnstone and John Hughes, my accountant, who worked for a company called Ballantyne & Co. We had not prepared any figures and I had not done any homework. The meeting started in a light-hearted manner but it soon became clear to me that, if I wanted to continue with the Bank of Scotland, then I would have to lay everything I had on the line. I could not understand what the fuss was about as our assets were far greater than our liabilities and the bank had lots of collateral in place as well as cross-company guarantees. The position of the bank was solid and there was no way that they were exposed.

The guy shouting out the demands was a director of the bank and he wanted my shirt. 'We will take your house as well,' he stated without any sense of negotiation, 'and we also require personal guarantees from all the directors including the spouses. I take it you have no problem with that?'

I shook my head to signal that everything was acceptable and he stood up and walked out of the room, leaving me stunned and his subordinates totally embarrassed. That day taught me never to trust any bank because when you need them most, they will take what they can and just move on as if nothing has happened.

I was now concerned with the way things were going with the business and this resulted in sleepless nights and a lot of stress. The strange thing about being in that situation is that there are not a lot of people with whom you can discuss your problems. A lot of people wouldn't believe you even if you told them you were under pressure. I once told a friend that I was really depressed.

'You? Depressed?' was the reaction. 'What a cheek! How can you be depressed with all the things that you have?'

The truth is that I have never felt that I have achieved anything or that what I have done in my life is anything out of the ordinary. There is always a belief that there must be more to life than this. That is why I strive to reach some point where I will feel a sense of achievement. I know that point of self-satisfaction will not be reached until, one day, I say to myself that this is all life has to offer and learn to appreciate the wonderful things I have, and the sooner I drop out of the rat race the sooner I will achieve self-satisfaction.

I remember just a few years back, walking down Byres Road in Glasgow's west end when I stopped to watch a new sign being fitted to a shop front. A young couple, whom I assumed were the new owners, stood back at the edge of the pavement and watched with great pride as the letters of the sign went up one at a time. I could sense their anticipation and the tears in their eyes showed how emotional this moment was and that it would be one they would remember for the rest of their lives. This scenario took me back to my first restaurant and how lovingly each picture had been put on the wall and each little plant moved from corner to corner to achieve the best result. I had polished each glass and each piece of cutlery myself and I could remember the butterflies in my stomach as I put the first bill into my till. It had been a long time since I had felt those emotions and I wanted to feel them again. I needed my fix; I needed the excitement that this young couple were experiencing.

Someone once said to me that the feeling that I am trying to achieve is similar to that felt by a cocaine addict. The first time you take the drug it gives you a great hit and a fantastic feeling. The more you snort, the less you feel the hit and then you have to do more and more to try and get that feeling again. Whether it is cocaine or business, to get the same initial satisfaction you just have to do more and more. Therefore, ultimately, there is no way to reach the end of the road because there is none. We all just kill ourselves trying to find it. For me, it was time for the next challenge, which was to boost my restaurant profits enough to repay all the debt I had accumulated. I could only do that through expansion.

Chapter Thirty-Two

THE KAMA SUTRA

It was 1995 and I was looking for my next fix, desperate to feel the high that I used to experience, and the only way to do that was to involve myself in something more unusual. The Gandhi restaurant in Sauchiehall Street was an institution. It had originally been run by the Purewals who had opened it in the late sixties. They ran it for many years very successfully and then sold it on to a guy called Bassi. I always thought that they were a little stuck-up because if you ever went to the Gandhi restaurant in those days, the attitude was condescending. I went in a couple of times with friends who knew them, aware there was no point in me going in by myself as they would not have given me the time of day. Mr Bassi was a businessman who had built himself a good reputation within the Indian community. I used to call him The Chairman because he always wanted to be on every Indian committee or organisation ever set up and he always seemed to end up being chairman. He had owned a couple of restaurants that he had bought from the Purewal family. One of these was the Amritsar in Bearsden and the other was the Gandhi.

He had sold the Amritsar to Manjit Singh for a rumoured £750,000 and was now trying to offload the Gandhi. He had got his timing right when selling the Amritsar but got it wrong with the Gandhi. He told me that he was once offered £900,000 for it but had held on to it as he believed that it would top the million-pound mark. We have all been there, thinking that we are on a roll and that we just can't lose, then bang! the whole thing starts to go belly up. Due to an increase in interest rates leading to a crash in property prices, he was now trying to sell it for £450,000. It had been on the market for months and there were no takers.

I went to see Mr Bassi and took along a mutual friend, Ashy Aziz, to witness the conversation. We had a couple of beers and talked business. Within the hour we had agreed a price of £425,000 and shaken hands on the deal. I told him that I would have a formal offer to him within forty-eight hours. Mr Bassi told me that as far as he was concerned, the restaurant was now mine and that his word was his bond. When I told him that I needed a set of drawings because I wanted to start the refurbishment as soon as possible he said he would look them out and asked me to collect them the next day. I went back to the Gandhi the next day as arranged and an embarrassed-looking Mr Bassi told me that the deal was off.

'What do you mean, "the deal is off"?' I asked in disbelief. 'Yesterday we shook hands and you told me that your word was your bond.'

He confessed that he had been negotiating with a brewery company for the past few weeks but, because the brewers had been dragging their heels, he did the deal with me. He had called the brewers that morning to tell them that he had sold the place to me and they offered him an extra £50,000. 'I will sell it to you but you will have to raise your offer to match theirs,' he said.

I told him that I had always seen him as a role model, looked up to and admired him and I just could not believe that he was the type of guy who would go back on a deal for the sake of £50,000. I insisted that as far as I was concerned the deal had been done and I would not pay him any more money. I was not sure at that point whether what he said was true or if it was ploy to get me to raise my bid. Either way, I was not going to bite.

I left the Gandhi that day with a heavy heart, having added to my experience of how business is done in the real world.

I wanted the place so much but out of principle, refused to raise my bid. My head told me that even at £475,000 it was a good deal for me and I knew if I didn't pay the extra £50,000 I would regret it in later years. It is not every day that one gets the opportunity to buy property in Sauchiehall Street but I still decided not to up my offer.

I got to know through the grapevine that Mr Bassi had indeed done a deal with a brewer and they were just sorting out the final details. Word was also on the street as to the way Mr Bassi had shook hands on a deal and then reneged. I did not have many sympathisers within the restaurant business community, though. They were all happy that I was not taking the place over so, although they knew that what Bassi had done was wrong, they were not openly condemning him. They did not like what he had done but, against that, they did not like me at all.

Three weeks went by and I was in my office with Ashy Aziz when I got a call from Mr Bassi. 'I have been giving a lot of thought to the situation and I have decided to sell the place to you. I have lived in Glasgow for many years and I have a reputation that I don't want to lose as I am planning to emigrate to Australia. I realise that it is not worth losing everything I have built for the sake of fifty thousand pounds. Let's do the deal at four hundred and twenty-five thousand.'

I agreed to get an offer in to his lawyers the very next day and turning to Ashy I said, 'Mr Bassi has just been let down by the brewers and is back to do the deal. The Gandhi is mine.' I packed up for the day and we headed down to the pub.

I decided to call the new restaurant the Kama Sutra. My wife said it was just an excuse for me to read the book. Little did she know that I had already read the book from cover to cover and I'd also seen the movie. To be honest, most men don't need to read that stuff – just show them a naked woman and they will soon figure out what to do with her. The Kama Sutra was going to be sexy and sultry without being sleazy and the designers did well to interpret my thoughts into reality and they gave me a really cool restaurant. The reason for choosing the Kama Sutra as a name as opposed to another Ashoka was that there were still a lot of people who didn't eat at the Ashokas for whatever reason and I decided that Harlequin should supply them with an alternative place to go. It was also a name that, once heard, would never be forgotten. In an industry full of boring, insignificant and inconsequential names such as The Passage to India and The Kashmir, the Kama Sutra was a breath of fresh air. I knew that just due to the name, most people would try it at least once.

The first St Valentine's Day we had, the Kama Sutra was packed for the 6 p.m. sitting and the 8.30 p.m. sitting. The phones were still red hot when I came up with the idea to do a late-night sitting at eleven. No one believed that we would have people wanting to book in at that time of night on St Valentine's Day but the staff were told to tell customers that we were doing an eleven o'clock sitting and that they should try to fill as many spaces as possible. At first we had no takers and I decided that we would have to be a bit more innovative. I told the staff not to call it an eleven o'clock sitting but to tell the customers that we were laying on a special 'Candlelit Midnight Lovers' Feast', complete with a romantic violinist, and that tables could be reserved from 11 p.m. I also put the price up by a fiver. Within a couple of days, all 130 seats were booked.

The Kama Sutra was also a fun place to market. Another year, as St Valentine's Day approached, I decided to launch my new St Valentine's Day aphrodisiac menu. The *Daily Record* were told about the challenge that I had set for couples wishing to spice up their lives and asked if they wanted to run the story exclusively. I was looking for fifteen couples from all over Scotland to come and stay for one night in the Moat House Hotel. A coach would then drive them to our restaurant where they would be wined and dined on our new menu. Then they would all be taken back to the Moat House for a night of unreserved passion and unconditional lust.

The next morning, at breakfast, the *Daily Record* reporter interviewed the couples and asked if they had been affected by the aphrodisiac qualities of our dishes. I had hoped that the wine and the executive rooms would have been enough of a backdrop to get them going at it like bunnies and also that the guys would exaggerate the number of times they had got the leg over just to impress their mates. It was a great fun promotion. Once again, we had more people in through the door than we could handle because I had managed to generate almost six full pages of publicity in a national newspaper. Once all the frustrated guys had read about the aphrodisiac qualities of the Kama Sutra curries and how they would drive their woman mad with passion, they felt that £25 a head to get their leg over was well worth the money.

The Kama Sutra was a complete success but it had been hard work. Leading up to the opening, I got totally immersed in making sure that the opening night would go well. Perhaps I should have left some of the heavy lifting to someone more able but, a couple of nights before the opening, I felt a crack in my back and I couldn't move. The pain was excruciating and when I finally made it to an osteopath he told me that I had a slipped disc. The opening night came and I remember hobbling about with a walking stick showing customers to tables.

I tried all the remedies over the next few weeks and then went to see a specialist at Ross Hall Hospital. He confirmed that my problem was indeed a slipped disc and all he could do was to operate. He recommended that I should not have the operation unless I felt it was completely necessary and recommended that I try other methods and cures before going back to him. He told me that he would be my last resort. It didn't fill me with great enthusiasm knowing that he was chasing business away and it made me realise the seriousness of having an operation done to the spine.

I spent the next eleven weeks on my back and only went to work when really necessary. It got so bad that I had to use a Zimmer on a lot of occasions and I was also having meetings with my staff and suppliers in my living room with me lying on my back. There was no alternative: the show had to go on. I finally decided to go for the operation and was taken into hospital three days later. The surgeon warned me that even after the operation there was a strong possibility that I could be left with the pain and also a bad limp. My mind was made up though and I told him to do what was necessary.

I am glad to say that the operation was a success and that I was able to go back to work, though I still get a few pains now and then. That, of course, is the difference between being self-employed and having a job: I could not just send in a sick line. I read recently that one out of five adults living in Glasgow who are of an employable age are actually receiving incapacity benefit and this figure shocked me. I wondered if I would have been a statistic had I not been self-employed.

The other thing that shocked me which is relevant to these facts is the perception some foreigners form of Scotland as a country when they hear about the numbers receiving incapacity benefit. I was in India recently and was in a bar in New Delhi when the funny stories and the jokes started to fly. On realising that I was from Glasgow, one guy from Malaysia told a story of an Irishman, a Japanese man and a Scotsman all drinking together in a bar when another customer came in and sat at the far end of the bar. They all recognised the stranger and were struggling to remember his name when the Irishman said, 'I know who that is – it's Jesus Christ!' They all agreed that it was indeed Jesus and decided to send over some drinks to show their appreciation for what this great man had done for the world. The Irishman sent over a pint of Guinness while the

Japanese man and the Scot sent over a saki and a whisky. After consuming the drinks, Jesus approached the three men to thank them and reached out to shake each of them by the hand.

When Jesus shook the hand of the Irishman, he cured him of his arthritis. 'Thank you, Lord,' said the Irishman, 'the pain in my limbs has disappeared.'

Jesus then shook the hand of the Japanese man who had suffered back pain for many years. 'Lord!' cried the man. 'The pain in my back is gone! This is wonderful – thank you so much.'

Jesus then turned to the Scotsman who leapt over the bar counter and shouted, 'Don't touch me – Ah'm oan disability!'

The whole bar burst into laughter, including myself, because I must admit that I found the story funny. Back in my room, as I lay in my bed and reflected on the story told by the Malaysian in a Delhi bar in front of an international audience, who all understood the punch line, I felt great sadness that this was how some people of the world perceived us. Something had gone seriously wrong with the Social Security system that was once the envy of the world.

Chapter Thirty-Three

GOING POSH

The next restaurant on my shopping list was the Amritsar, which was located in Bearsden, a posh Glasgow suburb where you had to be a really bad operator in order to mess up a restaurant. I would not say that Mr Singh was a bad operator but business was dire. He had bought the restaurant for a small fortune from Mr Bassi when the market was at its peak, which was around the same time as I had bought the nightmare in Paisley. When he took it over the business was performing well but within a few years it was struggling badly. So much so that the week that I took it over, the restaurant turned over £5,000, which was not even enough to cover the wages and repayments to the bank.

The place had been totally mismanaged. I would have thought that Mr Singh would have realised, after he had run a Paisley restaurant called the Shezan into the ground over a period of a few years, that perhaps he was not cut out to be a restaurateur. The industry was full of people like Mr Singh who had become successful by running shops and who all felt that the next step for them was to sell up the shops and move into the restaurant business. They didn't appreciate that running restaurants was very different from shops as the emphasis on quality, service and customer focus was paramount to becoming successful. They were not used to dealing with staff and had no perception of training, reward or motivation. I can't think of many who were successful. The family who eventually bought out Balbir in Elderslie Street for well over a million pounds eventually lost all their money. They ran a fantastic business into the ground and the restaurant closed down.

I had by now realised that there was no such thing as a straightforward or simple deal in business. All deals start off as if there will be no complications but once you get into the nitty-gritty, the horror stories start to emerge. The deal for the Amritsar was no different. Mr Singh was a nice enough guy and I had known him for a number of years and I liked him a lot. It was only when the lawyers got into the bones of doing the transaction that we realised that Mr Singh could not sell the place. There were inhibitions against the property which meant that until he resolved the outstanding matters, he could not sell the restaurant. Once again I had all my team standing by to move in to give the place a facelift and all my staff were ready to go and start operating the new unit. The problem dragged on for months until one day I told Singh that if the situation was not resolved that week I was going to walk away from the deal. I thought that I had been perfectly reasonable and was willing to buy his place if he could just deliver a clear title.

'If you can't deliver a clear title' I reasoned, 'I will have to move on to some other deal because I have been waiting around for five months.'

Singh's response to my request was unbelievable. 'Right then!' he shouted down the line. 'I will see you in the park and we will have a square go, just you and me!'

'What the hell are you on?' I asked, totally shocked. 'The last time I had a square go with someone in the park was when I was fourteen. Are you sure this will resolve the situation of your inhibition?'

I could hear him thinking. 'You are right,' he said, 'no square go then. You bring down your gang and I will bring down mine – we fight until the last man is left standing.'

I just could not believe the conversation I was having with a forty-year-old man whom I had always thought to be mature.

As they say, you don't really know what someone is like until you have dealt with them at first hand. I got to know later that Singh had been under a lot of pressure and the possibility of the deal falling through had snapped him. Years later I met him at the Sikh temple and he had grown a beard and was wearing a turban. He told me he was a much happier and less aggressive person since he got out of the restaurant business.

I decided to be patient and give him more time and the deal was eventually done. I ended up buying the freehold property for the Amritsar for £525,000 and renamed it the Ashoka Bearsden. I spent a small amount of money to freshen up the restaurant as it was in quite good decorative order when I bought it, and in the first week of opening we took more money from takeaways than our predecessor had taken for the whole business.

I had just about completed the deal for Bearsden when I got a call from a guy called Darrar who was running a restaurant in Kirkintilloch, only a few miles from Bearsden. The restaurant was called the Regent Brasserie and had a very good reputation. It was well established and had a good turnover. The problem was that the two partners were not getting along too well and they had also spent beyond their means, which I found later, when I worked with his brother Cammy, was a Darrar family trait. They were looking for a quick deal and the great thing for me was that there was very little money involved for me to take over the Brasserie. This deal was done very quickly as I was willing to cut corners that I would not normally cut because my exposure was so little. I renamed the place the Ashoka Kirkintilloch. The empire was growing once more and I was beginning to feel reasonably comfortable about my business prospects again.

My brother Sukhdev had lived in Bellshill for many years and he had spotted a site which was on the market that he felt would do really well. I didn't know Bellshill that well but

I bought the site on his recommendation and we opened a restaurant called the Ashoka Bellshill. I kept the bar below the restaurant, which I named Whisky Galore, and it provided me with a place to keep my whisky bottles that I had bought from a Christie's auction. The restaurant was never one of the star performers but it did not lose any money and in fact made a small contribution to the overall bottom line.

Chapter Thirty-Four

MEETING THE QUEEN

I could hear my mobile phone ringing as I struggled to open the door to my office. The polystyrene cup of coffee was beginning to feel uncomfortably hot and I almost dropped my roll and bacon as I struggled with the door handle. Typically, the ringing stopped just as I located my mobile buried under a pile of that morning's post. As I sat back to open the mail, my mobile bleeped to signal that someone had left a message. I put down the brown envelope from the Inland Revenue, instinctively reached for the phone and dialled 123.

'Hello, Mr Gill, my name is Angela and I have been trying to get hold of you for some time. Could you please call me back at Downing Street?' She left a phone number with a London city code. I checked the date to make sure it wasn't the first of April and then wondered who would want to wind me up first thing on a Monday morning. Still, my curiosity got the better of me and I dialled the number as my eye once again caught sight of the brown envelope. Was it a demand for more money from the Chancellor? Was he asking me to send him a cheque asap? The phone was answered after a couple of rings by a girl calling herself Angela and I was taken by surprise as I struggled to swallow a mouthful of hot coffee.

'It's Charan Gill here, Angela. I got your message and I'm just returning your call.'

Angela was pleasant and efficient at the same time. 'Mr Gill,' she started, 'we wrote to your home address some months ago and as yet we have not received a reply. Did you get the letter from Downing Street?'

After asking her where the letter had been sent, I told her that I no longer resided at that address and had moved to Pollokshields some time ago. I told her I wasn't very impressed by MI6 and that someone should be getting his or her knuckles rapped.

Angela showed that she had a sense of humour and responded with a bubbly laugh. 'Well I need this letter signed and returned as a matter of urgency. If I fax it to you, could you sign it and send it back?'

Again, my curiosity got the better of me and I asked her what this was all about. She explained that my name had been put forward for an MBE and that the Prime Minister had recommended it for the Queen's approval. The letter had to be signed to say that, if the Queen were to approve the nomination, then I would accept it as opposed to throwing it back in her face and humiliating the monarchy.

I had just taken the second bite out of my bacon roll as her words came down the line. 'Did you say an MBE?' I spluttered, choking on the fat of the bacon.

She confirmed everything she had said again and asked for my fax number. I blurted out three different numbers until I finally managed to calm myself down and tell her the right number. She told me that the Queen's approval would just be a formality once they had received my signature. I thought that might have been the case as I was sure that the Queen didn't know me from Adam – or from Ali for that matter. I don't think she was going to turn round to Philip and ask, 'Did you enjoy that curry from the Ashoka, dear? I do hope it didn't give you the runs because that fellow Charan Gill has been nominated for an MBE. Do you think I should grant it?' Somehow, I don't think that conversation would have taken place so I reckoned the MBE was in the bag.

Angela went on to explain how I should not tell anyone about the nomination and that the press were only told on

30 December so that they could print the New Year's Honours List on New Year's Eve.

I put down my half-finished roll and walked over to the fax machine. I watched it closely as the thoughts about a watched kettle never boiling crossed my mind. I lifted the receiver and placed it back again just to make sure it was properly on the hook. In fact, I think I did that about three times in as many minutes. After what seemed to me like an eternity but in actual fact was no more than five minutes, I saw the fax machine come to life and watched closely as it spewed out a sheet of paper which confirmed everything that Angela had told me on the phone just minutes earlier. I signed it immediately and sent it back down the line in record time. Remembering how Angela had sworn me to secrecy, I turned to Teresa Doherty and said, 'Tess, I am getting an MBE. Make sure you don't tell anyone because it's top secret.'

I have to confess that for me, the month of December 1997 had a real Christmas feel to it. The MBE was a wonderful present to get and I was chuffed to bits – as were Parminder and the children. I told my son Sampuran, who had just turned seven at the time, about my award.

'What is an MBE, Dad? What does it mean?' he asked, wondering what all the excitement was about.

'What it means, son,' I said, picking him up and throwing him in the air, 'is More Bhoonas for Everyone!'

It was around three o'clock on 30 December. I had just collected a couple of suits from Slater's Menswear and was walking back to the car when I got my first phone call from the press. It was a reporter from the *Daily Record*.

'Congratulations, Mr Gill! I have just seen the New Year's Honours list and I see that you have got an MBE. How does it feel?'

I told him the same thing that I told all the reporters who called me that afternoon and for the next two days – it felt marvellous. Getting the MBE for my 'Services to the Catering Industry' meant so much to me. It was not the same as getting it for community service or charity, which would have been fine too, but somehow it just felt much more significant to have been awarded it for something that I was so passionate about and an industry that I absolutely loved.

When one considers it, food is vital to all living things, including human beings. Without waxing too lyrical or mystical about it, some things we can live without: alcohol and cars, for instance – some say even sex, though I would rather starve if ever faced with the choice – but grub is a necessity. So, to be awarded an honour for 'feeding the people' was great. It was a fantastic feeling to know that my efforts had been recognised and I was now being given an almighty pat on the back. The other reason that I was pleased was that I had no idea how I got nominated or by whom. There had been no canvassing done and it was totally out of the blue. An MBE is not something that one strives for in life and even if one did, it was not always the case that one would get it. For those reasons, I felt really proud of myself and all those who had worked with me over the years to make this happen. I particularly enjoyed working in the restaurant that New Year because of the number of extra kisses I got from customers congratulating me on my achievement.

I had to wait until the following summer to collect my 'gong' and, on 1 July 1998, I went along to the Palace of Holyroodhouse with Parminder and the kids, all dressed up, to meet the Queen. Each recipient was only allowed three guests to accompany them into the main hall to watch the ceremony so we had to get the kids to draw straws to see who would accompany Parminder. Sampuran was given a short straw because it was decided by the girls that he would not appreciate what was happening anyway. Ceetl and Preetpal won and got to come with me to see the Queen. Basant, Jaspreet and

Sampuran had to stay in the gardens and wait for us to come out. I told them that they could watch the video later but I don't think that was much consolation. The video captured the moment the Queen pinned the medal on to my lapel. We exchanged a few pleasantries and then I must have said something funny because she burst into a laugh. Everyone who has looked at the photographs has asked what I had said to make her laugh but, being a gentleman, I have not repeated the story that I shared with Her Majesty to anyone.

As I walked out of the palace and into the gardens, the kids ran over to get a closer look at the medal on my lapel.

'What did the Queen say, Dad? Was she nice?'

I told them that as I approached Her Majesty that there was a lot of bowing and curtsying. I could tell from the excitement in their eyes that they were visualising the scene. I said to them that I had to ask the Queen to stop doing it as I found it most embarrassing. Following the investiture, we all went for a posh lunch and I popped a bottle of champagne. No one else wanted any so I just had to drink it myself. We got home early that evening after an exciting day and, as I put up my feet and settled back into the couch, I looked over at Parminder and said, 'Do you know what I think? I think I am going to take the day off work. Do you fancy celebrating with a fish supper?'

Years later, in 2003, I received a letter about bestowing a new honour on me. The offer came from the University of Paisley and they asked if I would accept an honorary doctorate from their Faculty of Entrepreneurship. I accepted the honour. For my family it was another great day and for myself another milestone on life's road. I had always wanted to wear one of those graduation robes and the one that I was given was a beautiful red one, different from all the other students who were graduating at the same time as myself. I also had to make a speech and I felt very honoured and privileged standing in front of all those students who were just setting off on life's journey.

As I imparted some of my experiences, I had a wee lump in my throat as my mind went back to the days when I was sixteen years old and my mother would come home from the Sikh Temple on a Sunday to see me playing Monopoly with my brothers. She would slap her forehead to signal her bad fortune, look up to the ceiling and ask God what bad thing she had done in a previous life to merit such a useless bunch of boys. 'Do you know that Mrs Dhammi's son got eight O levels and is going to be a doctor?' The next week it was Mrs Malhotra's boy who was going to be an accountant.

'Why don't you boys study more and be doctors and accountants too so that I can also tell my friends how well you are doing?'

I glanced at the row of hotels that I had managed to put on the Monopoly board and noticed that I also had Park Lane and Mayfair. I pointed to the board and said, 'Look, Mum, I don't think I am doing that bad.'

Many years after my mother had been taunted and tormented by her friends, she managed to get even with them. This came about after I had been made a non-executive director of the Southern General Hospital Trust. One of my duties was to sit in on interviews when the hospital had to employ a new consultant or surgeon. My role, of course, was purely to observe but that is not how my mother saw it. She went to the temple the following Sunday and after she was sure that everyone was listening, she told them how I was one of the top guys at the hospital and that just a few days earlier I had been interviewing Mrs Dhammi's consultant son who had come to see me about a job.

Chapter Thirty-Five

THE CALL CENTRE

A majority of the restaurants which I had opened were located in residential areas or suburbs which meant that, while our lunchtime business was non-existent, our takeaway and home delivery services were extremely popular, with some of our restaurants doing more than half their turnover from food consumed by customers in their own homes. I was keen to be the best at it, because most of the other local restaurants also provided this service. I always believed that in order to survive in business one must always be innovative. I have always said that if something stops evolving then it will inevitably die. In order to keep expanding one must always be ready to embrace change and adapt to new systems. One of the most innovative things that I did was to open up our own call centre.

I was approached by Billy Hall with an idea that he had for a home delivery service that was apparently working well in London. He knew we were good at delivering food to people's homes and he came to me with an idea which would enhance our turnover without increasing our costs: something that I am always prepared to make time for. He was going to set up a central telephone number, which he would advertise in a variety of ways, to take orders for a number of restaurants in Glasgow including Chinese, Indian and Italian. The telephone order would be passed on to one of the member restaurants which would prepare the meal. The food would then be collected by one of Billy Hall's drivers and delivered to the customer's home. The restaurant would pay a small commission and the customer a delivery charge, and that would be how Billy would make his money.

This service could be attractive to restaurants that were not doing any takeaway business, as it was all extra revenue. We talked through the pros and cons of the idea and I knew right away from my experience that it would be a logistical nightmare and very difficult to implement. His drivers would be running around all over the place and if a customer wanted three different types of food from three different restaurants, then the coordination of this would be impossible. I came up with a different idea that I thought might be easier to launch using the existing Harlequin takeaway business as a starting point.

Harlequin restaurants were always getting calls from customers from outwith our delivery areas who lived too far from the restaurants. In those cases, we would have to ask the customer to collect the food themselves, something that a lot of them were unwilling to do. They would then order from a restaurant closer to their homes and we lost the business. My idea was to sign up restaurants in areas that we were unable to service and pass orders to them as our agents. In return, we would get a percentage of their turnover. They would have to meet certain standards; to create the brand, we had to ensure that the service delivered consistent quality which was the key to the success of the venture. For instance, we would ensure that the restaurant becoming a member was popular in their area and the food was of a good standard. They would use a certain style of packaging and would charge standard prices, which were on our call-centre menu. Our costs would be controlled and could be kept down to marketing and call-centre operation only. Also, we would not have the hassle of employing drivers as these would be the responsibility of the member restaurants.

The service would be called Curries Direct and I would endorse it with advertising across the country. The idea was simple and I felt that we could make it work well for ourselves and our partners. All that was required was a bit of hard work and together we could provide a fantastic service to homes right across the west coast and central Scotland. Once we had the Scottish market covered then expanding it out across the entire country seemed like a manageable proposition. It should not be difficult to get partner restaurants on board with the idea as their outlay was minimal and all they had to do was put in a dedicated telephone line and buy a printer for the orders which the call centre would send down the line. After this they just had to make the order, pack it and get it sent out to the customer.

We decided to go with my idea and, as predicted, getting restaurants to be our agents was not too difficult as they saw it as extra revenue. The other reason that they wanted to be involved in Curries Direct was that if they signed up they were assured exclusivity in their area and that meant they were keeping out their competition. We launched the new service by doing a mailshot to over a million people followed by adverts on television. The service was quite successful but started to have problems shortly after going live as the members started to grudge paying our commission and would do sneaky things like ask the customers to phone them direct the next time. They just did not share my vision and within six months I decided that it was not worth the hassle. From then on I would use the call centre exclusively for my own restaurants. The call centre would not have been possible without the calm and focused way that Billy Hall functioned. Billy did not believe in speculative information and was a person who made all his decisions based on the information that he collected through the call centre and analysed himself. This required great patience and it is a quality that I personally lacked. He was very systematic in his marketing approach and most of the initiatives at the call centre were his. The good thing about

Billy was that he always delivered on his promise and never let anyone down so he became a key member of the Harlequin organisation.

Over the years, the call centre became a powerful tool for growing the home delivery business and our turnover went through the roof. The main increase came during existing peak times and this was due to the fact we now had twenty lines, meaning that customers were now able to get through first time and were not faced with an engaged tone. I was amazed to learn that we had been losing numerous calls just because our customers could not get through. The call centre also allowed us to build a fantastic database that was regularly updated. It also allowed us to get to know our customers through their spending patterns.

We got to know, for instance, the ones that lived on their own because they only ever ordered one dish. From this information we were then able to be more productive when it came to mailing special offers to our regulars. I knew that there was no point in sending out a two for the price of one offer to someone who only ever ordered one dish, so we decided to offer him or her free starters with every main dish. We were also able to profile our customers by using their postcodes, which allowed us to look at the areas to open new sites. Due to the call centre, our service levels in the restaurants also improved as the staff were more focused on serving the customers as opposed to being stressed out taking phone calls and making up all the bills.

Another really cool thing we could do was tell which customers were regular and the system was programmed in such a way that if the customer was regular and used the service on more than a certain number of occasions, the order slip that printed in the kitchen had stars on it to let the chefs know that this was a priority order. If we were ever short-staffed and orders started to run late then the staff knew that the priority customers should be looked after before the ones who only ordered sporadically. If I was going to piss off a customer then I would rather piss off one that only gave me £20 every couple of months as opposed to £20 every week. The call centre was certainly one of the most innovative things we did at Harlequin and worth every penny that I spent on it.

Although the home delivery service provided Harlequin with a good chunk of its turnover, it was not without hassle. Quite often we would get calls from customers claiming that things were missing from the order and that because of this their whole evening had been spoiled, so we should replace the whole order next week. The genuine cases rarely made ridiculous demands but there were many scammers out there who thought that by making these demands they would be able to eat free for weeks. The call centre kept a note of the ones who complained about missing items on a regular basis. These orders were checked and double-checked but customers would still make claims of missing items. Our last resort was to ask the customer to order their food from someone else as we obviously could not meet their standards.

We got a lot of complaints about the presence of foreign bodies in the food and when the customer claimed that it was a beetle we knew right away that it was a black cardamom that was used to flavour the fried rice. Due to the ignorance of the customers of this spice and the fact that it looks like a creepy-crawly complete with legs, the cardamom is normally removed prior to serving the rice but sometimes one would get through. We would get calls from hysterical customers who would have crunched into one of these bitter pods and no amount of convincing would pacify them. Normally the manager would have to go to the customer's home with a handful of cardamom and show it to the shaking hysterical customer. Only then would they believe that they had indeed bitten on a spice.

I remember once being told of a story of a restaurant owner whose customer had complained of finding a cockroach in his food. The owner went to the table and on close inspection realised that it was indeed a cockroach. The restaurant that night was full of customers and everyone was now looking over to see what the outcome of the situation would be. The owner calmly picked up the cockroach on a spoon and with a smile turned to the whole restaurant said, 'It is only a spice. It is very tasty,' and he put the cockroach into his mouth and swallowed it. If you are wondering if that story was actually about me, let me assure you that it wasn't. Let me also tell you with my hand on my heart that if I were ever in the situation where I had to eat a teeny-weeny cockroach to save my business, I would not hesitate for a second.

I once got a call from the call centre and was told that a customer had phoned to complain that he had found a mouse in his curry. I could not believe that this was possible but all the same, was very concerned. I called the customer who told me that he had the evidence lying on his kitchen table and that the next day he would be calling in the environmental health. I asked him if he was sure that what he had was indeed a mouse and suggested he might be mistaken. He told me that he was a biology teacher who had dissected many rats in class at school and knew what he was talking about.

I was stunned to hear this and asked if I could go over and see him at his home and also see the mouse for myself. He refused, saying that he would rather just call in the environmental health and that I was not welcome. I called him an hour later and told him that I would not be able to sleep unless he allowed me to go over to his home and he eventually agreed to let me go up to his house. I had called Mukesh, the manager of the restaurant that had made the delivery, and he told me that there was no way a mouse could have got into a curry. I asked Mukesh to meet me outside the customer's home so that we would go in together. It was almost midnight and I had received the initial call from the call centre three hours before but I was glad that I had the chance to talk to the customer and wondered how much it would take to keep him quiet.

Walking up the stairs to the flat, the thought of me picking up the mouse by the tail and swallowing it whole flashed before my eyes. I then looked at Mukesh and wondered if he valued his job enough to swallow it instead. We entered the flat and got the story about the customer's credentials and the fact that he had been teaching biology for ten years. We walked into the kitchen and he pointed to an item of food on the table and said, 'That's it there.' Mukesh and I were totally bewildered, because without even close inspection we recognised it as the bottom corner of a nan bread. I told the customer that it was part of his nan and he just said, 'Aw, is that right? Looks like a mouse to me.' I was relieved with the outcome but the teacher did not even have the decency to apologise.

We also got some funny calls that I didn't mind, one of these being when a woman called and asked if we could send out a home delivery. 'No problem,' I said. 'Where are you?'

She thought about it for a minute and said, 'Ah'm at ma sister's.'

I realised that restaurants were very much a profile business and I set myself a target to feature regularly in newspapers and magazines. Our marketing was different; it was unique and a lot of times it upset our competitors. But the popularity contest amongst our competition was one I wasn't interested in winning. And we also did a lot of in-house stuff, such as launching the Ruby Murray Club Card.

I named this after the famous singer from the fifties whose name was now used as rhyming slang for curry. The card could be used in any of our restaurants and had twelve boxes on it, each of which when ticked entitled the holder to an increasing level of giveaway. The twelfth box gave away a complimentary meal for two people. The take-up was phenomenal and our regulars appreciated getting something back.

Another idea was the launching of an in-house magazine, the *Delhi Record*, which, while getting the message across, was also tongue-in-cheek, featuring headlines like:

'Some You Win, Some You Vindaloos'
'Brotherhood of Nan'
'Tikka Look at Us Now'
'Rice and Shine'

and our Christmas slogan,

'Korma Ye Faithful'.

I once had a meeting with Martin Clark, who was the editor at the *Daily Record* at the time, and he told me that my publication had actually been discussed at their board meeting where some of the people present thought it was an infringement of their trademark. I would have absolutely loved it if they had taken me to court.

January was always a quiet time for the trade so we had our 'January Sales' – two curries for the price of one. I just thought that, if it was good enough for all the shops, then it was good enough for me and our January was busier than December. The two for one offer is something that is perhaps looked upon by a lot of restaurateurs as going down-market, taking the wrong road, but believe me when I say this: if you put enough time and thought into doing such promotions, you will win customers without jeopardising margins, but you must get it right. It is important to think through any promotional activity as it is easy to send out the wrong message which could be detrimental to the business.

I realised early in my career that the pen was mightier than the sword and treated the press with the utmost respect. Most journalists have a genuine interest in reporting positive news stories and were always happy to know and print what I was up to. It was important for me to be as honest as possible and deliver on the promises that I made in the press because too often people make up all sorts of stories to get a newspaper headline which has short-term benefits but serious long-term implications. No journalist likes to write a story only to discover some time later that what they had been told was just a pack of porkies. If you get on the wrong side of the press then they will come after you and if they do, more often than not it can mean curtains for a business.

There is a downside to being high profile and always being featured by the media and that is, when a negative story comes out to which your name is even remotely linked, then the headlines could be manipulated by the press to make it seem that you were the real culprit, as that is the headline that will sell more papers. There was a classic example of this when the press went to town on Michelle Mone who was the person behind the Ultimo Bra.

The story was that Michelle had been using a manufacturer in China that employed cheap labour and the article was very detrimental. The facts that the Chinese workers were being paid a normal wage for that country and that most of the other high-street retailers were buying their goods from the same or a similar manufacturer were completely ignored. The factory used by MJM was state of the art and it was regularly inspected by an independent auditor. Although it was given a clean bill of health, that is not always good enough when the media sense a juicy story. The reality is that, if one wishes to use the press as a promotional tool, then one must be prepared to take the flak, no matter how distorted this may be. If you live by the sword, then the chances are that you will one day die by the sword.

There was no point in me claiming that my restaurants were good just to get a customer through the door once. It was important to ensure that the product was good and our service was tip-top so that the customer would return time and time again. Repeat business is the lifeblood of any firm without which it is impossible to survive. I had always stressed the importance of looking after our regular customers – not that we didn't look after the first-timers, but my regulars always got priority.

I was once in a restaurant called the Taj International located just next to George Square. This was a good location for a restaurant but it was completely dead. I was negotiating with the proprietor to take over the site and visited it on a number of occasions at times that should have been peak time for business. But the restaurant was always empty. I asked the proprietor if he had many regulars and he just gave me a blank stare. I said, 'Surely you must have people who come in regularly and you know them by name or by what they eat or drink?' He told me that he didn't have a single customer whom he could call a regular. It was unbelievable that someone like him should be running a restaurant. Suffice to say, he is not running it any longer.

Chapter Thirty-Six

SATTY SINGH

The most unusual takeover of a restaurant happened when I took over Mister Singh's India. This was another one of Balbir's old restaurants that had been bankrupted by some novices and then taken over by Satty Singh who rebuilt the business back to the boom days of Balbir. The reason for it being unusual was that the boss of that particular restaurant, Satty Singh, wanted to be included in the deal. He asked that I buy his restaurant and then employ him in a managerial role. Satty Singh ran the place extremely well and I had always admired him as a restaurateur. He was very popular with his customers and the restaurant was a haunt for all the football stars, especially the ones who played for Rangers. Satty was a mad Rangers fan who described himself as a Jaffa Cake, that is, brown on the outside and orange in the middle. For some reason he was also very fond of 'guarding Old Delhi's walls'. His strength lay in his networking ability and he had the most amazing memory for people's names.

To be honest, to this day I still have no idea why Satty wanted to be a part of Harlequin. I am a very strong believer in the fact that once you have had a taste of self-employment and been your own boss then it is very difficult to go back and work for someone else. He told me that it would be good for him to get the exposure and experience of working with me and that he saw this as the best way forward for himself. I thought long and hard about taking on Satty but I honestly didn't think that it was the right move for me. I knew that it wasn't the right move for him either. I didn't think that there was much that

I could teach him because he had done all the right things since he had opened Mister Singh's. After much deliberation, I told him that I thought he was doing a great job at Mister Singh's and he should really work away on his own and I had no doubts that one day he would be a great success.

It is said that if one wishes to be a success then tenacity and perseverance are just two of the qualities that one has to possess, and Satty had both in abundance. He was back knocking on my door a couple of months later, saying that he wanted to help Harlequin to grow and believed that through that ambition he would also grow himself. Eventually I gave in and a deal was done for Harlequin to buy Mister Singh's and for Satty to come and work for me as head of operations and help to grow the company.

The idea was that I would not then be involved in making day-to-day decisions on the shop floor as he would take on that role. He saw this as a way to buy into the company and I felt that I could have groomed him to one day take over the business when I was ready to hand over the reins. I think our interest was mutual because I believed that one day he could have taken over and I saw this as an exit route for me. For him, it was his opportunity to place himself firmly in pole position, where if I were to sell he would be in the right place to get first bite at the cherry.

It was not long before Satty realised that it was difficult working for someone after he had been his own boss for years and I knew that it would just be a matter of time before he moved on. I also wanted to change my strategy as to how responsibility would be delegated in the years to come and Satty would then have a lesser role. It was good working together and we both got on really well and tried to make it work. Eventually Satty bought back Mister Singh's but decided to still remain as a part of the group for PR and marketing activities. The split was very amicable. Satty went on to greater things and continues to show his diversity in the many new challenges he overcomes in his new businesses.

The biggest restaurant I purchased was the Ashoka at the Mill and although its location meant that it was in a great catchment area, close to affluent suburbs like Newton Mearns, Pollokshields and Whitecraigs, the site was just not working as a pub. It has been my belief that people will travel a few miles to a good restaurant but not necessarily to a pub. Maclay the brewer owned the pub and I did a deal with their director, Steve Mallon, to take it over. The only hitch with this deal was that Balbir had also looked at the site and apparently had it surveyed. He called me to tell me that he had negotiated a deal and asked me to back off but I told him that it was not possible for him to have the deal in the bag because, as far as I was concerned, I had also done the deal. If Balbir had not come into the equation then I am sure that I would have gotten the site a bit cheaper. I wanted the Mill pretty bad so I put in an offer that Steve could not refuse. The other reason I wanted to keep Balbir at bay was that the Ashoka South Side, another of my restaurants, was not too far away and I didn't want him affecting my business. I knew how good he was and, if I could keep him out, then I would.

Even after all the experience of opening numerous restaurants, I didn't get this one quite right. The reason was that I had no idea that the place would be so busy. We opened as usual, without any real publicity, but no sooner had we opened the doors for business than the place was full to the brim. That may be all right if the restaurant has ninety seats but the Ashoka at the Mill could take almost 300. On top of this there was also a big demand for takeaway food. Although we had recruited plenty of staff, they just didn't have the experience and after two days, it was so busy that we had to close for a couple of days just to let the kitchen catch up with their preparations. Dishes that should be marinated for twenty-four hours were only getting done for four and quality was being compromised. It is possible for new restaurants to be taken by surprise if they advertise heavily prior to opening but I was amazed to be so busy because we hadn't really told anyone. The power of the brand was now evident.

I also had to draft in some friends to help out behind the bar. I asked one of them, Danny Doherty, for a jug of lager as I rushed past the bar to bring out some more food from the kitchen. When I came back he gave me a confused look and said, 'I have looked everywhere behind the bar and I have even checked through the wine list but I just can't find it. What the hell is a Jaggalagga?'

This reminded me of when I first started working as a waiter and Balbir had asked me for a bottle of Coke with ice. It was my first night and I was as nervous as hell. When he came back to the bar, I avoided eye contact and pretended to be busy. 'Where's the bottle of Coke with ice?' he asked.

I had looked at him sheepishly and told him that I had no idea how to get the ice into the bottle. Although the incident made me laugh, it was also a reminder to me that, if I wanted to remain in business, then I would need to find more quality staff.

Chapter Thirty-Seven

BRICKS AND MORTAR

I don't know if it is an Asian thing but we love bricks and mortar. Why pay rent when you can buy? When my father and his friends first came to Scotland they only rented for as long as it was necessary. Their first objective was to buy the house that they lived in. They would stay four to a room and even share their bed with a stranger if they had to, though no doubt with that sort of closeness they would not have remained strangers for very long. Then, once they had saved enough money for a deposit, they would buy their own little pad.

I had dabbled in the domestic property market briefly in the past purely through necessity. I was trying to sell my wee Wimpey house in Bishopbriggs as I had bought a bigger pad in Bearsden. A distant cousin was interested in buying my house but was having problems selling his own flat, so before I had even heard of the part-exchange idea, I proposed that I would take his flat in as part of the deal. I had now ventured into the domestic letting market and soon had it let out to some students. It was not something I was good at because I just felt that the return was not worth the effort. Perhaps it was not a good flat but I hated dealing with the tenants so much that I eventually stopped letting it out and for years just left it empty. I knew that a lot of people had built up nice portfolios of domestic properties and I had often thought about dabbling in the domestic property market once again, but the trauma of running that one flat was enough to put me off ever moving in that direction.

Many years prior to this, when I worked in Ashoka as a part-time waiter, a customer once gave me a lift home in his sports car. I asked how much such a car would cost me as I was determined to save up and buy one. He said he had paid £3,000 for it but he then went on to give me some advice which I remember to this day. 'If £3,000 is all you have,' he said, 'don't even dream about buying a car with it. Invest it in a business or an appreciating asset. The car will depreciate within a few years and you'll be left with nothing. If you invest your money into a business and make it successful, then you will be able to buy great cars whenever you want.' I reflected on those words years later when I drove out of a car showroom in my Bentley Arnage.

When Sandy Majhu, brother of Sanjay, came in to see me about building a small portfolio of flats which he would buy and manage on my behalf, I was immediately interested. Once again, it was just instinctive. Sandy had been buying and selling flats for some years and knew the market. He had a knack of buying flats for below valuation and he said that to start off the portfolio, he had a small flat in mind which required a £20,000 deposit. 'The flat will double in value over the next five years,' he said confidently.

We started to talk about his aspirations and future plans and I was impressed by his honesty and simplicity. He wanted to build a portfolio for me and was willing to be rewarded on results. If I didn't make money, then Sandy would not make money either. We agreed a formula that we were both happy to work with and shook hands on the deal.

That agreement was never documented but some years later I honoured it and Sandy was a happy man. Sandy had come to me for a £20,000 deposit but by the time he left a couple of hours later I had agreed that I would give him a pot of £2,000,000 with which he could buy me flats. The initial target was to buy around thirty-five flats around the periphery of the west end of Glasgow, an area that Sandy knew well. The west end itself was too expensive but he had identified a few pockets that were just ripe to invest in. I told him that we should target to buy these within eighteen months and if, after using up the £2 million, the project seemed successful then I would give him more money to expand the portfolio even further. The one thing that I had not told Sandy as he skipped out of my office was that I actually didn't have any money as yet, and this small inconvenience would be the next thing that I would have to address.

I called my own bank, which was the Bank of Scotland, and told them that I required an extra overdraft facility of £400,000, as I wanted to upgrade the restaurants over the next eighteen months. They were not unhappy with this as they saw it as reinvesting in the business. I then met with the Royal Bank and told them of my ambition to start a new business that would be purely buying to let, with a portfolio consisting of flats around the west end. I asked them for an overdraft facility of £2 million and they were happy to put this in place as long as every time I made a purchase and drew down on the facility provided I would put 20 per cent of the purchase price into the account. The gearing for borrowing would have to be kept at an eighty–twenty ratio and by the time the portfolio reached £2 million, my contribution would be £400,000. I now had the £2 million facility in place for Sandy without having to put a penny into the pot from my own pocket.

Over the next eighteen months Sandy spent the money as if he were a woman whose lover had just given her his Gold American Express card and by the end of that period he had spent all my money. Unlike the lover on a spending spree though, Sandy had spent wisely and when we revalued the portfolio two years later, it had enough equity to allow me to gear up and borrow another £2 million without any cash input from myself. I told Sandy that the prices we were buying at were still good and told him to make sure that he bought at least three flats every month for the next twelve months.

One year later the money was spent again and, once again, after waiting about six months, I got the portfolio revalued. The uplift was fantastic and it not only allowed me to take out the £400,000 that was owed to Harlequin Leisure and the Bank of Scotland, but also to borrow a further £2 million to expand the property company. I repeated this formula a few more times and stopped buying in 2004 when I felt that the market was getting too hot. At that point, the portfolio value stood at well over £12 million and if I were to have sold it and repaid the bank, I would have been left with a profit of £3 million; not bad for starting off with no money but a guarantee.

Was this all luck? I know for a fact that our timing to start the portfolio was spot on and had we tried to do this a few years later, we would not have achieved the same results. I guess there was luck involved, but the fact that I decided to take the risk was still the key to success. It also proved to me that people should take a leaf out of Sandy's book and that if they have a moneymaking idea, they should not be shy in approaching those who they think might be willing to invest in their ideas. The worst that can happen is that they can get a negative response but most times, in order to be successful, one has to persevere to get the results.

I have always felt that business should be conducted with a certain amount of credibility and honesty. On the whole, most people I have come across just want to make an honest living but, now and then, you experience transactions which leave a very sour taste – of course, this is even worse when you get turned over by people you've respected all your life. One of these was a deal which I had verbally agreed with one of Sandy's uncles, a man I had known for many years and had also been very friendly with. I should have remembered about doing business with men calling themselves 'Uncle' but this was different – or so I thought. I always knew that he had a reputation of being a shrewd businessman which, in my mind, is perfectly all right but he was also one of the men who let me down and disappointed me in the way that he conducted business with me.

We all get ourselves into situations in our business when cash flow can be tight. At times like that it becomes necessary to juggle things around by refinancing the borrowings or even selling something off. Sandy's uncle got himself into a situation where he had a cash-flow problem. He had put down a deposit for some new flats which he had bought off-plan. When the time came to settle, 'Uncle' found himself unable to raise the cash in time. Through Sandy, he approached me to ask if I would take one of the properties off his hands to help him out. I told Sandy that I would not buy the first property unless he also sold me the second one which was due to settle three weeks later. I believed that the first property was only worth buying if the second one, which was a better buy, was also a part of the deal.

Sandy called me back to say that his uncle had agreed to sell both the properties and on that basis I paid him for the first flat. Sandy and I both agreed that we didn't need anything in writing.

'It is your uncle that we are dealing with and I have known him all my life,' I told Sandy. When a month had gone by and I had heard nothing, I asked Sandy to call his uncle to see when the second property was due to settle. He called me back to say that his uncle had turned him over and bought the second property himself by using the profit from the first sale to me.

Normally I would walk away from these situations but I felt that 'Uncle' had to know what a sad guy he was and how he had not only let down his nephew who had so much respect for him, but also gone down so much in my own esteem. I told him that I had looked up to people like him all my life and had aspired to be like him and he had shattered my illusions. He told me straight out that things like that didn't concern him and, as I had nothing in writing, so far as he was concerned there was no deal. I told him that for the sake of a small amount of money he had lost the respect of many people. He told me he didn't care. I could perhaps have understood if he stood to gain hundreds of thousands but we are talking small change here. I cannot understand how a man could possibly do such a thing, especially when the money would have made no difference to his life. I have never spoken to him since.

A guy called Charlie Hamilton built the house that I moved into in Pollokshields and over the next few years Charlie and I became quite friendly. He came to me with an opportunity to invest in house development and told me that he had a couple of sites all ready to go. I had never been involved in house building but, as long as it was bricks and mortar, I was interested. Over the next four years, we built a lot of quality houses, spending a lot of money on each house. I found that Charlie was a bit of a perfectionist and would not cut corners. I think that is a good trait, and when one is building houses worth over £300,000 then the finishing should be of a good quality. Charlie would want the best even for houses that we were selling at under £100,000 and, although we built some great houses, we made very little money. It took a while for Charlie to get the balance and, by that time, we had both decided that it was time for us to part company but still remain friends. The house that Charlie had built for me was indeed one of quality as I sold it for three times what I had paid for it seven years after moving in.

Chapter Thirty-Eight

PUTTING SOMETHING BACK

Charity had never been my thing, I guess, though I was much the same as most people who gave a few quid whenever there was a major disaster. Disasters all over the world are happening with such frequency nowadays. One just has to switch on the television and we are treated to pictures from some poor part of the world which has been ravaged by floods, earthquakes or hurricanes. Every day we are shown harrowing scenes of people dying of AIDs or children starving to death. I am not sure whether there are now more disasters in the world or, due to the media, we just get to hear about them more often. When I was young, I hardly heard of any of the disasters facing the world and therefore the only charity I had really heard of was Oxfam.

People really did believe that charity began at home and I had heard the expression used so often that I started to believe that it was how it should be. I did set up a standing order at my bank for £5 a month payable to Oxfam back in 1985 when I had little or no money. The same amount still goes out of my bank today and, although I give as much as I can to numerous charities each month, that £5 is one fixed amount that I have never changed. I think it is a reminder to me of how far I have come in my life. The other thing I did was give away a few meals every now and then for raffle prizes when someone was doing a fundraiser but even these were few and far between. To show how things have changed, nowadays the head office and all the restaurants get bombarded with requests for free meals every week.

The first Charity Night that we organised through Harlequin was in 1997 and it was really a networking evening with the purpose of raising the company's profile. The office and a lot of the restaurant staff pulled together to make the event a success. It was held at the Edmiston Suite next door to Ibrox Stadium, home ground of Glasgow Rangers FC. Sanjay was instrumental in helping put the event together and he booked Tommy Docherty, the legendary football manager, as our guest speaker. Due to the venue and the speaker, it was very much a 'man's night' and 85 per cent of the turnout was male. The night was a great success in every way and we even had a couple of thousand pounds surplus. We decided to give this to a local charity and for the first time I felt really great giving away money.

The following year the event was moved to a bigger venue and we chose the Moat House Hotel as the venue. This time it was attended by 400 people and we were left with a £10,000 surplus. We decided that the year after we would make it an official charity night and came up with a brand name for the evening. We called it 'The Hottest Night of the Year'. Under this name and with more focus on fundraising, the night just went from strength to strength and we were now faced with another problem. All the 650 seats were getting sold within a week of announcing the date and we were now faced with telling a lot of our regular supporters that there were no places left. We were victims of our own success. The 'Hottest Night of the Year' was now one of the hottest nights in town, raising hundreds of thousands of pounds for charities all over the world.

Over the years stars from sport and the media graced the night. We had politicians, entrepreneurs and professionals all wanting to be seen at the event and we had some real fun nights. We held auctions to raise money and one year Darren Jackson, who was playing for Celtic at the time, put up his signed football strip as one of the prizes. The bidding on that particular item was a bit slow as Darren had not been playing too well recently and was struggling to get a first-team game. He ended up bidding for his own shirt and paid a small fortune for the privilege. The newspapers got hold of the story and reported that the only way that Darren could get back into the first team and get his strip was to pay for it.

I am pleased to say that the most expensive thing to be sold at an auction was a meal for twelve, cooked by none other than myself. If only they knew that I couldn't cook! The prize involved a meal for twelve to be cooked in your own home and served up by the Curry King himself. The bidding for that particular lot went higher and higher until it was eventually bought by Jim McColl of Clyde Blowers for the princely sum of £17,000. That is over £1,400 per head for a curry and I was particularly pleased. He paid for it immediately but the strange thing is that he never actually took the meal. Perhaps he had got to hear about my cooking and changed his mind, deciding just to cut his losses.

The reason that the Hottest Night raised so much money for good causes was the generosity of my friends. People like John and Kate McGuire who regularly gave me a free car to sell as a raffle prize, Chris and Mary Gorman, Alan Revie, Gordon White, Ann Rushforth and John Boyle to name just a few. If I started writing down the names of the people who gave hard-earned cash away at our fundraiser, the list would be endless. Sometimes it was not what they were buying but the very fact that they were giving that made them buy things. On one occasion, Fernando Ricksen, the Rangers player, stole my Indian shoes that I had taken off and left under the table as they were very tight. The next thing I knew he was on the stage auctioning them off! They were bought by Satty Singh, who later in the evening gave them back to me as a present. I didn't think they were so bad that he wouldn't want to keep them.

The 'Hottest Night' also allowed me to have reunion gigs with my band, Bombay Talkie, and the boys would fly in just to play at the function. I know it sounds sad but the only way I could get a gig was to organise it myself.

The generosity of the Scottish people never ceased to amaze me. Sometimes they are portrayed as tight-fisted by cartoonists who try to generalise the Scottish character, but from my personal experience nothing could be further from the truth. Whenever there was a need, anywhere in the world, the Scots always dug deep and gave as much as they could. This was especially true in the year 2005 when the world seemed to have more disasters than any other year.

First there was the Asian tsunami, for which the Scots raised more cash per head than any other country in Europe. I organised a small fundraiser at the Curry Karaoke Club and due to the limited capacity, had only a hundred people present, but even with this small number I managed to raise £100,000. A few months after raising this cash I went out to Sri Lanka where I met the most wonderful people. I saw complete devastation in many areas and a lot of people had lost their entire families, yet there seemed to be an acceptance of their fate and the belief that whatever happens in life happens for a reason. There was a serene atmosphere about Sri Lanka that I had never experienced before. There I met many people from different parts of the world who had given up their time, putting their everyday lives on hold to try and help the unfortunate victims.

I met the actor David Hayman and his friend Ronnie Bridges, who were there with a small team of volunteers. The great thing about David's team was that they were getting in amongst the people who needed the most help. They provided people who were living in makeshift tents with basic utensils to cook what little food they had or boil water. Sometimes we forget what is really needed as there is no point in giving someone food if they have no way in which to cook it. They were doing the things that some of the larger charities were still thinking about doing. It was also in Sri Lanka that I met the volunteers of the charity 'Glasgow, the Caring City'. The commitment and dedication of these volunteers was a humbling experience for me and made me want to do more. When I got back to Glasgow I got in touch with them and helped them to raise funds for their causes.

After the tsunami, the world was rocked by the earthquake in Kashmir which killed hundreds of thousands of people and made millions homeless. I worked with Glasgow, the Caring City, and through Billy Hall, who was in charge of the Harlequin call centre, set up a hotline for donations within hours. The first donation of £20,000 came in from Sir Tom Hunter, one of the most generous men I know. Our hotline took almost £200,000 within a week and again most of the money came from ordinary Scots, many of whom were pensioners and had barely enough for themselves. The other thing that I was able to do was encourage communities to work together, and when I took the Lord Provost of Glasgow, Liz Cameron, around the Sikh temples, they rallied to her call for help and within hours raised £27,000 for their Muslim brothers in Kashmir. It was a true show of unity from the people of Glasgow and something that pleased me very much.

The charity event that did the most for my ego was one that was organised by Michelle Mone of MJM International. During her auction, a dinner with Rachel Hunter, then wife of rock star Rod Stewart, was snapped up for £10,000. The next item to be auctioned was a dinner with Charan Gill and I was thrilled when it surpassed the previous bid and was sold for £11,000. That really made my night. The one thing about prizes that people have bought at auctions is that they are seldom used and I don't know whether people bid because they get carried away with the atmosphere or whether they see it as just another charitable donation. I don't know but, whatever the reason, long may it continue.

Lawyers and accountants are the only people I know who don't get carried away and place bids at charity auctions; they are always careful and guarded. Although they always supported my nights by taking tables, I couldn't actually recall them giving me any cash. I decided that they should not get off so lightly and when I was creating a charitable trust status for Harlequin, I asked McClure Naismith, my lawyers, and PKF, my accountants, to carry out the work. I first called Charles Burnett at PKF and asked him to do the accountancy work required to set up the trust. I then told him that Nick Naddell at McClure's was doing his part for no charge and I wanted PKF to do the same. Charles really had no option but to agree. I then called Nick and told him that PKF were not charging as the work was linked to charity and that I hoped his firm would do the same. After a short pause, Nick also agreed to waive his charge. It would have cost a couple of thousand to set up the trust and perhaps it is not a lot of money. The way I saw it, it was enough to give over a hundred people with cataracts the gift of eyesight.

Chapter Thirty-Nine

SHAK ATTACK

I enjoy going to the movies from time to time although the idea of sitting in a cinema watching two Bollywood movies for the price of one is not anything I would regard as remotely entertaining nowadays. I remember as a schoolboy going down to the pictures with my brothers on a Saturday morning and queuing up to see a Western. I loved to sit in the front row and boo and hiss when the Red Indians came over the ridge and stamp my feet loudly and cheer when the cavalry arrived to save the day. I grew up believing that the Red Indians were horrible people who attacked wagon trains and scalped good white people for no reason other than the fact that they enjoyed it. The first movie I saw which started to show the true picture of the plight of the Native American was *Soldier Blue*. After seeing that movie and its scenes of atrocities carried out by the cavalry on some of the peaceful Indian villages, I didn't stamp my feet at the movies any more.

It was on a visit to a multiplex cinema in the year 2000, in an area called Linwood, that I got my next flash of inspiration. The cinema was a typical out-of-town multiplex that had the usual mix of food outlets that one could see regularly at such sites. There was the usual Pizza Hut, Burger King, Brewers Fayre and a Harry Ramsden's. I noticed as I drove into the site that the Harry Ramsden unit was all boarded up and at first I thought this was due to a fire. On closer inspection, I saw that it was closed through choice and thought to myself that it was not the best of ideas for that site in the first place. I had visited it before as a customer and had found that it was overpriced and the food was pretty rank.

I had often wondered how it survived but had always figured that it was being subsidised by one of the other Harry Ramsden units. The following day I made some enquiries as to who I should talk to regarding the closed-down unit and was given the name of Derek Statt, who I was told owned the Scottish franchise rights for Harry Ramsden's. The following day, I went to visit Derek at his main site near the Quay cinema complex in Glasgow. It was a midweek day, just after lunchtime, and as I walked through the busy restaurant I saw that the average age of the customer was well over sixty. Derek was frank and open and he realised that I was much the same because my opening line to him was, 'Mr Statt, where do you think your future business will come from once all your regular customers are dead?'

I don't know whether I made that statement to be funny or to bring home to him that the days of Harry Ramsden's as a concept were numbered. He told me he knew there was little future for the Ramsden brand in its current form and that things would have to be changed. I got the impression that the changes would not be made by him as he already had an offer from someone to buy him out. I felt that Derek had had enough and was looking forward to spending more time on the golf course. Derek went into sales mode and told me that he thought it was a fantastic site, but he was trying to salvage what he could, and we both knew it. He knew that I was his only buyer but still he was trying to get the best deal he could and I think that in the circumstances he did very well.

We met on-site the following day and shook hands on a deal. All I had to do now was to think what I was going to do with the place. The press had already made up their minds as to what I should be doing and the headlines read, 'Curry King versus McDonald's'. Just because the site was located next to a

McDonald's and a Kentucky Fried Chicken, the assumption was that this was going to be a drive-through. The fact that there was no way to even adapt the building to enable it to house a drive-through didn't deter the media from spreading the word. It was now labelled as a fast-food drive-through joint and, though we got some fantastic press, it took me years to shake off the perception. The power of the press was realised when the Ashoka Shak opened its doors and we had all these people driving around the car park looking for a window at which to place their orders.

For many years I had wondered how I could grow the Ashoka into a national brand. There were no Indian chains in the same mould as Frankie and Bennies, Pizza Express or Nandos. I didn't think that Frankie and Bennies did great food and I don't think I have ever met anyone who has told me that they had a good meal there. The one thing I did know was that they were very busy and they were all making money. To my mind, the fact that the food they served was mediocre only proved that if the concept was correct and all the boxes which delivered to the customer whatever his needs were at that time were ticked, then the concept was bound to be successful. It was horses for courses and these particular locations were never going to be suitable for fine dining.

The challenge for me had always been finding good staff. I suppose that problem is not just mine but it is the same for most businesses looking to expand. One of the biggest hurdles is human resources and getting the right personnel is never easy. My new concept would solve those problems once and for all, or so I thought.

I wasn't really sure what exactly the Shak would be and for weeks I was in turmoil as to where it should be pitched. I toyed with the idea of making it a fast-food joint that would sell hand-held Indian food like chapatti wraps, and the newspapers had already told everyone that was what I was doing. I thought about developing a menu that would feature things that people could eat in their cars without having to park up. I had always fancied the idea of having an Indian drive-though but that idea could not be realised at this particular site. The same menu could have been offered to customers wanting to eat at the table, served on disposable plates. That way I would not need anyone to wash the dishes.

Knowing that the structure and layout of the building made this impossible, I then thought that we could charge more money by serving the dishes on proper plates. A quick calculation told me that the extra revenue would easily pay for the dishwasher. Whatever the concept, one thing that I really had to do was to try and deskill as much of the cooking as possible. I reckoned that if I could do away with expensive chefs and make do with line cooks, people who would work to simple recipes using sauces prepared in our central kitchen, the scope to expand would increase. Not only would the costs come down but it would be easier to source staff. The other reason that I wanted to have a central kitchen was to control the quality of the food. I knew that if all the sauces were prepared in a central kitchen, then there would be consistency of product in all the future Shaks.

I eventually decided to go for a middle-of-the-road approach and provide good service and good food at great prices. I wanted to give value for money and to get the message across I priced all the curries at £4.95. I didn't go to the expense of opening a central kitchen right away and decided to use the kitchens of one of the existing restaurants as our preparation base. The Linwood Ashoka Shak opened without any advertising taking place. I had just put up a banner outside telling people when we would be opening and on the opening day, the banner was replaced by one that read, 'Now Open'. I usually avoid advertising prior to an opening because I don't like being busy in the first few days. I always believe that it is important to get the teething problems out of the way before you start telling too many people that you are open.

The other thing that I always did was to avoid having an opening on a weekend. I much preferred to open on a Wednesday as this allowed the staff to get their days off out of the way for the first week and it was also easier to prepare for a midweek opening as the mood is generally relaxed. Wednesday and Thursday usually allowed the staff to settle down and the restaurant could also be fine-tuned in these first days before getting hit with a weekend rush. The first few weeks were pandemonium and business was much better than I had anticipated. This is quite normal, as a lot of people will try out a new place out of curiosity.

The normal trend for an Ashoka opening was that they were extremely busy for the first few weeks after which the sales would start to drop. They would bottom out after a couple of months, start to climb again and after about six months they would stabilise. The first wave would be due to curiosity and once a lot of the one-off punters fell away you would be left with a core of regulars, which you would then have to build the sales on.

This was a new idea and the central kitchen was working fine. The only thing that was not going down well was the nan bread that had been bought in from a company that supplied them to multinationals. Although we had spent a considerable amount of time working with this company, we were having real problems with quality and size. Eventually, I was forced to put in a tandoori oven on-site to make the bread fresh and my idea of total deskilled staff took its first knock.

I had tried to train local chefs to cook the curries, which should not have been difficult as the sauces and the meats were all cooked in the central kitchen. All the cook had to do was to mix the meat with the sauce in a frying pan, heat it until the texture was right and then serve it on a plate. It should not have been hard but we were struggling with the finished product and I reluctantly brought in a chef from one of the other restaurants. I didn't see this as defeat as he was still instructed to work according to the kitchen manual and not to start adding his own recipes.

I experienced some reverse racism when we first tried to introduce white staff to serve in our restaurants. Many years earlier, customers had felt uncomfortable being served by young Scottish waiters and waitresses as they thought that they didn't know what they were doing. Some customers would place the order and then ask one of the 'Asian' waiters to make sure that the order was taken correctly. Even though the Asian waiter knew little English and could not tell the difference between a pakora and a popadam, the customer just assumed that because he was Asian he would know everything about Indian cuisine. It's a bit like expecting every Scot to know about Scottish game and fish. It was even more difficult with chefs. If the customer knew that the chef was a local Scot then they would complain about the food before it even came to the table. Again, it has taken a long time but we seem to have now overcome that particular challenge.

The first Shak took a lot of changing and tweaking, with the menu being changed twice within the first three months until I eventually felt that everything was falling into place. I was happy enough with the figures and decided that this was the concept with which to expand the group. I started to look for more sites and over the next couple of years I opened up in Coatbridge, Dundee and Livingston. The Shak could be rolled out across the nation but I still had serious problems finding the right qualified staff to support the growth. I was desperate to grow my company but the problem of finding suitable staff was becoming critical. I decided that the only way I was going to solve this problem would be to go and find staff in India.

Chapter Forty

INTERVIEWING IN DELHI

Teresa Doherty had been working with me at Harlequin for many years. She had started working in the bar as a part-time waitress and as we expanded she played a vital role in the growth. Over the years she rose up the internal ranks and was eventually appointed company secretary. Whenever a job came up that needed to be handled with care and caution, I usually gave it to Teresa. I told her that I wanted to get staff from India to come and work for me and asked her to look at how this could be made to happen. She came back a couple of weeks later and told me that it could be done but it would not be easy.

The process of bringing staff from abroad is not a simple one. First, the job has to be advertised locally, nationally and in Europe to ensure that the labour we are looking for is not already available. Once the adverts have been placed then there has to be a period to allow for responses. If we cannot find anyone suitable to fill the post, then we have to advertise in India and wait for the response before setting up interviews and then flying over to carry them out. Once that is done, there is a need to ensure that all the paperwork is filled in properly, then along with references and qualifications these are sent to the Home Office who will assess them and hopefully issue a work permit. Well, if you think that's bad enough, once the work permit has been sent over to the prospective employee, the employee has to attend a further interview at the British Embassy in Delhi who will assess the employee according to their own criteria before issuing a visa to enter this country for a specified period of between one and three years.

I knew that the process would not be easy but there was no other way forward for me and it was the only route that I could take. It was an important task and one which I would have to give to someone who would be methodical and systematic and work to the letter of the law because if there was the slightest error at any stage the application would be refused. I asked Teresa to handle it herself and freed her up from other jobs so that she could concentrate on the task full-time. More cost to the company but I had to swallow it.

I can say this now as I have no need of their services but the process was made hard by officials who looked for reasons to knock back applications. There are so many inconsistencies within the system that, quite often, it depends on the person handling a particular application if it gets approval or not. The work permit system is a great idea and allows companies to bring expertise from overseas but I think it is very selective in the areas where the government wishes to see it being applied, and the catering industry is not one of their favourites. It was a little bit easier, if that is the right word, prior to Poland joining the EEC, to have the work permits processed but once Poland was on board we were told to employ staff who were coming from that country and were looking for work in Scotland. In making this suggestion, the government was missing the point that our industry was not looking for numbers, and that we required expertise in a specific field.

When we first placed an advert for kitchen staff in both a national and a European newspaper at a cost of thousands of pounds, we got one application. Compare this to the 3,000 emails we received when we placed a similar advert in a Delhi newspaper and you get the picture that the talent we required was available in abundance in India, and the type of people applying for the posts were highly qualified and well-educated individuals who would be a benefit to Scotland and its future economy.

We were told time and time again that we should be trying to recruit locally. My answer to that was always the same: who in their right minds would go to the extraordinary lengths that my company were willing to go to if we could find the same staff locally? Why would I go to such vast expense to try and cut through the red tape that was put in my way? How I wished I could place a local advert and have even three or four people who could cook Indian food applying to fill the vacancy. My life would be simple and my job one hundred times easier.

Teresa took on the task and, after going through the arduous process of travelling to India herself along with my fellow director Gurmail Dhillon, we eventually managed to get over our first batch of staff from India. It was great having these guys over and I felt that there was a certain change in the atmosphere of the restaurants – a change for the better. I had some real talent in our kitchens as well as front of house and these guys saw the opportunity to work for Harlequin as a great career move. One of them was Rajesh Saraf whom I met in Delhi. He had worked for the Oberoi Group of hotels for ten years and had only come to chat to me out of curiosity. He had been offered jobs in Dubai and in America but had refused them all. We had a long chat about the industry in general and I asked him if he would come to Scotland. He considered it for some time and eventually said yes. He came to Glasgow to work as a manager and I was so impressed that I eventually had him looking after all my restaurants.

Over a period of three years, Teresa and Gurmail and, sometimes, I, myself, travelled to India to find new talent to bring to Scotland and breathe fresh life into our industry. We were so successful, and Teresa was doing such a terrific job, that we were getting approached by other restaurant and hotel chains that were facing the same challenges as ourselves in recruiting for the industry. Teresa ended up placing staff in the Hilton, DiMaggio's and many other restaurants across Scotland. The workload was so high that we eventually had to open an office in Delhi to keep up with the demand.

Chapter Forty-One

CEETL'S WEDDING

It was around the time that I opened my second Shak, in Livingston, that I got an answer to a question I had asked myself for many years: how would my children choose their spouses? Indeed, I was often asked a similar question when being interviewed by press or radio: 'Are your daughters going to have arranged marriages?'

There is never an easy answer because you just don't know what life has in store and what awaits you round the corner. I have always been of the opinion that one must never expect things to turn out in certain ways, because it is only when you expect something that you are disappointed. Be ready for whatever life throws at you and no matter how hard or harsh it seems at times, try to embrace it. It is important for any parent to make their views known and if they feel that their children are making a wrong decision then they should try and convince them that they should rethink their decisions. Even with the knowledge of hindsight and the experience of age, I still make big mistakes; therefore, I know that it is easy for children to make choices that they may one day regret. Some may argue that they will learn by their own mistakes but I think that if they can learn from yours, or the mistakes of others, then it is a lot less painful for all concerned. I believe that even if children make choices that are against your own wishes then, once all the convincing has failed to change their minds, it should be a parent's duty to support them.

Too often in the Asian community I have seen families torn apart because the children have decided to choose their own partners. Love for one's children has to be unconditional and, no matter what they do, they can never be treated as outcasts because those are the times when they most need your love. You have to guide them to make the right choices, not bully them to make the choices that suit you.

I was pleased with the way all my girls had grown up and felt they were 'well balanced' and prepared for whatever life had to throw at them. Ceetl, Basant and Preetpal had all been good at school and had gone on to the University of Glasgow, gaining degrees in various subjects. Jaspreet had been under pressure to emulate her sisters and get that university degree but, with all that pressure, I could see that she was buckling. They had all had the best education that I could provide them with and were educated at Glasgow Academy. The fees were high as there was one period when all five of our children were attending the school at the same time. I was looking to pick up some kind of award for that feat because I am sure I must have set a school record and that no other family has had five kids attend at the same time.

I was pleased that they had done well at school but, though education was important, I would never force my children to do something that they didn't want to do themselves. When Jaspreet struggled during her first year at college and I could see that this was affecting her personality I told her that I didn't want her to go to college and that she should come and work with me in one of my restaurants. The change in her was immediate and she became a much happier girl knowing that she did not have to be academically brilliant to make me happy. She started to work in the Ashoka at the Mill and enjoyed her job very much. The following year she was back at college of her own free will and now, without any baggage, is enjoying college and is motivated to do well.

The work ethic that my father instilled in me is one that I wanted to pass on to my children. That is more important to me than education. I think if one can have both then that would be fantastic, but it can be easy for children whose parents are financially well off to lose all appreciation of money, coming to think that everything is available in the shops and all you need is a credit card that daddy will pay off at the end of each month. I didn't want to ever spoil my kids and if you were to ask them now they would tell you that although they had everything in life that they needed it was never excessive. They rarely wore branded clothes as Parminder always felt that they were a rip-off and that you were only paying for the label.

I also made sure that they got a taste of employment and earned their own money and I had them all working in the Harlequin call centre as soon as they were old enough. They had to start to make their own way in life. All I was willing to do at this stage was provide them with the means to earn. They also got a taste of working in the restaurant and were all very capable of serving tables as well as any of the waiters that I employed. There was one Christmas Day in particular when we had a lot of staff call-offs and I brought in the whole family to work on Christmas Day. The day was enjoyable (at least it was for me!) and I felt a great sense of pride to see them rushing around keeping customers happy when a lot of kids in their position would have thought that they were the ones who should be getting served.

They were always aware that work came first and that the customer was king. They knew for instance that they were not to go into any of the restaurants at busy times and take up tables in case we had to refuse customers. Even if they wanted to order a takeaway, they would do it at times when they knew that the restaurant would be quiet. Home deliveries were also a no-go at the weekends as it was more important for the paying customer to get their food hot and on time than it was for our household so, more often than not, they would have to go and collect the food themselves. When Sampuran turned fourteen I had him working at the Ashoka making teas and coffees at the weekend. He hated it and would try to make excuses for not going but that was one thing I would not let him off with, even though I fell out with his mother over it on a number of occasions.

When the kids were very young and money was tight at home, Parminder and I had made a conscious decision that, no matter how bad things got financially, it was important that she would stay at home with the kids and be there for them going to school and also when they came home. With the very small age gap between the four girls, most of Parminder's day was taken up going from nursery to school and back at different times of the day. It would not have been so bad but for many years Parminder didn't have a car as we couldn't afford a second one and she had to do it all on foot. I think the fact that she was always there for them has certainly made a difference to the way that the children have turned out in life.

Mr Sewa Singh Kolhi has always been around and has been a man to whom I have turned for advice on many occasions. We went through a lot of challenges together and had a lot of fun times at the Asian Arts Centre and various other projects that we did together. The climax to our relationship came when the two of us went to Holyrood Palace at the same time to get our MBEs from the Queen. I think that Mr Kolhi was more pleased for me than he was for himself. He always seemed to be there when I needed someone to bounce ideas off or, more importantly, when we were thinking about a marriage.

'My brother in Coventry has found the ideal boy for Ceetl,' he said without any greeting or introduction. He always phoned early in the morning and was never one for idle gossip or long chats. There was rarely a 'good morning' either because he told me that one should always get to the point. I always tried to prepare myself when he called because I never knew what he was going to say or ask me to do. If Mr Kolhi asked me to do something then I would normally do it; I had developed a lot of respect for him over the years, having known him since I was a little kid.

I told Parminder what Mr Kolhi had said on the phone and she said that we should talk to Ceetl and all have a think about it. This was not the first call we had had regarding Ceetl, for it is very common for women to talk to one another and pitch their relatives' sons or daughters as prospective partners. Parminder had been through this before and so had Ceetl. I don't believe in arranged marriages and, nowadays, there are few, if any, in the Indian community in Scotland. The most common way for children to meet future husbands or wives is through introduction. If one takes the time to consider this, most people meet their partners through some form of introduction, even in western culture. Whether it is someone that you are introduced to at work or by family or even a blind date, it is still an introduction. I know lots of people who try to set up their friends with people they know and sometimes romance blossoms.

Parminder and I were due to go to Birmingham for a wedding and decided to take the opportunity to go and meet the boy, Chandeep Bains, and his family. It was just coincidence, and had it not been for the wedding we might not have gone. We went to Chandeep's house and spent a very pleasant afternoon chatting with all his family and left feeling as if we had known them for a long time. We felt very comfortable. We told Ceetl on our return that we felt that she should meet with Chan and see how they felt. I think the term used is to see if they would 'click'.

Chan's family all came to Glasgow for an overnight visit and Ceetl and Chan went for a meal so that they could be alone. She told us that she thought he was nice and that they had exchanged phone numbers and would like to see how the relationship developed. It took another few meetings and nightly phone calls and after a few months, they both said that they would be happy to get engaged.

The wedding was a fairly large affair and numerous customs had to be adhered to. Most of these involved a party of some sort with lots of drink and plenty of dancing. The final wedding had a guest list of 580, but by Indian standards that was not a particularly large wedding – I have been to some weddings where there were over 800 guests. In India, the number of people coming to a wedding can be taken as a measure of the family's standing within the community and I have heard of weddings where they have had over 5,000 guests. A lot of people send out invites just for the sake of it and because they want everyone to talk about how large the wedding was.

I am not for large weddings and believe that they should be small family affairs with only a limited number of close friends, and I was for chopping the numbers right down. However, Parminder's intervention made sure that the list was still quite large. We cut back on the numbers as much as we could for Ceetl's wedding and in the process a number of people that we had known for many years were not invited and have not talked to us since. The wedding went off without a hitch and, after moving to Coventry with Chan for about six months, they both came back and settled in Glasgow, which was good news for both Parminder and myself.

As I write, we are in the process of organising the wedding of my third daughter, Preetpal. She met a boy at the University of Glasgow when she was studying there and asked if we would meet him. Parminder and I went to meet the parents of the family and we said that, if Preet was happy, then we had no objection to them getting married. I was happy that everyone had agreed to a small wedding and Preet has actually decided to have a small lunch at home for the marriage party as opposed to having hundreds turning up at the Hilton. Parminder and I started to butcher our wedding list and we asked Bobby's parents to do the same. After many arguments between Parminder and me, we decided that, no matter how hard we tried, it was just not possible to get the list down below 300. The marquee would not be able to take the numbers and we convinced Preet, whose own guest list was just fourteen people, that we should have the wedding at the Hilton.

Two down, three to go.

Chapter Forty-Two

SINGING ALL THE WAY TO THE BANKS OF THE CLYDE

I have to confess that I have one of the worst memories around when it comes to remembering names, and I am even worse when it comes to faces. I have great admiration for those who can recall the names of people they have only met for a brief moment, and quite often I am even envious as I have always felt that if I had this talent I would be a far better networker, but, as it is, I am completely useless. I sometimes tell the story that when I go out with my wife to dinner or to an event where we will meet many people whom I know, I ask her to save me embarrassment by immediately introducing herself when people say hello, so that I don't have to make the introductions. On one such occasion, as we entered a hotel foyer I turned to her and said, 'You know what I am like with names and I might have to introduce you to folk, so tell me one last time: what is your name again?'

I once met a guy at a petrol station and he came over and greeted me like a long lost friend. 'How are you?' he asked, thrusting out his hand for me to shake.

I told him I was well and, trying to fish for clues as to who he was, I asked, 'I have not seen you for ages, man, where have you been?'

'Mr Gill,' he replied, 'I spent a couple of hours with you the other day when we were taking new food shots for your menu, remember? I'm the photographer.'

It was most embarrassing and all I could say was, 'God! You look so different without the camera.'

I was once watching the engagement ceremony of a friend's son on video and I said to Parminder, 'Was I at that engagement? I can't seem to recall being there.'

She told me that she was sure I had attended. We had a bit of healthy debate and I maintained that there was no way I would not have remembered if I had been there.

'It's not the type of thing one forgets,' I argued.

I was just getting ready to place a heavy bet with her when the video camera panned out to take a wider shot and there was me, dressed in my finest suit, standing next to the future groom and handing him over the engagement ring which I had been trusted to carry.

In contrast to that, I have always had a unique gift that allows me to remember certain conversations and situations that I think will be good for my business. I could be in a restaurant and notice small things like how a drink gets poured or how the tables are laid. At the time I don't realise that these things are registering because I make no mention of them and indeed, I might even seem oblivious to them. But years later, when I am looking to do things differently and want to make changes in our operating methods, something happens and all this information, which for a lot of people would have been useless, just comes pouring out.

One such example was how I came to open the Curry Karaoke Club. It all started when I was invited by the *Sun* newspaper to join them for a night out which they were having in a place called the Shanghai Shuffle, a Chinese restaurant with a unique selling point, which was that it was big on karaoke. When people booked into this restaurant it was not for a couple of hours but for the whole evening, so vast amounts of money were spent on drinks. It was very well established and it was so popular that if you wanted a table for one of the busier nights you would have to wait a month before you could even get in. The evening I was there it was extremely busy and I was told that this was the norm. There was a great atmosphere, the wine was flowing freely, and everyone seemed to be having a fabulous time. As I watched people singing, dancing and enjoying themselves, I noticed the price of the drinks being served and something inside me thought, 'If this can work with Chinese food, then it can work with Indian. Maybe one day I will open a Curry Karaoke restaurant.'

That day came two years later. Once again, the opportunity landed on my lap and, once again, I was not slow in seizing the moment. I took a call from Derek Statt, the man who had sold me the closed-down Harry Ramsden unit which became my first Ashoka Shak. He had a business proposition for me and told me that after the experience he had had with our first deal he felt comfortable to put another opportunity my way. He said he knew that if I agreed terms with him verbally then I would not mess him around and the deal would go through without any hitches.

It reminded me how important it is when doing business that one does it with integrity and honesty. I feel that too many think business is about ripping people off or conning your way through a deal to make money; believe me, that happens all the time and one has to be wary. Sometimes if you are not sharp and don't keep your wits about you, you are going to get shafted. I have always believed that there has to be positive benefits to both sides, and that once the dust has settled on a deal, everyone should be able to look back and think to themselves that they're happy with what has been achieved. It is not always the most money that is made or paid which makes deals sweet or palatable: there are other parameters like staff jobs, tax benefits and future growth plans which all play a major role in the final outcome. If one conducts business with a certain simple dignity then your reputation is created and opportunities will come to you first, as opposed to those that have been rejected by numerous other parties, and this was why Derek was on the phone.

He told me that he was one of the directors of a trust that was responsible for operating the Tall Ship project next to the old Pump House restaurant. They also had a lease to operate the restaurant but their current tenant had decided to lock the doors. Although the tenant was still paying the rent, the board were not happy that the place had closed down and wanted another operator. 'Would you be interested in coming in to look the place over and operate it?' he asked hopefully.

This was not a place that would be easy to rent to a good operator as many had tried and failed. It was out of the way and not easy to find. There was no passing trade as it was located in a dead end on the banks of the River Clyde. It had a history of failure and whoever came in would have to do something special to get customers to travel to it. The only way to make this happen was to turn it into a destination venue which punters would be keen to travel to. I saw the club's isolated location as an advantage for the type of operation I had in mind.

I knew the place well. It had opened many years previously as a restaurant complex that had housed three restaurants – one Italian, one seafood and, ironically, an Indian. Although it had been initially successful, after a few years it had gone into receivership. It then changed hands a number of times until it was taken over by Willie Haughie, who spent a great deal of money to refurbish it and opened it as an entertainment venue. It had a good kitchen, a fabulous lighting system, a nice stage and was extremely well fitted out. Most importantly, it also had a really good sound system and the latest karaoke equipment. As Derek told me about the situation of the Pump House, I could already visualise myself singing Frank Sinatra's 'New York, New York'. The deal was done within days and I asked my eldest daughter Ceetl and her husband Chan if they would come into the deal as partners. They agreed immediately and, with the help of my other daughters, they launched the Curry Karaoke Club within a few months of my having the initial conversation with Derek Statt.

The club was an instant hit and within a few months people had to book weeks in advance to be sure of getting a table. Although Chan had experience in the food and bar trade due to his father having a pub in Coventry, it was the first real experience that the girls had of running their own business. It was good to see that they had no qualms about putting in the long hours to make the business work and, as far as I could see, they were enjoying it very much. The fact that it was a karaoke club and they all loved to sing was an obvious bonus.

Ceetl and Preet had been a part of a band called Only Kismet and they had also released a single that did reasonably well. When they took up singing, hoping to make it into a career, I encouraged them and told them that if they put their minds to it then they could become stars. Deep down, though, I was hoping that they would just enjoy the experience for a while and then settle down to real jobs and that is exactly what happened. But their singing was sure coming in handy at the Curry Karaoke Club.

Chapter Forty-Three

THE ENTREPRENEURIAL EXCHANGE

Since I had given up singing on stage on a regular basis, I was beginning to feel a void in my life that no amount of restaurant openings could fill. When you get used to being on stage and the applause of an appreciative audience, the buzz is difficult to emulate and I had a craving to perform on stage and hear that applause once again. I got the opportunity when I was asked to speak at a lunch held by one of the local enterprise companies. I prepared for the twenty-minute talk feeling a little nervous as I had never spoken on stage before. It is so much easier to go up there and sing, because when you are singing, you can actually pretend to be someone else and your character undergoes a complete change. That is why a lot of performers are very shy people when they are not on stage or in front of camera.

This brings me to an old myth about Scots people being unhappy in service jobs because they think it demeans them having to call customers 'sir' and 'ma'am'. The trick is to approach the job as an actor might. It's not *you* being a waiter, but you acting the role of a waiter. Let's face it, John Wayne never served in any war and actually didn't like horses, but he still had a reputation as a tough guy. It's amazing what you can achieve when you take your personality out of the equation.

That first speech went remarkably well and when the applause came at the end of it I felt a similar buzz to the one I used to feel on stage. After that, many other speaking engagements followed and these varied from bankers' dinners to speaking at schools and colleges. I also enjoyed after-dinner speaking and was thrilled to be asked to go along and speak at Burns Suppers. I once spoke at a charity dinner called the Wags Dinner where they had five speakers all doing a ten-minute slot on a topic that they were given just a few days before the event. At the end, the guests all voted for the best 'wag' or speaker, the one that they found most humorous and entertaining, and I was thrilled when I was announced as the winner. This gave me the confidence to do more events and I really enjoyed after-dinner speaking. Although I was getting asked regularly to speak at events, I decided to limit these, as it is so easy to get distracted from your day job.

The one conference that I really wanted to speak at was the Entrepreneurial Exchange annual conference that is held at the prestigious Gleneagles Hotel. I had never actually got around to joining the Exchange and my application form had been lying in my desk drawer for many months. I had been to a couple of their events and was very impressed by the organisation and its list of high-profile members. I think one of the reasons for me not joining was that I actually felt that I was not good enough. Most of the people that I knew to be members were, in my opinion, much better entrepreneurs than myself and they had businesses that turned over money that I could never imagine. I had also felt that it was a very tight-knit organisation and that you had to be one of the gang to be accepted. I thought of it as an organisation for high fliers and not for wee guys like myself. I suppose that was an image problem that the Exchange had and if it deterred me from joining then I wondered how many other people it was keeping out because of its perceived superiority complex.

When the opportunity came and I was asked to be one of the speakers, I was flattered and nervous at the same time. What would I say to an audience made up of the top Scottish entrepreneurs? Would they have anything to learn from my experiences?

In the front row were Tom Hunter, Chris Gorman, Jim McColl, Gio Bennedetti, Willie Haughie and Brian Johnstone, no relation to Alan Johnstone my old bank manager, who was representing the Bank of Scotland. Elsewhere in the room were Ann Gloag, Paul Slater, John McGuire, John Boyle, Gerald Weisfield, Richard Emmanuel, David Moulsdale and 250 others.

My grandfather had always told me how my singing would open many doors for me and bring me introductions to people whom I would otherwise never talk to. He had never known that to speak to an audience and be able to connect with them was also great for winning friends. I knew within the first few minutes that my speech was going well. I had no PowerPoint presentations, I told my audience, no special effects that were used by other speakers to help hold the audience's attention. My story was a simple one that came from the heart. It was a journey that had started in a small village in the Punjab, where my grandfather had told me that once I had moved to Scotland I would do so well that I would own my own scooter with a glass visor, all the way to Gleneagles, where I was being given the honour of sharing my story with my business heroes.

Most people in that room already knew my story because, really, it was no different from any of their own. I knew that people like Sir Tom Farmer, whom I spoke with later, could relate to my story. I could sense that they were reminiscing about some of their own experiences and reliving their own roller-coaster rides as I spoke of my life's journey since arriving in Scotland.

I enjoyed my day at Gleneagles and the highlight came when Sir Tom Hunter invited me and Parminder to his fortieth birthday bash which was taking place two days later in Monaco. Parminder was apprehensive about going as she didn't know anyone who was going to be there and, of course, she had nothing to wear. But we went along, had a fantastic weekend and Parminder told me that she had never felt so comfortable in her life. She had been expecting pompousness and snobbery. After all, I had taken her to some dinners before where a lot of the people had been snooty and condescending. She could not believe how down-to-earth everyone at that party was. The reason for this was quite simple: all the people in that room, including Sir Richard Branson and Phil Green, had made their money the hard way and we had all walked the same road. There was a true sense of camaraderie. We were even given a lift back from Monaco in John Boyle's private Learjet.

I joined the Entrepreneurial Exchange a few weeks later and have enjoyed meeting people from all sorts of backgrounds chasing the same dream, which is to build businesses of substance and become successful in their own right. I came to realise that the Exchange was not exclusive to the Scottish business elite but that a third of the membership had businesses with turnovers of less than £1 million. The criterion for membership is not what size of business one is running on joining but, more importantly, what size of business one wants to be running in the foreseeable future. Potential members must have the aspiration and the desire to grow their business.

I would say to anyone who is in business, whether they are just starting out on their own or have already successfully built their business, that they should join the Exchange because no matter which stage of our business life we have reached, we all need friends and mentors along the way. If you are already successful then it is important to give something back and help those businesses that are just starting out and need all the help and advice they can get.

Within a couple of years I was elected to the role of vice chair and I am pleased to be playing an active role and providing whatever help I can to whoever asks for it. The most important thing about being part of any organisation is to put into practice what you know has worked for others. At the last annual conference one of the speakers had talked about writing his autobiography. He talked about how much he had enjoyed doing this and spoke about the important role that a book can play in raising one's profile. He urged everyone to think about writing a book and I knew as I listened to him speak just last year that, before the next annual conference at Gleneagles came around, I would have written my own book.

In the bar that evening, I declared my intention to complete my autobiography within the year and my announcement was met by scepticism and sarcasm from my drinking associates. They all knew that I had left school without a single O grade and my typing skills left a lot to be desired. Even I knew it would be a struggle.

Michelle Mone was more sympathetic. 'I have no doubt in your ability but you'll never have the time to do this,' she said.

It was a throwaway remark but I said that, if she bet me a fiver, it would give me an incentive to write the book. After clarifying that I would write the book myself and not get a ghostwriter to do it, she put forward her right hand to seal the deal. I shook her hand and accepted the challenge. I am sure that was the last Michelle thought about the conversation.

The morning after the night before is when most of us forget the bar bets and move on to more pressing matters but that is the difference between achievers and talkers. I dusted down my old laptop and sat down to write my autobiography. One of the driving forces was to win that five-pound bet.

I also learned through the Exchange that it was not always good to get sentimental about your business and that, when the time is right, one has to start thinking about an exit. Selling up was something that I had never considered but it was something that came up in conversation whenever I spoke with serial entrepreneurs. A lot of them had been successful because they had never got attached to their businesses which they bought and sold without any emotion. I realised that it was important to have an exit route but I knew that I had failed to plan for it. As time went on, my thoughts turned to selling my restaurants and moving on to something else. I had opened enough restaurants and I knew that the sense of adventure within the industry for me was now gone.

There was a choice for me to make: the first alternative was that I should push ahead with my expansion plans and expand a lot faster than I had been doing; the second was that I should hand the baton over to someone else who would. Standing still was not an option for Harlequin because, as I have said before, to stand still is to die.

I did consider my first alternative and in fact almost made a couple of acquisitions, which would have more than doubled the size of the company, and I would have ended up with another eighteen restaurants. One of these was a local chain of pizzerias called Leonardo's. A guy called Mike Conyers was operating them and, unfortunately, things had not gone to plan for Mike and the bank had called in the receivers. I had done a deal with the Bank of Scotland for the whole chain and the bank had verbally agreed to this, but at the eleventh hour they had reneged on the deal and brought in a management company to trade the units as they did not want to take such a large hit on the debt. This incident left me a bit disillusioned with the bank and it left a very bitter taste in my mouth. If they had been able to look into the future, they would have taken the money from me because the management company who were supposed to be the experts at running restaurants went bankrupt themselves within a few months. I have never brought up the subject with the bank, as I have never been the type to gloat.

The other deal which I almost completed was for a national chain of restaurants called Fatty Arbuckle's and the attraction for me in doing this deal was that it would have turned Harlequin into a national chain overnight. If I was fully committed to my aspirations to be a really serious player within the industry then this was a great opportunity to realise my ambitions. Again the deal fell through at the last minute and, when I think back, I wonder if it didn't happen because my heart was no longer in it. I think I knew within myself that it was time for change. I knew that I didn't want to continue working in the industry I had once loved. The enthusiasm was not the way it used to be.

I remember the days when I would go to bed and could not wait for the morning to come so that I could go back into work and finish off some unfinished business. It is passion like that which grows small insignificant businesses into major brands. I have always preached that, if you are not one-hundred-and-fifty per cent passionate about your job, then you will never do it well. One has to enjoy going to work or that work is just a chore. I knew I was not giving it the same commitment that I once had done and that lack of enthusiasm soon begins to show. If the man at the top is not driven and motivated then everyone else in the team will be affected. I could already sense apathy. The thing about being the boss is that nobody can sack you and when your performance level goes down that decision has to be taken by yourself. It is not an easy thing to put up your hands and admit that you can no longer cut it and that someone else can actually come in and do better. I recognised the changes in myself and I knew that whether I owned sixteen restaurants or sixty I would still not be happy; so, after some careful consideration, I started to plan my exit.

Once I had decided that I wanted to leave the industry that had been my life for the past twenty-five years, I told Parminder that I was seriously considering selling up but she just dismissed it as a mid-life crisis. There was no way she could ever see me selling. I then had a meeting with Gurmail and told him that I felt that the time was right for me to move on and that he would always have the first option to buy my shares and own Harlequin outright. His son, Sukhvir, had been working in the business now for almost two years and I told Gurmail to consider running the company with his son. Gurmail told me that he was not interested in keeping any of his shares and that if I wanted to sell then he would also want to move on. That said, I started to look for the best way out.

Chapter Forty-Four

SHIPSHAPE TO SELL

Once the decision to sell had been made, the challenge was to find a buyer who would not only want to run a company like Harlequin but also someone who could raise the finance to pay for it. If I had built a chain of bars then my exit would have been much easier as one of the brewers would surely have snapped it up. The problem was that the market I was in only had a few players with the balls to do the deal. A lot of them thought that I *was* Harlequin and that if I were to move on then the business might not last much longer after my departure. None that I knew were looking to buy; in fact, there were more looking to sell. The only way I was going to find someone to take over was to identify a person who had the emotional desire to own Harlequin.

I believe that most businesses are bought for commercial reasons and commercial reasons only, but there are also times when emotions and ego can encourage someone to buy or invest into enterprises that most others would not touch. The classic example of this is when people invest in football clubs which they supported as kids. These guys wear their hearts on their sleeves, and the need to show their peers that they have achieved an impossible dream often overrules commercial judgement. I would not say that this was the case with Harlequin but I know that there were only a few people who would have bought me out, one of their reasons being to show the world that they were now the top people as far as the Indian restaurant scene was concerned.

Harlequin is a great company that has always been profitable but I still needed someone who knew the real value of the brand and that person had to be someone close to the organisation. I needed someone whose need to own Harlequin had been a childhood dream and that man, for me, was Sanjay Majhu. Sanjay had always wanted to show what he could do if he were in my shoes. When he was a Harlequin franchisee he had the weakest performing restaurant in the group. This had led to ridicule from other franchisees and managers and Sanjay had always been desperate to prove them all wrong. The commercial case for someone to take over my business was always there but it would be the emotional aspect that would close the deal.

I sold Mister Singh's India back to Satty Singh. I then sold another of my restaurants, the Ashoka in Bellshill, to the manager who had been running the unit. This was the start of my tidy-up operation that I had devised with some input from my company accountant, Narinder Aggrawal. Narinder had been working with me for about two years and I had hired him fully aware that the company that he had worked for before coming to me had gone into receivership. I felt that lightning would not strike twice and gave him the chance to prove himself. When Narinder came on board, I was able to have reliable day-to-day information on which I could base my decisions and having him made my life a lot easier when it came to the sale. I also had the issue of the Ashoka in Johnstone to resolve and I decided that I would sell my shares in that company to my brother Sukhdev. I think he got a good deal because two years after he bought me out, he was offered 50 per cent more for the same unit. I knew I was going soft but what the hell? He was family and I knew that he had worked his butt off for many years and deserved everything he had. I often wish I had spent more time with him as he was a great operator and we could have done so much more together. As it turned out, he is now one of the main players in Sanjay's new regime and the fact that I sold up and moved on has probably opened a lot more doors for Sukhdev because he almost certainly finds it easier to talk business with Sanjay than he did with me. Anyway, you can't keep a good man down and he has certainly started to shine and his confidence is at an all-time high.

Sanjay already owned the Spice of Life restaurant in Argyle Street that I had sold to him just three years before. He had since got himself into the pharmacy business and was now the proud owner of six pharmacies, a fantastic achievement in a short space of time. He was also a shareholder, along with Rajan Kaura, in an electrical wholesale company which Rajan had built from scratch and the company was doing extremely well. I knew that if the deal could be structured in a way that would make it possible for Sanjay to arrange the funding then he would bite my arm off to get control of my business.

Before I could decide anything at all, I had to make sure that my tax position was looked into, because it was no use selling off my life's work just to see the taxman walk away with all my money. I have always believed in paying my taxes and would never consider involving myself in schemes that would mean evading tax. This said, there is always a danger that if one is not careful and does not get the proper professional advice then one could end up paying too much. It is therefore imperative that in these situations one should get all the necessary tax clearances before selling or buying to avoid heartache later on. I called Charles Barnett, my accountant at PKF, to look at the deal and they soon had all the necessary clearances.

After some more days of soul searching I made the telephone call that had Sanjay dashing over to my house. I told him that I had decided to sell and told him that he was getting the first chance to acquire the business. I told him how much cash it would take to make me relinquish my shareholding. He told me there and then that he would take the deal and that one way or another he would have the funds in place within three months. Sanjay was as good as his word. He did come up with the money and I felt a sense of relief and sadness at the same time.

Chapter Forty-Five

TAKING TIME OUT

I had always wanted to take out some time for myself and laze around the house. Time was a luxury that I could never afford because I was always on the move. Months after I sold my business, I was still going into the office. I had managed to keep myself a small room upstairs, out of everyone's way so that I had somewhere as a base. I had considered working from home but I knew that would have driven Parminder crazy and, within a few months, I too would have gone insane. When you have been in the habit of going to work for so many years then it becomes a habit that is hard to break. I was also getting lots of calls again from organisations and charities wanting me to become a board member and there were also a lot of people who started to come and see me for free advice.

There were also those who knew that I had sold my business and therefore would have some spare cash, so I was sent through a number of business ideas in which to invest. Most of these I just ignored. I did invest £25,000 in one scheme but the money had been used up within months and my investment turned into zilch. It is very easy to get sucked back into a very busy schedule and I felt that I was busier than ever but not really doing anything constructive.

I refused to become a board member for anyone except the local charity called Glasgow, the Caring City because of my belief that one should only join committees if one has a genuine contribution to make. So many times I have come across people who only wanted to be chairmen of organisations because it helped to massage their egos. I, of course, had no problems in the ego department – it had always been big enough and was massaged often.

I decided that I would go and spend a bit of time in India and see what was happening in the land of my birth. I knew that the economy of the country was booming and, apart from getting a feel for India as a place to do business, I also wanted to go on a spiritual trek into the foothills of the Himalayas. I had another few friends who wanted to go to Hemkund Sahib, a spiritual destination for Sikhs situated 14,000 feet up the mountain. Why do they have to put spiritual places so far away? I went to India about a month before the trek and told the rest of the guys that I would have everything organised for them by the time they arrived. The six weeks I spent in India were just what I needed to get me out of my routine in Glasgow. I got to know a few people in Delhi and I was hoping to touch base with Ajit Caur but could not find her phone number. I made a mental note to catch up with her next time around; perhaps she would still be interested in launching my pop career.

My son Sampuran, who was now fifteen years old, also joined me and we went to see the Taj Mahal and visited the backstreet industries responsible for making all the beautiful marble ornaments that were available at exorbitant prices in the Delhi tourist shops. We visited many cities and made lots of new contacts and, for the first time, I started to feel Indian again. I enjoyed being there but I was also homesick for Glasgow and missing my family and friends. I didn't think that I could ever leave Scotland to live in another country.

When my friends joined me for the trek, the timing was just right as I had seen as much as I had wanted and was ready to leave the hot and dusty Delhi for the cooler climate of the Himalayan foothills. Ramesh and Anil joined me from Bournemouth and Inderjit and Harjit joined me from Kuala Lumpur. I had got myself reasonably fit and felt ready for the walk. The first 8,000 feet were easy, probably because we went that distance in a car. I had managed to hire the eight-seater minibus along with a driver, who would stay with us for the duration of the trip, for about £280, including the petrol. With the help of our Delhi office manager Yashwant Deval, who worked for Teresa's recruitment company, I also managed to get hotels booked along the way to the top. The hardest and also the most enjoyable part of the journey was the part we had to do by foot but being up on those hills and far away from telephones was distressing.

I was able to think clearly for the first time since the sale and I soon started considering my next venture. India was certainly a country whose economy was booming. I had noticed vast changes and the country had so much development going on it was difficult not to start noticing opportunities. I thought how great it would be if all my entrepreneurial friends could see what India had to offer and I started to think of ways to make this possible.

I had visited Estonia recently with my friend John McGlynn, who owns a company called AirLink specialising in long-term car parking near Scottish airports. He had just opened an office in Estonia and called it Scotland House. The purpose of this office was to introduce Scots and Scottish companies to the opportunities available in Estonia and vice versa. I liked his idea and asked if he thought it would be a good model for an office in Delhi. John thought it was a great idea so I decided that this would be something that I would like to do. I felt that with my knowledge of Scottish business and knowing the difficulties and challenges that Scottish entrepreneurs faced, it might be possible for me to introduce them to partners in India with whom they could work and gain mutual benefits.

To test the theory John asked me to have my Indian office carry out some research to see if he could obtain land near

India's international airports to provide long-term car-parking facilities for people flying off on business or holidays. He had reckoned that with India's booming economy and the sheer numbers of people using airports, there must now be a market for his product. I didn't have to carry out any research. If we were just to look at the numbers then it was possible to see a picture that would suggest that John would make lots of money. However, knowledge of local customs and culture is of the utmost importance when investing in foreign lands. I told John that his car park would not work because in India most people who owned a car also employed a full-time driver and that when people went to the airport, they would always get dropped off by their driver. If they didn't have a driver then a member of the family would insist on seeing them off and then picking them up on their return. With this in mind, I told him that long-term airport parking is not seen as necessary in India. I wondered how much this advice was worth to John in monetary terms but he made do with a pint of Guinness.

I had promised John that I would look at the possibility of setting this up on my trip to India and while I had been there I had looked at a number of office options. I settled on premises in Greater Kailash 2, an established part of Delhi, and decided that I would open a Scotland House within the next six months. I was back from my trek and feeling totally rejuvenated. My friends and I were in a restaurant in Delhi and we were still talking about our adventure and the effects that our 'pilgrimage' had had on us when my phone rang.

The call was quite unexpected and I had to ask again who it was. 'Charan, it's Jack McConnell here – the Scottish First Minister. Do you have a minute to chat?'

Chapter Forty-Six

MY WEEK IN POLITICS

Jack told me that there was an urgent matter that he wished to discuss and asked when I would be flying back into Glasgow. I told him that I would be back that Friday morning and we set up a meeting for him to come around to my house that afternoon. I wasn't sure why he wanted to see me and I didn't question him on it as I decided it would be better to talk face to face. I didn't have to wait long though, because the next day while I was still in Delhi I got a call from a journalist from the *Evening Times* who said, 'Mr Gill, I guess that by now you already know that Mike Watson has pled guilty to setting fire to the curtains in an Edinburgh hotel. He has also resigned from his position as MSP for Cathcart. Your name has come up in a number of conversations as the man who will be fighting for that seat. Do you have any comment to make?'

I told him that the Mike Watson resignation was news to me as I had not watched any television or read any newspapers for the past fortnight. I had not considered running for Cathcart and that was the only comment that I had to make. I was not surprised that the press had called me so soon: I was only surprised that it was the only call I had got.

Jack McConnell came to see me a couple of hours after I had arrived home and got straight to the point. He asked if I would consider standing in the forthcoming by-election and suggested that I should. I was not quite sure that this was what I wanted, having always been happy to work on the periphery of politics. For the next hour we discussed the pros and cons of the by-election over a couple of vegetable parathas and I told him that I would need to sleep on it and also discuss the matter with my family. Jack told me that I would have to make up my mind over the weekend and then, if I was going to go for it, throw my hat into the ring on the Monday morning.

Parminder has never been keen on my profile in the media and has never enjoyed being interviewed or photographed herself. She knew that if I were to go into politics then there would be a lot of media attention and she was not happy about this. I spent a lot of time talking to my family about a future for me in politics. This was not just another venture to go off and do by myself. If I was going to be an MSP then I would need the support of my family. They knew that I would be putting myself in the firing line for many reasons, not least from members of the Labour Party itself. Parminder and the children all gathered round and the eventual outcome of our family meeting was that they felt I should go for it. All their lives I had told them to follow their instincts and search for new horizons and this was the same advice my kids were now giving me. I had always told them that too many people die with the song still in their hearts and that they should not reach the end of their lives and regret not doing the things that they had always wanted to do. I should listen to my heart and do what I felt was the right thing and they promised that they would stand beside me no matter what.

I had told Jack that I was not a member of the Labour Party and, indeed, I had never been a member of any party. I told him that I feared a backlash from party members. The main support came from the business community from all over Scotland and also from a lot of the political editors of newspapers. The general consensus was that I would be a breath of fresh air and that my experience of life in general would bring a new, much-needed dimension to Scottish politics. These were words similar to the ones used by Jack McConnell when he had met me at my home. I received many phone calls from members of the general public who encouraged me to take on the challenge and said that if there was anything that they could do I should just ask.

I was also pleasantly surprised when I spoke to some of the local Labour members and the constituents of Cathcart. Their feedback and encouragement convinced me that I should consider this opportunity seriously. My mother called to wish me luck, something that she had never done before in her life – so that felt special. Further up the Labour party political pecking order the mood was different. I spoke with Alex Mosson, a man who had been involved in Labour politics all his life, and he told me that there were people who had worked for the party for many years and felt they had served their time. They would not be happy if Jack McConnell tried to parachute me in. It wasn't the opposition that I would have to worry about but the party members themselves, and Alex, being one of the old guard, seemed to sympathise with this attitude.

Although I understood where Alex was coming from, there was a part of me that was very confused. There is a hierarchy in politics that would not be adhered to in the world of business. Just because someone had been working with me at Harlequin for many years did not mean that they would get automatic promotion when the chance came along for a better job. I argued that there were many cases where I had people working in my restaurants but when I had to hire at a senior level, the door would be thrown open to all who were interested and the best person would get the job. That is how the commercial world operates but, as I learnt, it is not so in politics and that could be seen from the profiles of the MSPs. The majority of them were councillors before moving up the ladder to take up their well-earned seats at Holyrood. The sad thing is that a lot of these people are career politicians who have not served their time at the 'university of life', which to my mind far outweighs the need to have been a party member for a given number of years. There is not enough diversity in either the councils or in the Scottish Parliament and this cannot be good in modern politics.

I was advised that, if I joined the Labour Party, then a case could be made under special circumstances to allow my name to be put forward to the National Executive, who would then decide on the shortlist of candidates. I decided to join the party and put myself forward, believing that I would be given the opportunity to present myself to local party members and put my fate in their hands. Alas, it was not to be and within twenty-four hours I learnt that I had not even made the shortlist. Whatever the reason, I knew that representation from the Labour Party members who thought they were in line for the job because of the number of years they had been hanging around the peripheral corridors of power certainly had something to do with it.

My political career was over before it had even begun and I didn't know whether to laugh or cry. I know that Parminder was certainly relieved as politics is not something she regards as an area in which I should be involved. I was pleased to see the Tory Party acknowledging the need for fresh blood and giving the opportunity to David Cameron to lead the party over those who had a lot more experience and were higher up the pecking order.

I rarely regret anything that I do in life and my week in politics was no different. I enjoyed the experience and I had the opportunity to meet so many new people with backgrounds I was unfamiliar with. I am not quite sure if it is something I would want to pursue in future but I learnt a long time ago never to say never and always be prepared for the unexpected.

Chapter Forty-Seven

TAKING SCOTLAND TO INDIA

The time I had spent in India over the summer was wonderful. I had been back on numerous occasions to the land of my birth but I had always been too busy to notice the changes that had taken place in the country. I always had other things on my mind and the summer of 2005 was the first time I had been in India when my mind was totally free from the usual business stresses that had become a part of my personality. I had always admired the enthusiasm of the Indian people; they were entrepreneurial in every sense of the word and nothing was ever a problem. If you wanted something sourced then they all had a cousin who could deliver. The energy I felt in the air and the dynamism of the masses of people just took my breath away. I was free from all stresses and my mind was now receptive to new challenges and opportunities that this massive country with its 1.3 billion people had to provide.

I managed to get so much information through the Internet and the statistics were fascinating, especially for a boy who had grown up and spent all of his life in a country of less than five million people with a declining population. I learnt that India had eighteen official languages (and over 320 unofficial languages) with over 1,650 dialects. It was an educated nation with an increasingly literate population. It churned out over two million graduates every year and, interestingly, I learned that 38 per cent of the doctors and 36 per cent of NASA scientists working in the United States were Indian.

To satisfy the news-hungry nation there were 5,600 daily newspapers and 15,000 weeklies. There were 20,000 periodicals, printed in twenty-one languages. India was a nuclear power and was only one of three countries in the world to have built its own supercomputer. The GDP was fast approaching 10 per cent and manufacturing was on the way up. I discovered that India was the largest producer of motorcycles in the world as well as the second-largest manufacturer of tractors. By 2010, India is set to supply half a million cars a year to Korea and is currently supplying fifteen of the world's major automobile makers in the car industry with components.

The figures go on and on. The pharmaceutical industry is growing at a rate of 10 per cent every year and there are more than two million new subscribers for mobile phones every month. Even the rickshaw drivers have mobile phones, seeing modern technology as an investment because their regular customers can now phone them whenever they require their services. India was now also encouraging foreign investment and barriers that made it difficult for overseas companies to invest in India were being brought down.

This progress had not gone unnoticed and the number of friends and associates in Scotland asking about the opportunities in India was starting to grow. More and more people wanted to know about India. Some were looking to outsource services in call centres and technology. Others were interested in sourcing products from marble, slate and furniture to computer chips. Still others were looking for joint-venture opportunities that Indian companies had to provide and there was also a lot of interest from colleges and universities looking to bring Indian students to Scotland and provide much welcome revenue in the form of fees. A number of them were turning to me with their questions.

It was difficult not to get sucked in by the enthusiasm and I felt that I had to do something to help bring companies wishing to do business in the two countries together.

Considering the best way to do this, my thoughts went back to a recent trip I had taken to Tallinn in Estonia with some friends from the Entrepreneurial Exchange that had been organised by fellow Exchange board member John McGlynn. As I said in an earlier chapter, John had been trying to encourage trade between Estonia, a country he had become very fond of, and Scotland and he had opened his Scotland House office in Tallinn, the Estonian capital, to provide a base for Scottish companies wishing to acquire information in the Estonian market. I had liked this idea and I felt it would be the ideal model for launching my initiative to encourage dialogue and contact between companies and individuals wishing to meet and do business between India and Scotland.

I had already established some good contacts in Delhi and, with an old friend, Mohinder Goyal, who was already exporting from India to Scotland, I decided to open an office in Delhi. The office would be the link between the two countries and we would provide the necessary know-how to help companies assess whether they could do business in the other country. I coordinated the opening with a Scottish Trade mission that had been organised to go to India through the Scottish Council for Trade and Industry as I felt it would give me extra exposure that would not have been possible if I had just opened the office on my own. It was also nice to have lots of friendly faces at the opening and the support of the SCTI was very encouraging and most welcome.

I opened the office in February 2006 and got a fantastic turnout to the ceremony. We even had representatives from the British High Commission turning up to see what I was up to. I think that the fact the office had been named Scotland House was perhaps a bit misleading because it could be seen as a political initiative and linked to the Scottish Government. I met a guy who worked in Brussels who told me that there had been a debate about the opening of Scotland House in India and people in Brussels were wondering what was going on. I just felt that the name reflected what the operation was all about and the fact that we had people sitting up and taking notice was proof of that very fact.

My friend Mohinder agreed to manage the Indian side of the operation and took it upon himself to find a good administrator who could follow up and answer the enquiries that were bound to come in. These were humble beginnings and it reminded me of my first business venture. This was not the first time that I had started a business with one employee and turned it into a company employing hundreds. I was feeling the buzz and I knew that I wanted to spend more time in India because that would be the only way I could identify opportunities that I could then notify to keen investors in Scotland. I was starting to look forward to my time in India.

I was also considering my personal life and whether I should be making changes in that department. I had discussed my intentions of spending time in India with Parminder and she was quite open to the suggestion of having a pad in Delhi. She was probably thinking how that would make life easier when shopping for all the outfits for the girls' weddings. I also considered my son's future, wondering what was in store for him and whether he should get some more exposure to India. I met many people in Delhi and was always aware that education was a key area for their children. Indians invested heavily in the future of their kids and didn't compromise when it came to education. I started to research the schools in India and was very impressed by the standards of some of the top boarding schools, so much so that I started thinking about Sampuran going to one of these schools for his last two years of school education before returning to Scotland to go to university. When I came back to Scotland after the opening of Scotland House, I discussed my vision with Sampuran and told him that I felt a couple of years in a school in India would be good for his future prospects.

I don't think he was totally focused on what I was saying because he said yes without once looking up from his Xbox. It was only later, when I had managed to get him away from his computer game, that he realised what I was suggesting and at first he was not pleased. The thought of leaving home had never occurred to him. He had always felt that he would stay with the family until at least he went to university and even then, perhaps, he would still be at home. It took a week or so of discussing the pros and cons of the move before he eventually started to come around. He checked out the school website and he was most impressed. We discussed how the world was shrinking fast and how future success depended on being able to operate on the global market and see the world as one country.

His first objection was that he was too young and I remembered once using those words, to no avail, to avoid getting married. I told him that he was old enough and that only sixty years ago he would have been drafted into the army and sent off to fight in Germany at his age, so going to a boarding school in the foothills of the Himalayas was no great test of character. He eventually agreed and, in fact, started to talk about it excitedly whenever he got the chance. Life is indeed mysterious and we just don't know where we may end up. I had come to Scotland as a wee boy and now my son was thinking of going back to India to study and perhaps start doing business in India. This is something that my grandfather would never have foreseen but my feeling is that he would have been very proud.

I have no idea what the future has in store for me. I love Scotland and I enjoy the buzz of India. I also miss the buzz of the restaurants and at times still feel like working the tables on a Saturday night. Will the lure of the restaurant business, which is in my blood, be too strong for me to ignore? Who knows? If I ever open a restaurant again I am sure you will all get to hear about it and I hope you will pop in and say hello.

I think that my life has been full of twists and turns and I believe that there will be many more surprises in store that will astonish even me. It has been a wonderful journey that has kept me moving and shaking for over forty years and I would change none of it. Even the blunders that took me to the edge of bankruptcy were incidents without which I would not be half the man I am today and I am happy to have experienced them.

As the plane takes off from Glasgow airport to take Sampuran and me to Delhi, where I now plan to buy a house, I sip my champagne and my mind wanders back to my first plane journey that landed in Glasgow and I thank my good fortune and my kismet for all that it has provided me. If someone had given me a blank sheet of paper back then and asked me to write down how I would like my life to turn out, I don't think I could have done a better job than what fate had in store for this boy from the Punjab. I could not have imagined this in my wildest dreams.